W.H. Wilkins

The Romance of Isabel Lady Burton

The Story of Her Life. Vol. II

W.H. Wilkins

The Romance of Isabel Lady Burton
The Story of Her Life. Vol. II

ISBN/EAN: 9783744771511

Printed in Europe, USA, Canada, Australia, Japan

Cover: Foto ©ninafisch / pixelio.de

More available books at **www.hansebooks.com**

THE ROMANCE OF ISABEL LADY BURTON

VOL. II

THE ROMANCE OF
ISABEL LADY BURTON

THE STORY OF HER LIFE

TOLD IN PART BY HERSELF
AND IN PART BY
W H WILKINS

WITH PORTRAITS AND ILLUSTRATIONS

VOLUME II

NEW YORK
DODD MEAD & COMPANY
1897

University Press
JOHN WILSON AND SON CAMBRIDGE USA

CONTENTS OF VOL. II

BOOK II
(*Continued*)

CHAPTER XI
IN AND ABOUT DAMASCUS 375

CHAPTER XII
EARLY DAYS AT DAMASCUS 387

CHAPTER XIII
THROUGH THE DESERT TO PALMYRA 403

CHAPTER XIV
BLUDÁN IN THE ANTI-LEBANON 425

CHAPTER XV
GATHERING CLOUDS 448

Contents

CHAPTER XVI
JERUSALEM AND THE HOLY LAND 469

CHAPTER XVII
THE RECALL 493

CHAPTER XVIII
THE TRUE REASONS OF BURTON'S RECALL . . . 510

CHAPTER XIX
THE PASSING OF THE CLOUD 524

CHAPTER XX
EARLY YEARS AT TRIESTE 535

CHAPTER XXI
THE JOURNEY TO BOMBAY 554

CHAPTER XXII
INDIA 574

CHAPTER XXIII
TRIESTE AGAIN 604

CHAPTER XXIV
THE SHADOWS LENGTHEN 625

CHAPTER XXV
GORDON AND THE BURTONS 645

Contents

CHAPTER XXVI
THE SWORD HANGS 677

CHAPTER XXVII
THE SWORD FALLS 698

BOOK III

WIDOWED

CHAPTER I
THE TRUTH ABOUT "THE SCENTED GARDEN" . . 719

CHAPTER II
THE RETURN TO ENGLAND 739

CHAPTER III
THE TINKLING OF THE CAMEL'S BELL . . . 749

INDEX 773

LIST OF ILLUSTRATIONS

VOL. II

	PAGE
ISABEL BURTON	*Frontispiece*
THE BURTONS' HOUSE AT SALAHÍYYEH, DAMASCUS	376
THE COURT OF THE GREAT MOSQUE, DAMASCUS	384
ARAB CAMEL-DRIVERS	422
BA'ALBAK	430
"THE MOON," LADY BURTON'S SYRIAN MAID	442
MOSQUE OF OMAR, JERUSALEM	472
THE DEAD SEA	484
TRIESTE	540
RICHARD F. BURTON	550
PORT SAID	562
ARAB CAMEL-DRIVERS	566
THE CAVES OF ELEPHANTA	574
PANORAMA POINT AND THE BHAO MALLIN HILLS, MÁTHERÁN	578
THE BORAH (NATIVE) BAZAR, BOMBAY	590
GOA	598

List of Illustrations

	PAGE
SUEZ	612
THE BURTONS' HOUSE AT TRIESTE	638
CAIRO	662
FACSIMILE	672
LADY BURTON IN 1887	686
A NATIVE LADY, TUNIS	694
FACSIMILE	711
THE ROOM IN WHICH LADY BURTON DIED	770
THE ARAB TENT AT MORTLAKE	770

BOOK II.—WEDDED

(CONTINUED)

CHAPTER XI

IN AND ABOUT DAMASCUS

(1870)

Though old as history itself, thou art fresh as breath of spring, blooming as thine own rosebud, as fragrant as thine own orange flower, O Damascus, Pearl of the East!

DURING the first weeks at Damascus my only work was to find a suitable house and to settle down in it. Our predecessor in the Consulate had lived in a large house in the city itself, and as soon as he retired he let it to a wealthy Jew. In any case it would not have suited us, nor would any house within the city walls; for though some of them were quite beautiful —indeed, marble palaces gorgeously decorated and furnished after the manner of oriental houses — yet there is always a certain sense of imprisonment about Damascus, as the windows of the houses are all barred and latticed, and the gates of the city are shut at sunset. This would not have suited our wild-cat proclivities; we should have felt as though we were confined in a cage. So after a search of many days we took a house in the environs, about a quarter of an hour from Damascus, high up the hill. Just beyond it was the desert sand, and in the background a saffron-hued mountain known as the Camomile Mountain; and camomile was the scent which pervaded our village and all Damascus. Our house was in the suburb of Salahíyyeh, and we had good air and light, beautiful views, fresh water, quiet, and above all liberty. In five minutes we could gallop out over the mountains, and there was no locking us up at sunset. Here then we pitched our tent.

I should like to describe our house at Salahíyyeh once more, though I have described it before, and Frederick Leighton once drew a sketch of it, so that it is pretty well known. Our house faced the road and the opposite gardens, and it was flanked on one side by the Mosque and on the other by the Hammám (Turkish Bath), and there were gardens at the back. On the other side of the road were apricot trees, whose varying beauty of bud and leaf and flower and fruit can be better imagined than described. Among these apricot orchards I had a capital stable for twelve horses, and a good room attached to it for any number of *saises*, or grooms, and beyond that again was a little garden, through which the river wended its way. So much for the exterior. Now to come indoors. As one entered, first of all came the courtyard, boldly painted in broad stripes of red and white and blue, after the manner of all the courtyards in Damascus. Here too splashed the fountain, and all around were orange, lemon, and jessamine trees. Two steps took one to the *líwán*, a raised room open one side to the court, and spread with carpets, divans, and Eastern stuffs. It was here, in the summer, I was wont to receive. On the right side of the court was a dining-room, and on the left a

[From a sketch by the late Lord Leighton.

THE BURTONS' HOUSE AT SALAHIYYEH, DAMASCUS

[*Page 376.*

cool sitting-room, when it was too hot to live upstairs. All the rest of the space below was left to the servants and offices. Upstairs the rooms ran around two sides of the courtyard. A long terrace occupied the other two sides, joining the rooms at either end. This terrace formed a pleasant housetop in the cool evenings. We spread it with mats and divans, and used to sit among the flowers and shrubs, and look over Damascus and sniff the desert air beyond.

Of course this house was not the Consulate, which was in the city, close to the Serai, or Government House.

I think the charm of our house lay chiefly in the gardens around it. We made a beautiful arbour in the garden opposite—a garden of roses and jessamine; and we made it by lifting up overladen vines and citrons, and the branches of lemon and orange trees, and supporting them on a framework, so that no sun could penetrate their luxuriant leafage. We put a divan in this arbour, which overlooked the rushing river; and that and the housetop were our favourite places to smoke on cool summer evenings.

By this time you will probably have discovered my love for animals, and as soon as I had arranged our house at Damascus the first thing I did was to indulge in my hobby of collecting a menagerie. First of all we bought some horses, three-quarter-breds and half-breds. Thorough-bred Arabs, especially mares, were too dear for our stable, and would have made us an object of suspicion. In the East, where there are official hands not clear of bribes, an Arab mare is a favourite bribe, and I had many such offers before I

had been at Damascus long; but I refused them all.
Richard always gave me entire command of the stable,
and so it was my domain. Living in solitude as I
did very much, I discovered how companionable horses
could be. There was no speech between us, but I
knew everything they said and thought and felt, and
they knew everything I said to them. I did not
confine my purchases entirely to horses. I bought a
camel and a snow-white donkey, which latter is the
most honourable mount for grand visiting. I also
picked up a splendid Persian cat in the bazaars, and I
had brought over with me a young pet St. Bernard
dog, two brindle bull-terriers and two of the Yar-
borough breed, and I added later a Kurdish pup. I
bought three milk goats for the house, and I had
presents of a pet lamb and a *nimr* (leopard), which
became the idol of the house. The domestic hen-yard
was duly stocked with all kinds of fowls, turkeys,
geese, ducks, and guinea-fowls, and in the garden and
on the terrace and the housetop I kept my pigeons.
This collection was my delight. I cannot say that they
were a happy family. After a time I trained them
into living together in something like harmony, but it
took a very long time. I added to my family also
from time to time half-famished dogs which I had
rescued from the streets, or ill-treated and broken-down
donkeys, which I purchased from some cruel master.
In the course of time it became a truly wonderful
gathering.

The animals in the East seem to me to be almost
more intelligent than those at home. **They certainly**

have a way of showing their likes and dislikes very strongly. When I first came to Damascus, fond though I was of animals, I found that most of them shied at me. I do not think that they had been accustomed to an Englishwoman at close quarters. For instance, I went for a walk one day, and met a small boy leading a donkey laden with radishes, as high as a small tree. I suppose that I was strange-looking, for at the sight of me the donkey kicked up his heels and threw all the radishes about for a hundred yards around. The poor little boy set up a howl. I ran to help him, but the more I tried the more the donkey ran away, and at last I understood by signs that the donkey was shying at me, so I threw the boy a coin and retreated, and sent another boy to help him. We called to an old man riding a shabby-looking horse, but the moment the horse saw me it did exactly the same thing, and nearly flung the old man off. My sides ached with laughing. Fancy being so queer that the animals take fright at one!

I think before I go further I ought to give some general idea of the city of Damascus as it appeared to me. I have already said that my first sight of the city was one of disappointment; but when I got to know it better its charm grew upon me, and I shall never till I die like any place so well. Damascus, as I suppose every one knows, is the largest town in Syria. In shape it is rather like a boy's kite, with a very long tail. The tail of the kite is the Maydán, the poorest part of Damascus, but rich in ruined mosques and hammáms, and houses which at first sight look as though they were in decay. But when we got to know these houses better, we found that marble courts, inlaid chambers, arabesque ceilings, often lay behind the muddy exteriors. The city itself is divided into three quarters: the Jewish in the southern part, the Moslem in the northern and western, and the Christians in the eastern. The Moslem quarter is clean, the Christian quarter dirty, and the Jewish simply filthy. I often had to gallop through it holding my handkerchief to my mouth, and the kawwasses running as though they had been pursued by devils. Everywhere in Damascus, but especially in this quarter, the labyrinthine streets are piled with heaps of offal, wild dogs are gorged with carrion, and dead dogs are lying about. One must never judge Damascus, however, by externals: every house has a mean aspect in the way of entrance and approach. This is done purposely to deceive the Government, and not to betray what may be within in times of looting. You often approach through a mean doorway into a dirty passage; you then enter a second court, and you behold a marvellous transformation. You find the house thoroughly cleaned and perfumed, paved courts with marble fountains and goldfish, orange and jessamine trees, furniture inlaid with gold and ebony and mother-o'-pearl, and stained-glass windows. In the interior of one of the most beautiful houses I saw in Damascus the show-room was very magnificent, upholstered in velvet and gold, and with divans inlaid with marble, mother-o'-pearl, ebony, and walnut, and there were tesselated marble floors and pavements and fountains; but, *en revanche*, God knows where they sleep at all. One of the ladies I went to call on first in her house was a very young and pretty bride, only a fortnight married. She was gaudily dressed with about £2,000 worth of diamonds on her head and neck, but the stones were so badly set they looked like rubbish. She rolled from side to side in her walk, which is a habit very *chic*.

Notwithstanding her internal grandeur, Damascus is but a wreck of her former splendour, albeit a beautiful wreck. Ichabod! her glory has departed; not even the innumerable domes and minarets of her multitudinous mosques can reinstate her.

I think I ought to touch on the bazaars, as they form such an integral part of the life of Damascus. Many of them were very beautiful, all huddled together in a labyrinth of streets, and containing almost everything which one could want. I used to love to go with my Arab maid and wander through them. There was the saddlery bazaar, where one could buy magnificent trappings for one's Arab steeds, saddle-cloths embossed with gold, bridles of scarlet silk, a single rein which makes you look as if you were managing a horse by a single thread, and bridles of silver and ivory. There was a shoemakers' bazaar. How different from a shoeshop in England! The stalls were gorgeous with lemon-coloured slippers, stiff red shoes, scarlet boots with tops and tassels and hangings, which form part of the Bedawi dress. There was a *marqueterie* bazaar, where one found many lovely things inlaid with choice woods, mother-o'-pearl, and steel. And there was the gold and silver bazaar, where the smiths sat round in little pens, hammering at their anvils. Here one could pick up some most beautiful barbarous and antique ornaments, filigree coffee-cup holders, raki cups of silver inlaid with gold, and many other beautiful things too numerous to mention. There was another bazaar where they sold attar and sandal-wood oil; and yet another where one could buy rich Eastern stuffs and silks, the most beautiful things, which would make a fine smoking suit for one's husband, or a *sortie de bal* for oneself. Here also you can buy izárs to walk about the bazaars *incognita*. They are mostly brilliantly hued and beautifully worked in gold. There was also the divan, where one bought beautiful stuffs, gaudy Persian rugs, and prayer-carpets for furnishing the house. There was the bazaar where one bought henna, wherewith to stain the hands, the feet, and the finger-nails. And last, but by no means least, there was the pipe or narghileh bazaar, which contained the most beautiful pipe-sticks I ever saw, and the most lovely narghilehs, which were made in exquisite shapes and of great length in the tube. The longer the *narbish*, or tube, the higher your rank, and the greater compliment you pay to your guest. I used to order mine to be all dark chocolate and gold, and to measure from four to six yards in length, and I never had less than twelve narghilehs in the house at once, one of which I kept for my own particular smoking, and a silver mouthpiece which I kept in my pocket for use when visiting. I cannot hope in a short space to exhaust the treasures of these gorgeous bazaars. I can only say in conclusion that there were also the bazaars for sweetmeats, most delectable; for coffee, of which one never tastes the like out of Damascus; and every kind of *bric-à-brac*.

No account of Damascus, not even a bird's-eye view, would be complete without some mention of the great Mosque, whither I was wont now and again to repair. When I went, I of course took off my boots at the entrance, and put on my lemon-coloured slippers, and I was always careful to be as respectful and as reverent as if I were in my own church, and to never forget to leave a trifle for the poor, and to give a substantial tip when I went out. The Mosque was a magnificent building, with a ceiling of beautiful arabesques; the floor of limestone like marble, covered with mats and prayer-carpets. One of the most beautiful domes had windows of delicately carved wood, whose interstices were filled with crystal. There was a large paved court with a marble dome and fountain; and there were three minarets, which it was possible to ascend and from them to look down upon Damascus. It was up one of these minarets that the Duchesse de Persigny ascended, and when prayer was called she refused to come down. The Shaykh sent all kinds of emissaries and entreaties, to whom she replied: " Dites au Shaykh que je suis la Duchesse de Persigny, que je me trouve fort bien ici, et que je ne descendrai que quand cela me plaira." She did not please for three-quarters of an hour. She also visited *cafés* which Moslem women do not visit, and shocked the kawwasses so much that they begged the French Consul not to send them to guard her, as they were losing their reputation! But to return to our muttons. This superb Mosque has alternately served as a place of worship for many creeds: for the Pagans as a temple, for the Christians as a cathedral, and for the Moslems as a mosque. Like Damascus, it has had its vicissitudes, and it has been taken captive by Babylonians, Greeks, Persians, Assyrians, and Turks.

The Hammám, or Turkish Bath, is another feature of Damascus, and was one of my favourite haunts. I first went to the Hammám out of curiosity, and was warmly welcomed by the native women; but I was rather shocked. They squat naked on the floor, and, despoiled of their dress and hair and make-up, are, most of them, truly hideous. Their skins are like parchment, and baggy; their heads as bald as billiard-balls. What little hair they have is dyed an orange red with henna. They look like the witches in *Macbeth*, or at least as if they had been called up from out of the lower regions. They sit chatting with little bundles of sweets and narghilehs before them. An average Englishwoman would look like an *houri* amongst them; and their customs were beastly, to use the mildest term. The Hammám was entered by a large hall, lit by a skylight, with a huge marble tank in the centre and four little fountains, and all around raised divans covered with cushions. Here one wraps oneself in silk and woollen sheets, and after that proceeds to pass through the six marble rooms. The first is the cold room, the next warmer, the third warmer still, until you come to the *sudarium*, the hottest room of all. First they lather you, then they wash you with a *lif* and soap, then they douche you with tubs of hot water, then they shampoo you with fresh layers of soap, and

THE COURT OF THE GREAT MOSQUE, DAMASCUS.

[*Page* 384.

then douche again. They give you iced sherbet, and tie towels dipped in cold water round your head, which prevent you fainting and make you perspire. They scrub your feet with pumice-stone, and move you back through all the rooms gradually, douche you with water, and shampoo you with towels. You now return to the large hall where you first undressed, wrap in woollen shawls, and recline on a divan. The place is all strewn with flowers, incense is burned around, and a cup of hot coffee is handed and a narghileh placed in your mouth. A woman advances and kneads you as though you were bread, until you fall asleep under the process, as though mesmerized. When you wake up, you find music and dancing, the girls chasing one another, eating sweetmeats, and enjoying all sorts of fun. Moslem women go through a good deal more of the performance than I have described. For instance, they have their hair hennaed and their eyebrows plucked. You can also have your hands and feet hennaed, and, if you like it, be tattooed. The whole operation takes about four hours. It is often said by the ignorant that people can get as good a hammám in London or Paris as in the East. I have tried all, and they bear about as much relation to one another as a puddle of dirty water does to a pellucid lake. And the pellucid lake is in the East.

Then the harems. I often spent an evening in them, and I found them very pleasant; only at first the women used to ask me such a lot of inconvenient questions that I became quite confused. They were always puzzled because I had no children. One cannot generalize on the subject of harems; they differ in degree just as much as families in London. A first-class harem at Constantinople is one thing, at Damascus one of the same rank is another, while those of the middle and lower classes are different still. As a rule I met with nothing but courtesy in the harems, and much hospitality, cordiality, and refinement. I only twice met with bad manners, and that was in a middle-class harem. Twice only the conversation displeased me, and that was amongst the lower class. One of the first harems I visited in Damascus was that of the famous Abd el Kadir (of whom more anon), which of course was one of the best class. He had five wives: one of them was very pretty. I asked them how they could bear to live together and pet each other's children. I told them that in England, if a woman thought her husband had another wife or mistress, she would be ready to kill her and strangle the children if they were not her own. They all laughed heartily at me, and seemed to think it a great joke. I am afraid that Abd el Kadir was a bit of a Tartar in his harem, for they were very prim and pious.

So much for the city of Damascus.

In the environs there were many beautiful little roads, leading through gardens and orchards, with bubbling water, and under the shady fig and vine, pomegranate and walnut. You emerged from these shady avenues on to the soft yellow sand of the desert, where you could gallop as hard as you pleased. There were no boundary-lines, no sign-posts, nothing to check one's spirits or one's energy. The breath of the desert is liberty.

CHAPTER XII

EARLY DAYS AT DAMASCUS

(1870)

Though old as history itself, thou art fresh as breath or spring, blooming as thine own rosebud, as fragrant as thine own orange flower, O Damascus, Pearl of the East!

AS soon as we had settled in our house I had to accustom myself to the honours of my position, which at first were rather irksome to me; but as they were part of the business I had to put up with them. I found my position as the wife of the British Consul in Damascus very different from what it had been in Brazil. A consul in the East as *envoyé* of a Great Power is a big man, and he ranks almost as high as a Minister would in Europe. Nearer home a consul is often hardly considered to be a gentleman, while in many countries he is not allowed to go to Court. In the East, however, the Consular service was, at the time I write, an honoured profession, and the *envoyés* of the Great Powers were expected to keep up a little state, especially the English and the French. They had a certain number of Consular dragomans, or gentleman secretaries, in distinction to the travelling dragoman, who bears the same relation as a courier in Europe. They also had a certain number of kawwasses, who look like cavalry soldiers. The Consulate at Damascus was then quite like a diplomatic post, and I felt like a Minister's wife, and was treated accordingly. For instance, every time I went outside my door I was attended by four kawwasses, with swords and uniforms much ornamented, also a dragoman interpreter. The duty of these four attendants was to clear the way before and behind me, and I assure you it was far more pain than pleasure to me to see mules, horses, donkeys, camels, little children, and poor old men thrust out of the way, as if I were sacred and they were all dirt. How they must have cursed me! I told my kawwasses that I did not wish them to show themselves officious by doing more than was absolutely necessary for the dignity of the British Consulate and the custom of the country. But their escort certainly was necessary to a great extent. When the common people saw a kawwass, they knew one was of importance, and made way for one; otherwise a woman could not walk the streets of Damascus without being molested: even the famished herds of dogs seemed to know the difference between kawwass and no kawwass. The danger from dogs was that they collected and ran in packs, and you were almost caught in the eddy of wild and half-starved dogs if you were not guarded.

I hate pomp and ceremony of all kinds, except where it is absolutely necessary; but in this case I could not dispense with it. The French Minister's wife was hissed in the streets of Constantinople because she chose to dispense with her escort. A Protestant clergyman's wife was nearly struck by a Turkish soldier for brushing against him with her petticoats, thus rendering him, according to his religion, unclean. Besides, women in the East want a guard. A missionary young lady who came up in the *coupé* of the diligence from Beyrout to Damascus had an unpleasant experience. A Persian, who called himself a gentleman, was inside, and kissed her all the way up. She, poor little idiot! saw no way out of the transaction, but came and threw herself on Richard's protection several days after, and there was an ugly row. She had the Persian arrested, and tried him. If anybody had tried that sort of game on with me, I should have made an example of him myself, and taken the law in my own hands, whoever he was. An escort was therefore necessary. I can understand how some consuls' wives, sometimes vulgar, ill-conditioned women, might get elated at this newly acquired importance, and presume upon it until they became unbearable. I found the lack of privacy very trying at first, but I was anxious to bear it because I saw that English influence at Damascus required lifting a great many pegs higher than our predecessor left it. The only member of our English *noblesse* the people had hitherto known in Damascus was Lady Ellenborough, of whom more anon.

As soon as we were settled down I had to begin my receptions. I fixed my reception day on Wednesday; and it was no trifle, for the visitors came all day long. One native lady told me indignantly that she had been to see me three times on my reception day, and had been refused. I said, "When did you come? and how could it happen that I had never heard of it?" She answered almost angrily, "I came at daylight, and again at sunrise, and again at eight o'clock." I said it was rather early; and though I was an early riser, it was just possible that I had not made a suitable toilet to receive her. On my reception day the dragomans interpreted for me. The kawwasses, in full dress of scarlet and gold, kept guard by turns, and the servants were engaged incessantly in bringing up relays of narghílehs, chibouques, cigarettes, sweetmeats, sherbet, Turkish coffee and tea. My visitors sat on the divans, cross-legged or not, according to their nation, and smoked and chatted. If there were Moslem women, I had two separate reception-rooms, and went from one to the other, as the women will not unveil before strange men. It was a most tiring day; for not only did people come all through the day, but I was obliged to concentrate all my thoughts not to make a mistake in etiquette. There were many grades and ranks to be considered, and the etiquette in receiving each guest was different according to the rank. The dragoman in attendance upon me would whisper until I knew it, "One step," or "Two steps," or "Half across the room," or "The door." I thus knew exactly the visitor's rank, and by what term to address him, from the lowest to the highest. Of course, in receiving natives, the method of receiving men and women was different. I advanced to meet the women; we mutually raised our finger-tips to our hearts, lips, and foreheads. They then seized my hand, which I snatched away to prevent their kissing it (it sounds rude, but it isn't; it is the essence of politeness), and I kissed them on both cheeks. I personally removed their veils and their izárs. When they took their leave, I reveiled them, and accompanied them to the door. With the men I did not shake hands: we saluted at a distance. If my visitor was a well-bred man, he would not expect me to rise, but would come and kiss my hand, and had to be pressed two or three times before he would consent to sit down. The only man I was in the habit of rising for was the Wali, or Governor-General of Syria, because he represented the Sultan, and he in his turn paid me a similar respect. When he left, I accompanied him to the door of the room, but never to the street door. Moreover, it was *de rigueur* every time a visitor came that coffee, tea, or sherbet should be offered him, and that I should take it with him and drink first. It was a custom with the natives, and I could not omit it; but when I first held my receptions I found it a great tax upon me, and mixing so many drinks gave me indigestion. Afterwards I grew more wary, and merely moistened my lips. Another thing I used to do at my earlier receptions was to make tea and coffee and carry them round myself, while the dragomans would lazily sit and look on. I didn't understand this at all, so I told them to get up and help me, and they willingly handed tea and coffee to any European, man or woman, but not to their native ladies, who blushed, begged the dragomans' pardon, and stood up, looking appealingly at me, and praying not to be served. So I found it the easiest thing to wait on the native women myself, though I felt very indignant that any man should feel himself degraded by having to wait on a woman.

I must now mention three of my principal visitors, each of whom afterwards played a large part, though a very different part, in our life at Damascus.

First of all was the Wali, or Governor-General of Syria. I received him in state one day. He came in full uniform with a great many attendants. I seated him in proper form on a divan with pipes and coffee. He was very amiable and polite. He reminded me of an old tom-cat: he was dressed in furs; he was indolent and fat, and walked on his toes and purred. At first sight I thought him a kind-hearted old creature, not very intelligent and easily led. The last quality was true enough; for what disgusted me was that Syria was really governed by dragomans, and the Wali or any other great man was a puppet. For instance, if the Consul wanted to see the Wali, he had to send one of his dragomans to the Wali's dragomans, and they arranged between them just what they liked. The two chief men met each other, attended by two dragomans, who reported every word of the conversation round Damascus. These men easily made people enemies; and the lies, mischief, and scandal they originated were beyond imagination. I have said that my first impression of the Wali was as of a well-fed cat; but I soon discovered that the cat had claws, for he quickly became jealous of Richard's influence, and during our two years' sojourn at Damascus he was one of our worst enemies.

Another, and the most interesting of all the personages who attended my receptions, was Lady Ellenborough, known at Damascus as the Honourable Jane Digby El Mezráb.[1] She was the most romantic and picturesque personality: one might say she was Lady Hester Stanhope's successor. She was of the family of Lord Digby, and had married Lord Ellenborough, Governor-General of India, a man much older than herself, when she was quite a girl. The marriage was against her wish. She was very unhappy with him, and she ran away with Prince Schwartzenburg when she was only nineteen, and Lord Ellenborough divorced her. She lived with Prince Schwartzenburg for some years, and had two or three children by him, and then he basely deserted her. I am afraid after that she led a life for a year or two over which it is kinder to draw a veil. She then tired of Europe, and conceived the idea of visiting the East, and of imitating Lady Hester Stanhope and other European ladies, who became more Eastern than the Easterns. She arrived at Beyrout, and went to Damascus, where she arranged to go to Baghdad, across the desert. For this journey a Bedawin escort was necessary; and as the Mezráb tribe occupied the ground, the duty of commanding

[1] Miss Stisted speaks of her as "Jane Digby, who capped her wild career by marrying a camel-driver," and animadverts on Lady Burton for befriending her. The Shaykh was never a camel-driver in his life, and few, I think, will blame Lady Burton for her kindness to this poor lady, her countrywoman, in a strange land.]

the escort devolved upon Shaykh Mijwal, a younger brother of the chief of this tribe. On the journey the young Shaykh fell in love with this beautiful woman, and she fell in love with him. The romantic picture of becoming a queen of the desert suited her wild and roving fancy. She married him, in spite of all opposition, according to the Mohammedan law. At the time I came to Damascus she was living half the year in a house just within the city gates; the other half of the year she passed in the desert in the tents of the Bedawin tribe, living absolutely as a Bedawin woman. When I first saw her she was a most beautiful woman, though sixty-one years of age. She wore one blue garment, and her beautiful hair was in two long plaits down to the ground. When she was in the desert, she used to milk the camels, serve her husband, prepare his food, wash his hands, face, and feet, and stood and waited on him while he ate, like any Arab woman, and gloried in so doing. But at Damascus she led a semi-European life. She blackened her eyes with kohl, and lived in a curiously untidy manner. But otherwise she was not in the least extraordinary at Damascus. But what was incomprehensible to me was how she could have given up all she had in England to live with that dirty little black—or nearly so—husband. I went to see her one day, and when he opened the door to me I thought at first he was a native servant. I could understand her leaving a coarse, cruel husband, much older than herself, whom she never loved (every woman has not the strength of mind and the pride to stand by what she has done); I could understand her running away with Schwartzenburg; but the contact with that black skin I could not understand. Her Shaykh was very dark—darker than a Persian, and much darker than an Arab generally is. All the same, he was a very intelligent and charming man in any light but as a husband. That made me shudder. It was curious how she had retained the charming manner, the soft voice, and all the graces of her youth. You would have known her at once to be an English lady, well born and bred, and she was delighted to greet in me one of her own order. We became great friends, and she dictated to me the whole of her biography, and most romantic and interesting it is. I took a great interest in the poor thing. She was devoted to her Shaykh, whereat I marvelled greatly. Gossip said that he had other wives, but she assured me that he had not, and that both her brother Lord Digby and the British Consul required a legal and official statement to that effect before they were married. She appeared to be quite foolishly in love with him (and I fully comprehend any amount of sacrifice for the man one loves—the greater the better), though the object of her devotion astonished me. Her eyes often used to fill with tears when talking of England, her people, and old times; and when we became more intimate, she spoke to me of every detail of her erring but romantic career. It was easy to see that Schwartzenburg had been the love of her life, for her eyes would light up with a glory when she mentioned him, and she whispered his name with bated breath. It was his desertion which wrecked her life. Poor thing! she was far more sinned against than sinning.

Our other friend at Damascus was the famous Abd el Kadir. Every one knows his history: every one has heard of his hopeless struggles for the independence of Algeria; his capture and imprisonment in France from 1847 to 1852, when he was set free by Louis Napoleon on the intercession of Lord Londonderry. More than that, Louis Napoleon was magnanimous enough to pension him, and sent him to Damascus, where he was living when we came, surrounded by five hundred faithful Algerians. **He loved the** English, but he was very loyal to Louis Napoleon. He was dark, and a splendid-looking man with a stately bearing, and perfectly self-possessed. He always dressed in snow white, turban and *burnous*, with not a single ornament except his jewelled arms, which were superb. He was every inch a soldier and **a** sultan, and his mind was as beautiful as his face. Both he and Richard were Master-Sufi, and they greatly enjoyed a talk together, both speaking purest Arabic.

When I look back **on** those dear days and friends in Damascus, my eyes fill and my heart throbs at the memories which **crowd** upon me. When I think of all those memories, none is dearer to me than the recollection of the evenings which we four — Lady Ellenborough, Abd el Kadir, Richard, and myself — used to spend together on the top of our house. Often after my reception was over and the sun **was** setting, we used to ask these two to stay behind the others and have a little supper with us, and we would go up to the roof, where it was prepared, and where mattresses and the cushions of the divans were spread about, and have our evening meal; and after that we would smoke our narghílehs, and talk and talk and talk far into the night, about things above, things on the earth, and things under the earth. I shall never forget the scene on the housetop, backed as it was by the sublime mountain, a strip of sand between it and us, and on the other three sides was the view over Damascus and beyond the desert. It was all wild, romantic, and solemn; and sometimes we would pause in our conversation to listen to the sounds around us: the last call to prayer on the minaret-top, the soughing of the wind through the mountain-gorges, and the noise of the water-wheel in the neighbouring orchard.

I have said *we* smoked, and that included Lady Ellenborough and myself. I must confess to the soft impeachment, despite insular prejudices; and I would advise any woman who sojourns in the East to learn to smoke, if she can. I am no admirer of a big cigar in a woman's mouth, or a short clay; but I know of nothing more graceful or enjoyable than a cigarette, and even more so is the narghíleh, or even the chibouque, which, however, is quite a man's pipe.

I must add that when we were in the East Richard and I made a point of leading two lives. We were always thoroughly English in our Consulate, and endeavoured to set an example of the way in which England should be represented abroad, and in our official life we strictly conformed to English customs and conventions; but when we were off duty, so to speak, we used to live a great deal as natives, and so obtained experience of the inner Eastern life. Richard's friendship with the Mohammedans, and his perfect mastery of the Arabic and Persian languages and literature, naturally put him into intimate relations with the oriental authorities and the Arab tribes, and he was always very popular among them, with one exception, and that was the Turkish Wali, or Governor, aforesaid. Richard was my guide in all things; and since he adapted himself to the native life, I endeavoured to adapt myself to it also, not only because it was my duty, but because I loved it. For instance, though we always wore European dress in Damascus and Beyrout, we wore native dress in the desert. I always wore the men's dress on our expeditions in the desert and up the country. By that I mean the dress of the Arab men. This is not so dreadful as Mrs. Grundy may suppose, as it was all drapery, and does not show the figure. There was nothing but the face to show the curious whether you were a man or a woman, and I used to tuck my *kuffiyyah* up to only show my eyes. When we wore Eastern clothes, we always ate as the Easterns ate. If I went to a bazar, I frequently used to dress like a Moslem woman with my face covered, and sit in the shops and let my Arab maid do the talking. They never suspected me, and so I heard all their gossip and entered into something of their lives. The women frequently took me into the mosque in this garb, but to the harím I always went in my European clothes. Richard and I lived the Eastern life thoroughly, and we loved it.

We went to every kind of ceremony, whether it was a circumcision, or a wedding, or a funeral, or a dervish dance, or anything that was going on; and we mixed with all classes, and religions, and races, and tongues. I remember my first invitation was to a grand *fête* to celebrate the circumcision of a youth about ten years of age. He was very pretty, and was dressed in gorgeous garments covered with jewellery. Singing, dancing, and feasting went on for about three days. The ceremony took place quite publicly. There was a loud clang of music and firing of guns to drown the boy's cries, and with one stroke of a circular knife the operation was finished in a second. The part cut off was then handed round on a silver salver, as if to force all present to attest that the rite had been performed. I felt quite sick, and English modesty overpowered curiosity, and I could not look. Later on, when I grew more used to Eastern ways, I was forced to accept the compliment paid to the highest rank, and a great compliment to me as a Christian, to hold the boy in my arms whilst the ceremony was being performed. It was rather curious at first to be asked to a circumcision, as one might be asked to a christening in England or a "small and early."

For the first three months of my life at Damascus I only indulged in short excursions, but Richard went away on longer expeditions, often for days, sometimes on business and sometimes to visit the Druze chiefs. I have said that our house was about a quarter of an hour from Damascus, and whilst Richard was away on one of these expeditions I broke through a stupid rule.

It was agreed that I could never dine out or go to a *soirée* in Damascus, because after sunset the roads between Damascus and our house on the hillside were infested with Kurds. I was tired of being "gated" in this way, so I sent to the Chief of the Police, and told him I intended to dine out when I chose and where I chose, and to return at all hours—any hours I pleased. He looked astonished, so I gave him a present. He looked cheerful, and I then told him to make it his business that I was never to be attacked or molested. I showed him my revolver, and said, "I will shoot the first man who comes within five yards of me or my horse." I went down twice to Damascus while Richard was away the first time, and I found all the gates of the city open and men posted with lanterns everywhere. I took an escort of four of my servants, and I told them plainly that the first man who ran away I would shoot from behind. I came back one night at eleven o'clock, and another at two o'clock in the morning, and nothing happened.

When I knew that Richard was coming back from the desert, I rode out to meet him about eight miles. I did not meet him until sunset. He said he knew a short cut to Damascus across the mountains, but we lost our way. Night came on, and we were wandering about amongst the rocks and precipices on the mountains. We could not see our hands before our faces. Our horses would not move, and we had to dismount, and grope our way, and lead them. Richard's horse was dead-beat, and mine was too fiery; and we had to wait till the moon rose, reaching home at last half dead with fatigue and hunger.

Our daily life at Damascus, when we were not engaged in any expedition or excursion, was much as follows: We rose at daybreak. Richard went down every day to his Consulate in the city at twelve o'clock, and remained there till four or five. We had two meals a day—breakfast at 11 a.m., and supper at dusk. At the breakfast any of our friends and acquaintances who liked used to drop in and join us; and immediately after our evening meal we received friends, if any came. If not, Richard used to read himself to sleep, and I did the same. Of Richard's great and many activities at Damascus, of his difficult and dangerous work, of his knowledge of Eastern character and Eastern languages, of his political and diplomatic talents, all of which made him just the man for the place, I have written elsewhere. Here I have to perform the infinitely harder task of speaking of myself. But in writing of my daily life at Damascus I must not forget that my first and best work was to interest myself in all my husband's pursuits, and to be, as far as he would allow me to be, his companion, his private secretary, and his *aide-de-camp*. Thus I saw and learnt much, not only of native life, but also of high political matters. I would only say that my days were all too short: I wish they had been six hours longer. When not helping Richard, my work consisted of looking after my house, servants, stables and horses, of doing a little gardening, of reading, writing, and studying, of trying to pick up Arabic, of receiving visits and returning them, of seeing and learning Damascus thoroughly, and looking after the poor and sick who came in my way. I often also had a gallop over the mountains and plains; or I went shooting, either on foot or on horseback. The game was very wild round Damascus, but I got a shot at red-legged partridges, wild duck, quail, snipe, and woodcock, and I seldom came home with an empty bag. The only time I ever felt lonely was during the long winter nights when Richard was away. In the summer I did not feel lonely, because I could always go and smoke a narghileh with the women at the water-side in a neighbour's garden. But in the winter it was not possible to do this. So I used to occupy myself with music or literature, or with writing these rough notes, which I or some one else will put together some day. But more often than not I sat and listened to the stillness, broken ever and anon by weird sounds outside.

So passed our life at Damascus.

CHAPTER XIII

THROUGH THE DESERT TO PALMYRA

(1870)

> Who is this that cometh up from the wilderness, leaning upon her beloved?
> *The Song of Solomon.*

> The oracles are dumb;
> No voice or hideous hum
> Runs through the archèd roof in words deceiving.
> MILTON.

RICHARD had wished ever since he came to Damascus to visit Palmyra, or Tadmor, in the wilderness. It is about one hundred and fifty miles distant in the open desert. His main reason for going there was his private wish to explore, but it was also his official duty to open up the country, now infested with hordes of wild Bedawin tribes, who attacked, robbed, and killed right and left. Several Englishmen had been to Palmyra, but always with a large escort of the tribe of El Mezráb, and Richard wanted to break through the system which this tribe had of practically levying blackmail upon travellers, which often meant as much as six thousand francs, as each man in the escort costs about £2 a head. We decided therefore to go without any Bedawin escort, to show that it could be done, and thus to throw open this most interesting part of Syria to travellers. At first a lot of people wanted to join us in the expedition; but when it came to the point they gradually sneaked away, and many of them wept and wished us good-bye, and thought it madness. Indeed, so much was said that I set out with more than a suspicion that we were marching to our deaths. But Richard wished it, and that was enough for me. He never permitted any obstacle to hinder his progress. He made up his mind to travel without the tribe of El Mezráb, and he gave me the option of going with him, and I said, as I always said, "I will follow you to the death." It was rather funny to find the excuses which people made for not going with us. One had business in Beyrout, another was ill, the third had married, and so on. So when the day of departure dawned (April 1; I had been in Damascus three months) our faithful friends dwindled down to two—the Russian Consul, and a French traveller, the Vicomte de Perrochel.

On the morning of our departure we had a very lively breakfast. As I have said, it was our custom to let our friends drop in for this meal, and on this occasion we found ourselves surrounded by every kind of Eastern figure. They evidently thought us mad—especially me. My dress was very picturesque, and I was vain enough to turn myself round and round, at their request, that they might view it, which they did with cries of admiration. It consisted of large yellow button boots and gaiters, an English riding-habit with

the long ends of the skirt tucked in to look like their
Eastern baggy trousers, an Eastern belt with revolver,
dagger, and cartridges. My hair was all tucked up
under the *tarbash*, and I wore one of the Bedawin veils
to the waist, only showing a bit of face. The veil was
of all colours, chiefly gold braid, bound by a chocolate
and gold circlet near the forehead. Richard slung over
my back and round my neck a whistle and compass, in
case of my being lost. I had brought out two first-rate
horses, both stallions, one half-bred, the other three-
quarters; they were called Salim and Harpash. An
Arab was to ride one, and lead the second when I was
riding something else. The first stallion would be good
for travelling and fighting, and the second for bolting,
if needful. I knew I had to ride erect half a day at a
stretch, which meant about fifteen or twenty miles.

We set forth with great pomp and ceremony; for
the Mushir, or Commander-in-chief, and a large cavalcade saw us out of the city, and exchanged affectionate
farewells outside the gates, evidently not expecting to
see us again. This being the first day, we made only a
three hours' march; it cleared us of Damascus and its
environs, and we camped early on the edge of the
desert. I cannot convey to you the charm of a Syrian
camp. I shall never forget my first night in the desert.
The horses were all picketed about; the men were lying
here and there in the silvery moonlight, which lit up
our tripod and kettle; and the jackals howled and
capered as they sniffed the savoury bones. People talk
of danger when surrounded by jackals, but I have
always found them most cowardly; they would run

away if a pocket-handkerchief were shaken at them. It was the prettiest thing to see them gambolling about in the moonlight; but after we had turned in a strange effect was produced when a jackal, smelling the cookery, ran up round the tent, for the shadow on the white canvas looked as large as a figure exaggerated in a magic lantern. During my first night under canvas I was awakened by hearing a pack coming—a wild, unearthly sound. I thought it was a raid of the Bedawin rushing down upon us, and that this was the war-cry; but the weird yell swept down upon us, passed, and died away in the distance. **I grew to love the** sound.

The next morning the camp began stirring at dawn. It was bitterly cold. We boiled water and made some **tea. We** hurried our dressing, saw the animals fed and watered, tents struck, things packed up, and the baggage animals loaded and sent on ahead with orders to await us at Jayrúd. We always found it better to see our camp off ahead of us, otherwise the men loitered and did not reach the night-halt in time. We started **a** little later. The way to Jayrúd was across a sandy plain, with patches of houses here and there, and a village at long intervals. A village **on** the outskirts **of** the desert means twenty or thirty huts of stones and mud, each shaped like a box, and exactly the same colour as the ground. We breakfasted in a ruined mosque. After that we started again, and came to a vast plain of white sand and rock, which lasted until we reached Jayrúd. It was about fifteen hours' ride from Damascus. A little way outside Jayrúd we were caught in **a** sand-storm, which I shall never forget.

Richard and I were both well mounted. When it came on, he made a sign in which direction I was to go. There was no time to speak, and we both galloped into the storm as hard as we could pelt. The sand and wind blinded me, and I had no idea where I was going. Once I did not see that I was riding straight at a deep pit; and though Arab horses seldom or never leap, mine cleared it with one bound. After that I was wiser, and I threw the reins on Salim's neck, for his eyes were better than mine. This continued for three hours, and at last we reached Jayrúd, where we had arranged to halt for the night.

Jayrúd is a large clean village in the middle of the salt and sandy plain. We stopped for the night with Da'as Agha, who was a border chieftain, and a somewhat wild and dangerous character, though Richard knew how to tame him. His house was large and roomy, with spacious walls and high-raftered ceilings. While we were at supper crowds of villagers collected to see us, and the courtyard and the house were filled with and surrounded by all sorts of guests from different Bedawin tribes. Camels were lying about, baggage was piled here and there, and horses were picketed in all directions; it was a thoroughly oriental picture.

An unpleasant incident happened. I had engaged a confidential man as a head servant and interpreter. He was an Arab, but he spoke French. He was an exceedingly clever, skilful man, and Richard told him off to wait on me during the journey, and to ride after me when needful. When we got to Jayrúd, as soon as I dismounted, I took Richard's horse and my own and walked them up and down to cool. As soon as my man and another came up I gave them the **reins**, saying, "After our hard ride in the sand-storm take as much care of the horses as though they were children." He answered, "Be rested, Sitti"; but an unpleasant smile came across his face, which might have warned me. I ought to have mentioned that three times since we had set out from Damascus he had ridden short across me when we were at full gallop. The first time I begged him not to do so, as it was very dangerous, and the second time I threatened him, and the third time I broke **my** hunting-whip across his face. He merely said, "All is finished," and hung back. However, I did not think anything more of it, and I went in and had my supper. While we were eating, and my back was turned, he threw the reins of my horse to a bystander, and, drawing a sword, he cut the throat of the good, useful, little horse which I had hired for him, and which he had been riding all day. I saw people running, and heard a certain amount of confusion while I was eating; but being very tired and hungry, I did not look round. Presently somebody let it out. I rose in a rage, determined to dismiss the man at once; but Richard checked me with a word, and pointed out the unwisdom of making him an open enemy, and desired me to put a good face on the matter till the end of the journey. The explanation of the little beast's conduct was this. **He** had really wanted to ride a thorough-bred horse, but it was ridden instead **by** my dragoman's brother, and his rage had been uncontrollable when he saw **the** coveted animal caracolling before him. Moreover, he had a spite against me, and he thought that if he killed his own horse I should give him a better one, by some process of oriental reasoning which I do not pretend to understand. However, he was mistaken, for I mounted him after that on the vilest old screw in the camp.

Next morning we woke early. Mules, donkeys, camels, horses, and mares were screaming and kicking, and the men running about cursing and swearing. In such a Babel it was impossible to feel drowsy. I felt very faint as we set out from Jayrúd. The salt marshes in the distance were white and glistening, and the heat spread over them in a white mist which looked like a mirage bearing fantastic ships. We breakfasted at the next village, Atneh, in a harím, the women having all gone out. It was the house of a bride, and she had hung all her new garments round the walls, as we display our wedding presents *pour encourager les autres*. When the women came back, the men retired from the harím. Atneh was the last settlement, the last water, the last human abode between Jayrúd and Karyatayn—a long distance. After this we had a lengthy desert ride in wind and rain, sleet and hail, and the ground was full of holes; but it was a splendid ride all the same. The Arabs, in their gaudy jackets, white trousers, and gold turbans, galloped about furiously, brandishing and throwing their lances, and playing the usual tricks of horsemanship—*jeríd*. We met a terrible storm of thunder and lightning, and betweenwhiles the fiery sun sent down his beams upon a parched plain. The desert ground was alternately flint, limestone, and smooth gravel; not a tree or shrub, not a human being or animal, was to be seen. The colours were yellow sand and blue sky, blue sky and yellow sand, yellow and blue for ever.

We arrived at dusk at the spot where we had told our advance guard to pitch the tents. We found everything ready, and after our horses were cared for we dined. That night for the first time we slept in our clothes, with revolvers and guns by our sides. The men took turns to keep watch, so that we might **not be** surprised by a Ghazu, a tribe of six or seven hundred Bedawin, who go out for marauding purposes. The Ghazis charge furiously, with their lances couched. If you have the pluck to stand still until they are within an inch of your nose, and ask what they want, they drop their lances; for they respect courage, **but** there is no mercy if you show the white feather. **We** meant to say to them, "We are the English and Russian Consuls travelling on business. If you touch us, there will be consequences; if you want a present, you shall have it; but you are not to shame us by taking our horses and arms, and if you insist we will fight." There was a driving wind that night, and I feared the exposure and hardship if the tents were blown down and the fire blown out, as it threatened. We could scarcely keep a lamp or candle alight. No Ghazis came.

We rose next morning in the cold, dark, misty, and freezing dawn. We had some difficulty in starting our camp; the horses were shivering, and the muleteers and camel-men objected. We had a long and lonely ride through the same desolate valley plain as yesterday, banked on either side in the distance by naked, barren mountains, and we were very thankful when the sun came out. We breakfasted at a ruined khan, and changed our horses. Then we rode on and on, seemingly for an age, with no change; not a bird nor a tree nor a sound save the clattering of our horses' hoofs. At length, when within an hour of Karyatayn, we got a little excitement. On slightly rising ground about five miles off we espied, by the aid of field-glasses, something which we discovered to be a large party of mounted Bedawin. We sounded our whistles, and our stragglers came in till we all were collected. I ought to mention here that from the time of our leaving Damascus stragglers had joined us continually from every village. Naturally the number of our camp-followers became great, until we assumed a most formidable appearance, numbering nearly eighty in all. As soon as our stragglers reached us we formed a line, and the opposite party did the same. They then galloped to meet us, and we did likewise. When within a quarter of a mile of each other we pulled up, and they pulled up. We fully expected a charge and a skirmish, so we halted in a line and consulted; they did the same. Three of us then rode out to meet them; three horsemen of their line then did likewise. They hailed us, and asked us who we were and what we wanted. We told them we were the English and Russian Consuls passing to Palmyra, and asked in our turn who they were. They replied that they were the representatives of the Shaykh of Karyatayn, and his fighting men, and that they bore invitations to us. They then jumped down from their horses and kissed my hand. We were greeted on all sides, and escorted in triumph to the village; the men riding *jeríd*—that is, firing from horseback at full speed, hanging over by one stirrup with the bridle in their mouths, quivering their long lances in the air, throwing and catching them again at full gallop, yelling and shouting their war-cries. It was a wild and picturesque scene. So we entered Karyatayn, went to the house of the Shaykh, and dispatched a note to him.

His dwelling was a big mud house, with a large reception-room, where we found a big fire. There was a separate house for the harím, which appeared numerous, and I was to sleep there in a room to myself. Before dinner, while we were enjoying the fire and sitting round the rug, a fat young Turkish officer entered with an insolent look. Thinking he had come with a message from Omar Beg, a Hungarian brigadier-general in the Turkish service who was stationed here, we saluted in the usual manner. Without returning it, he walked up, stepped across us, flung himself on our rug, leaned on his elbow, and with an impertinent leer stared in our faces all round until he met Richard's eye, which partook of something of the tiger kind, when he started and turned pale. Richard called out, "Kawwasses!" The kawwasses and two wardis ran into the room. "Remove that son of a dog." They seized him, fat and big as he was, as if he had been a rabbit; and although he kicked and screamed lustily, carried him out of the house. I saw them give him some vicious bumps against the walls as they went out of the door into the village, where they dropped him into the first pool of mud, which represented the village horse-pond. By-and-by Omar Beg came down to dine with us. We all sat round on the ground and ate of several dishes, chiefly a kid stuffed with rice and *pistachios*. After dinner we reported to Omar Beg the conduct of his *sous-officier*, and he said that we had done very well, and he was glad of the opportunity of making an example of him, for he was a bad lot; and a Turkish soldier when he is bad is bad indeed. He had committed a gross insult against us, and it is always best in the East to resent an insult at once.

Our next day was a pleasant, lazy day, during which we inspected Karyatayn at our leisure. We rested, read, and wrote, and made a few extra preparations for the march. I went to call on the wife of Omar Beg, who was the daughter of the well-known German *savant* Herr Mordtmann. She was living with her husband quite contentedly in this desolate place, in a mud hut, and her only companions were a hyena and a lynx, which slept on her bed. The hyena greeted me at the gate; and though I was not prepared for it, I innocently did the right thing. It came and sniffed at my hands, and then jumped up and put its paws on my shoulder and smelt my face. "Oh," I thought, "if it takes a bit out of my cheek, what shall I do?" But I stood as still as a statue, and tried not to breathe, looking steadily in its eyes all the while. At last it made up its mind to be friendly, jumped down, and ran before me into the house. Here I found the lynx on the divan, which sprang at me, mewed, and lashed its tail till Madame Omar came. She was a charming German lady; but her husband kept her secluded in the harím like a Moslem woman. She told me I had done quite the right thing with the hyena. If people began to scream, it took a pleasure in frightening them. I found this out a little later, for it got into Richard's room, and I found him, the Russian Consul, and the Vicomte de Perrochel all sitting on the divan with their legs well tucked under them, clutching their sticks, and looking absurdly uncomfortable at the *affreuse bête*, as the Vicomte called it.

I had had a tiring day, and was glad to go to the harím that night and turn into my little room. But, alas! no sooner had I got in there than about fifty women came to pay me a visit. By way of being gracious, I had given a pair of earrings to the head wife of the Shaykh, and that caused the most awful jealousy and quarrelling among them. I was dying to go to bed, but they went on nagging at one another, until at last a man, a husband or a brother, came of his own accord to tell them to take leave, and upon their refusing he drove them all out of the room like a flock of sheep. Fortunately I had a bolt to my door, so that I was able to shut them out. My sleep, however, was very much disturbed, for they kept on trying the doors and the shutters nearly all night. They have an intense curiosity concerning European women, and during my toilet next morning I could see fifty pairs of eyes at fifty chinks in the windows and doors. It was really very embarrassing, because I could not tell the sex of the eyes, though I imagined that they belonged to my visitors of the night before. Dressing as I did *en Amazone* seemed to afford them infinite glee; and when I arrived at the cloth nether garments of my riding-habit, they went into shrieks of laughter. However, I put a bold face on it, and sallied forth to the square of the village, where I found the rest of our party. Our horses were being led up and down by the soldiers; our camels with water in goats' skins, and our baggage beasts, our camp-followers, and our free-lances, were drawn up on one side. Omar Beg accompanied us out of the village with a troop of cavalry, and started us with forty dromedaries, each carrying two soldiers. The cavalcade looked very fine, and when Omar Beg took his leave of us we were about one hundred and sixty strong.

We had a long day's march through the desert. It was very hot. We went through a wild defile, rested, and climbed up a mountain. We then returned to the plains, and in the afternoon we saw a mirage—castles and green fields. We were late in finding our tents, and very tired. Again we did not undress, but slept with our weapons by our sides.

The next morning we set out again at 6.30. We rode towards a mountain in the distance, and defiled by a picturesque and dangerous ledge amongst craggy peaks. We had heard that the Bedawin knew of a well hereabouts, and we determined to find it. We discovered it, and so abolished the worst difficulty which travellers had to undergo in visiting Palmyra. We rested by the well, which was full of the purest water. When sitting by it, we heard guns echoing like thunder in the mountains. We thought it might mean a Bedawin attack; but probably it was a signal, and they found us too strong. They were on our track the whole time. After an hour we descended once more into the arid plain, and rode on and on. At last we descried dimly the khan which was to be our night halt. It seemed quite close, but the nearer we rode the farther it seemed. We reached it at last, a fine old pile, deserted and solitary, which looked splendid in the sunset. Our camp by moonlight will ever live in my memory: the black tents, the animals picketed, the camels resting, the Turkish soldiery seated around, and the wild men and muleteers singing and dancing.

On this night, as on all nights, I had always plenty to do. It was Richard's business to take the notes and sketches, observations and maps, and to gather all the information. I acted as his secretary and *aide-de-camp*. My other business was to take care of the stable, see that the horses were properly groomed, and look after any sick or wounded men. My duties varied according to the place in which we halted for the night. If it were near an inhabited place, Richard sat in state on his divan, and received the chiefs with narghilehs and sherbet. I saluted, and walked off with the horses, and saw that they were properly groomed and fed. Sometimes I groomed my own horse and Richard's too, if I did not feel sure that they would be properly attended to. I would then go back to my husband, sit on the divan at a respectful distance and in a respectful attitude, speak if spoken to, and accept, if invited, a little sherbet or a narghîleh. I then saluted, went again to see that the horses were properly picketed for the night, prepared my husband's supper, and returned to his tent for supper and bed; and the next day the same over again. So far as I could I made myself useful, and adapted myself to my surroundings as an Eastern woman would have done.

The next day, our eighth from leaving Damascus, we went out of camp at 6.30, and rode over the hot stony desert for five hours. Suddenly we descried a small lake, but about one hundred and fifty Bedawin were there before us. At first we thought it was a Ghazu; but we found afterwards that it was only a party of one hundred and fifty watering their animals; they could not attack us until they had time to collect their men, and mustered some six hundred strong. However, they looked "nasty"; and as our stragglers were all over the place, to attract their attention, and bring us together, I asked Richard's leave to make a display of *tir*. We put an orange on a lance-point seventy yards off. I had the first shot. By good luck I hit it, and by better luck still they did not ask for a second, which I might have missed, so that I came off with a great reputation. Everybody fired in turns, and all our people came up by degrees, until we mustered enough to fight any Ghazu, if necessary. We then formed into a single line, and rode until the remainder of the day. We approached Palmyra thus, cheering and singing warsongs; and I am sure that we must have looked very imposing.

The first sight of Palmyra is like a regiment of

cavalry drawn up in single line ; but as we got nearer gradually the ruins began to stand out one by one in the sunlight, and a grander sight I have never looked upon, so gigantic, so extensive, so desolate was this splendid city of the dead rising out of, and half buried in, a sea of sand. One felt as if one were wandering in some forgotten world.

The Shaykh of Palmyra and his people came out to greet us, and he conducted us to his house. We approached it over the massive blocks of stone that formed the pavement and by a flight of broad steps. The interior of Palmyra resembles a group of wasps' nests on a large scale, clinging to the gigantic walls of a ruined temple. The people were hideous, poor, ragged, dirty, and diseased, nearly every one of them afflicted with ophthalmia. What have the descendants of the great Zenobia done to come to this? We dined at the Shaykh's house, and had our coffee and pipes. Later we returned to our camp, which consisted of our five tents and ten for the eighty soldiers. It was picturesquely placed, close to the east of the grand colonnade of Palmyra, for the sake of being near the wells, and the animals were picketed as much as possible in the shelter, for during our sojourn there we suffered from ice and snow, sirocco, burning heat, and furious sou'westers. We had two sulphurous wells, one to bathe in, and the other to drink out of. Everybody felt a little tired, and we went to bed early. It was the first night for eight days that we had really undressed and bathed and slept, and it was such a refreshment that I did not wake for twelve hours. My journal of the following morning contains a very short notice. We were considerably refreshed, and attended to our horses and several camp wants. We lounged about till breakfast and wrote our diaries. It was scorchingly hot weather. We were here for five days, so we did not begin serious work until noon.

So many travellers have described Palmyra that it is not necessary for me to describe it again, and I suppose that everybody knows that at one time it was ruled over in the days of its splendour by Zenobia, a great queen of the East. She was an extraordinary woman, full of wisdom and heroic courage. She was conquered by the Romans after a splendid reign, and the Emperor Aurelian caused her to be led through Rome bound in fetters of gold. The city must once have been magnificent, but it was now a ruin. The chief temple was that of the Sun. The whole city was full of columns and ruined colonnades. One of the great colonnades is a mile long.

I saw something of the inner life of Palmyra, the more so because I wore a dress very much like that of a man. So attired I could go almost where I liked, and enter all the places which women are not deemed worthy to see. My chief difficulty was that my toilet always had to be performed in the dead of night. The others never appeared to make any, except in the stream, which was too public for me, and I did not wish to appear singular.

In another way my masculine garment had its drawbacks, for I always used to forget that they regarded me as a boy, and I never could remember not to go into the haríms. Once or twice I went into them, and the women ran away to hide themselves screaming and laughing at my appearance; and I remember once or twice, on being remonstrated with, pointing to my chin to plead my youth, and also my ignorance of their customs. I passed at Palmyra as Richard's son; and though it was a little awkward at first, I soon fell into my part, and remembered always to be very respectful to my father, and very silent before him and the elders. Often in my character of boy I used to run and hold Richard's stirrup as he alighted from his horse, and sat on the edge of the divan while he talked to the Shaykhs of Palmyra. I always tried to adapt myself as far as possible to the customs of the country where I found myself, and I think I may say without flattery that I had a good many capabilities for being a traveller's wife. I could ride, walk, swim, shoot, and defend myself if attacked, so that I was not dependent on my husband; and I could also make myself generally useful—that is to say, I could make the bed, arrange the tent, cook the dinner, if necessary wash the clothes by the river-side, and mend them and spread them to dry, nurse the sick, bind and dress wounds, pick up a smattering of the language, make the camp of natives respect and obey me, groom my own horse, saddle him, learn to wade him through the rivers, sleep on the ground with the saddle for a pillow, and generally to rough it and do without comforts.

We spent five days at Palmyra. The first was devoted to a general inspection of the place. The second, we visited the Temple of the Sun and the Towers of the Tombs. These latter are tall square towers, four storeys in height; and each tower contains apertures for bodies like a honeycomb. I noticed that all the carving was of the rudest and coarsest kind. There was no trace of civilization anywhere, no theatre, no forum, nothing but a barbarous idea of splendour, worked out on a colossal scale in columns and temples. The most interesting thing was the Tombs. These were characteristic of Palmyra, and lined the wild mountain-defile entrance to the city, and were dotted about on the mountain-sides. It was a City of Tombs, a City of the Dead. I was much struck too with the dirtiness of the people of Palmyra, which dirtiness results in pestilence, ophthalmia, and plagues of flies.

The third day two officers, the Shaykh of Palmyra and another, dined with us in our tents, and after dinner we strolled about the ruins by moonlight, and when we were tired we sat down in a large ring on the sand, and the soldiers and muleteers danced a sword-dance with wild cries to musical accompaniments and weird songs. I shall never forget the exceeding beauty of the ruins of Palmyra by moonlight. The following day we explored the caves, and found human bones and things, which I helped Richard to sort, much to the disgust of the Vicomte de Perrochel, who was shocked at my want of sensibility, and said that a Frenchwoman would certainly have had hysteria. We also explored the ruins, and wrote descriptions of our journey to Palmyra. We had all retired to rest, when I was aroused by hearing a roaring like that of a camel. I ran out of my tent to see what was the matter; and being guided by a noise to the servants' quarters, I found the kitchen assistant in convulsions, and the rest holding him down. It was a Syrian disease, a sort of epilepsy. They all wanted to tread on his **back, but I** would not let them **do it.** I got some hot brandy and restoratives, and gave him a good dosing between his clenched teeth. The result was he came to in an **hour** and a half, sensible, but very tipsy; but he managed to kiss my hand and thank me. The last day was Easter Sunday. **We** performed our Sunday service in one of the ruined temples, we wrote our journals, and prepared for departure on the morrow. The next day **we** left Palmyra. We should **have** done better to have remained there **fifteen** days instead **of five.** I wish we had taken ropes and ladders, planks to bridge over broken staircases, **and** a crowbar. We might then have thoroughly examined three places which **we** could not otherwise do : the Palace of the Pretty, the Palace of **the** Maiden, and **the** Palace of the Bride, **the three** best Tower Tombs.

We left camp at dawn, and a terribly hot day it was. We encamped at 8 p.m. in a mountain defile. We were all dead-beat, and so were the horses. At night I had fever, and a hurricane **of** wind and rain nearly carried our tents away. **On** the second day we rode from dawn to sunset, with the driving wind and the sand in our faces, filling eyes, ears, nose, and mouth. I felt so cold, tired, and disheartened, that as I sat in my saddle **and** rode along I cried for about **two** hours, and Richard and the others laughed at me. Whilst I was crying we saw **a** body of mounted Bedawin dodging

ARAB CAMEL-DRIVERS. [*Page* 422.

about in the mountains. So I dried my eyes, and rode on as hard as I could pelt until we reached Karyatayn at sunset; but I had to be lifted off my horse, and could not stand for some minutes.

All clamoured to rest one day at Karyatayn. We had already been riding for two days hard, and were simply done up. The muleteers mutinied, and said that their backs were broken and their beasts dead-beat. There was only one person in the camp not tired, and that was Richard, who seemed made of cast iron. He said, "You may all remain here, but I shall ride on to Damascus alone, for on Friday the English and Baghdad mails come in, and I must be at my post." All the responsibility then fell upon me, for they all said if I would remain they would be glad. But the idea of Richard riding on alone through the desert infested with Bedawin was not to be entertained by me for one moment, so I said, "On we go."

The next morning we left early. I tried at first to ride in the panniers of one of the camels; but it bumped me so unmercifully that after half an hour I begged to be let down. Camel-riding is pleasant if it is at a long trot; but a slow walk is very tedious, and I should think that a gallop would be annihilation. When I got down from my camel, I mounted my horse, and galloped after the rest, and in time got to my place behind Richard. I always rode a yard or two behind him. In the East it would not have been considered respectful for either wife or son to ride beside a husband. We got to Jayrúd at dark, and we saw hovering near us a party of Bedawin, armed and mounted; they eventually retired into the mountains. But when we got back to Damascus, we heard that all through our journey the bandits had been watching us, and would have attacked us, only they were afraid that our rifles would carry too far.

The next day was the last. We started at sunrise, and rode all day, reaching home at 8 p.m. I had not realized the beauty of Damascus until then. After all those days in the desert it seemed a veritable garden of Paradise. First of all we saw a belt of something dark lining the horizon; then we entered by degrees under the trees, the orchards, and the gardens. We smelt the water from afar like a thirsty horse; we heard its gurgling long before we came to it; we scented and saw the limes, citrons, and watermelons. We felt a mad desire to jump into the water, to eat our fill of fruit, to lie down and sleep under the delicious shade. At last we reached our door. The house seemed to me like a palace of comfort. A warm welcome greeted us on all sides; and as every one (except Richard) and all the horses were dead-beat, they all stayed with us for the night.

CHAPTER XIV

BLUDAN IN THE ANTI-LEBANON

(1870)

Come, my beloved, let us go forth into the field; let us lodge in the villages.

Let us get up early to the vineyards; let us see if the vine flourish, whether the tender grape appear, and the pomegranates bud forth: there will I give thee my loves.

The mandrakes give a smell, and at our gates are all manner of pleasant fruits, new and old, which I have laid up for thee, O my beloved.

The Song of Solomon.

DURING the next few weeks at Damascus there was an outbreak of cholera, which gave me a great deal of trouble at the time. Several people died in great agony, and I did what I could to check the outbreak. I made the peasants wash and fumigate their houses and burn the bedding, and send to me for medicine the moment a person was taken ill. Fortunately these precautions checked the spread of the disease; but along the cottages at the river-side there was also an epidemic of scarlet fever more difficult to keep within bounds. I secured the services of a kind-hearted French surgeon, who attended the patients, and I myself nursed them. I wore an outside woollen dress when attending cases, and this I hung on a tree in the garden, and never let it enter my house. I also took a bag of camphor with me to prevent infection. However, after a time I was struck down by one of those virulent, nameless illnesses peculiar to Damascus, which, if neglected, end in death, and I could not move without fainting. An instinct warned me to have a change of air, and I determined to go to Beyrout. Two hours out of Damascus I was able to rise, and at the half-way house at Buká'a I could eat, and when I arrived at Beyrout after fourteen hours' journey I felt almost well. I had three weeks' delicious sea-bathing at Beyrout; and while there we kept Her Majesty's birthday at the Consulate-General with great pomp and ceremony. We also made several little expeditions. Richard went farther afield than I did, to Tyre, Sidon, Carmel, and Juneh. I was too weak to go with him, which I regretted very much, as I would have given a great deal to have visited the grave of Lady Hester Stanhope.

On June 14 we turned our faces homewards to Damascus, and as we journeyed over the Lebanons and descended into the plain I could not help feeling the oriental charm of the scene grow upon me. Beyrout is demi-fashionable, semi-European; but Damascus is the heart of the East, and there is no taint of Europeanism about it. As I was nearing Damascus in the evening I fell in love with it. The first few weeks I had disliked it, but gradually it had grown upon me, and now it took a place in my heart from which it could never be thrust forth. I saw how lovely it was, bathed in the evening sun, and it seemed to me like home—the home that I had dreamed of in my childhood long ago. I cannot tell what worked this charm in me; but henceforth my affections and interests, my life and work, knitted and grew to that Damascus home of ours, where I would willingly have remained all my days. I knew that mine was to be the wanderer's life, and that it is fatal for the wanderer to make ties and get attached to places or things or people; but in spite of this presentiment, I greedily drank in whilst I could all the truths which the desert breathes, and learnt all I could of oriental mysteries, and set my hands to do all the good work they could find, until they were full to overflowing.

Ten days after our return to Salahíyyeh we had a severe shock of earthquake. Richard and I were sitting in an inner room, when suddenly the divan began to see-saw under us, and the wardrobe opposite to bow down to us. Fortunately no harm was done; but it was an unpleasant sensation, like being at sea in a gale of wind.

As Damascus began to be very hot about this time, we moved to our summer quarters at Bludán, about twenty-seven miles across country from Damascus in the Anti-Lebanon. It was a most beautiful spot, right up in the mountains, and comparatively cool. We threaded the alleys of Bludán, ascended steep places, and soon found ourselves beyond the village, opposite a door which opened into a garden cultivated in ridges up the mountain. In the middle stood a large barn-like limestone hall, with a covered Dutch verandah, from which there was a splendid view. This was our summer-house; it had been built by a former consul. Everybody who came to see us said, "Well, it is glorious; but the thing is to get here." It was a veritable eagle's nest.

We soon settled down and made ourselves comfortable. The large room was in the middle of the house, looking on to the verandah, which overhung the glorious view. We surrounded it with low divans, and the walls became an armoury of weapons. The rooms on either side of this large room were turned into a study for Richard, a sleeping-room, and a study and dressing-room for me. We had stabling for eight horses. There were no windows in the house, only wooden shutters to close at night. The utter solitude and the wildness of the life made it very soothing and restful.

One of my earliest experiences there was a deputation from the shaykhs and chiefs of the villages round, who brought me a present of a sheep, a most acceptable present. Often when alone at Bludán provisions ran short. I remember once sending my servants to forage for food, and they returned with an oath, saying there was nothing but "Arab's head and onions." I don't know about the Arab's head, but there was no doubt about the onions. I often used to dine off a big raw onion and an oatmeal cake, nothing better being forthcoming.

In many ways our days at Bludán were the perfection of living. We used to wake at dawn, make a cup of tea, and then sally forth accompanied by the dogs, and take long walks over the mountains with our guns in search of sport. The larger game were bears, gazelles, wolves, wild boars, and a small leopard. The small game nearer home were partridges, quail, and woodcock, with which we replenished our larder. I am fond of sport; and, though I say it, I was not a bad shot in those days. The hotter part of the day we spent indoors reading, writing, and studying Arabic. At twelve we had our first meal, which served as breakfast and luncheon, on the terrace. Sometimes in the afternoon native shaykhs or people from Beyrout and Damascus would come and visit us. When the sun became cooler, all the sick and poor within fifteen or sixteen miles round would come to be doctored and tended. The hungry, the thirsty, the ragged, the sick, and the sore filled our garden, and I used to make it my duty and pleasure to be of some little use to them. I seldom had fewer than fifteen patients a day, half of them with eye diseases, and I acquired a considerable reputation as a doctor. We used to dine at seven o'clock on the terrace. After dinner divans were spread on the housetop, and we would watch the moon lighting up Hermon whilst the after-dinner pipe was being smoked. A pianette from Damascus enabled us to have a little music. Then I would assemble the servants, read the night prayers to them, with a little bit of Scripture or of Thomas à Kempis. The last thing was to go round the premises and see that everything was right, and turn out the dogs on guard. And so to bed. Richard used to ride down into Damascus every few days to see that all was going well; so I was often left alone.

I must not linger too long over our life at Bludán. Mr. E. H. Palmer, afterwards Professor of Arabic at Cambridge, and Mr. Charles Tyrwhitt-Drake, who had done much good work in connexion with the Palestine Exploration, came to us about this time on a visit, and we made many excursions from Bludán with them, some short and some long. We used to saunter or gypsy about the country round, pitching our tents at night. I kept little reckoning of time during these excursions. We generally counted by the sun. I only know that we used to start at dawn, and with the exception of a short halt we would ride until sunset, and often until dusk, and sleep in the desert.

One of our most interesting excursions was to Ba'albak, which is far more beautiful, though smaller, than Palmyra; and it can be seen without danger—Palmyra cannot. The ruins are very beautiful. The village hangs on to the tail of the ruins—not a bad village either, but by comparison it looks like a tatter clinging to an empress's diamond-bespangled train. The scenery around is wild, rocky, and barren.

When we arrived at Ba'albak, the Governor and the chief people rode out to receive us. Our horses' hoofs soon rang under a ruined battlement, and we entered in state through the dark tunnels. Horses were neighing, sabres were clanking; it was a noisy, confusing, picturesque scene. We tented for the night in the midst of the grand court of the ruins. In the morning the ladies of the Governor's harím paid me a visit in my tent. With their blue satin and diamonds, they were the most elaborately dressed women I had seen for

BA'ALBAK. [*Page* 430.

a long time. We stayed at Ba'albak several days, and explored the ruins thoroughly. It is the ancient Heliopolis. One of the most striking things amid its rocky tombs and sepulchral caves and its Doric columns and temples was the grand old eagle, the emblem of Baal. On Sunday I heard Mass at the Maronite chapel, and returned the call of the ladies aforesaid. In the evening we dined with the Governor, who illuminated his house for us. We passed a most enjoyable evening. I spent most of the time in the harím with the ladies. They wished me to tell them a story; but as I could not recite one fluently in Arabic, the Governor allowed me as a special favour to blindfold our dragoman, and take him into the harím as an interpreter, the Governor himself being present the whole time to see that the bandage did not come off. One night Mr. Drake and I lit up the ruins with magnesium. The effect was very beautiful. It was like a gigantic transformation scene in a desert plain. Every night the jackals played round our tents in the moonlight, and made the ruins weird with strange sights and sounds.

We left Ba'albak at dawn one morning, and rode to the source of the Lebweh. The water bursts out from the ground, and divides into a dozen sparkling streams. Of all the fountains I have ever seen, there is not one so like liquid diamonds as this. We picketed our horses under a big tree, and slept for a while through the heat of the day. At 4.30 p.m., when it was cooler, we rode on again to Er Ras. When we arrived we met with a furious, rising wind. We stopped there for the night, and the next morning galloped across the plain to Buká'a. We had a long, tiring ride, finally reaching a clump of trees on a height, where we pitched our camp. The Maronite chiefs were *jeríding* in the hollow. They came to dinner with us, and I gave them a present of some cartridges, which appeared to make them very happy.

The next day we continued to ride up a steep ascent. At last we stood upon a mountain-range of crescent form, ourselves in the centre, and the two cusps to the sea. Turning to the side which we had ascended and looking below, the horizon was bounded by the Anti-Lebanon, with the plain of Buká'a and the ruins of Ba'albak beneath and far away. From this point we could see the principal heights of the Lebanon, for which we were bound, to make excursions from the Cedars. We had a painful descent for an hour and a half, when we reached the famous Cedars of Lebanon, and camped beneath them. We pitched our tents among the Cedars, under the largest trees. They are scattered over seven mounds in the form of a cross. There are five hundred and fifty-five trees, and they exude the sweetest odours. We spent a very pleasant time camping under their grateful shade.

At last the day came for our party to break up, Mr. Palmer and Mr. Tyrwhitt-Drake *en route* for England, and Richard and I to return to Bludán. So we parted.

It took Richard and myself many days to get back to our home. After parting with our friends, we resolved to visit the Patriarch, Primate of Antioch and of all the East; and escorted by a priest and the shaykh we travelled by way of a short cut and terrible descent of three hours. It was no better than a goat-path. We at last arrived at Dimán, the summer residence of the Patriarch, a conventual yet fortress-like building on an eminence, commanding a view of the whole of his jurisdiction. We were charmed with the reception which his Beatitude gave us. We were received by two bishops and endless retainers. The Patriarch, dressed in purple, sat in a long, narrow room like a covered terrace. We of the Faith knelt and kissed his hands, and the others bowed low. His Beatitude seemed delighted with Richard, and at dinner he sat at the head of the table, with me on his right and Richard on his left. We then went to see the chapel and the monks, and the view from the terrace, where we had coffee. His Beatitude gave me a number of pious things, amongst others a bit of the true Cross, which I still wear.

After we left the Patriarch's we found a dreadful road. Our horses had literally to jump from one bit of rock to another. It consisted of nothing but *débris* of rocks. The horses were dead-beat long before we had done our day's work, and we had to struggle forward on foot. Night found us still scrambling in the dark, worn out with fatigue and heat. I felt unable to go another step. At last, about nine o'clock, we saw a light, and we hoped it was our camp. We had yet some distance to go, and when we reached the light we found a wretched village of a few huts. It was so dark that we could not find our way into the shedlike dwellings. We had lost our camp altogether. At last, by dint of shouting, some men came out with a torch, and welcomed us. Tired as I was, I saw all the horses groomed, fed, watered, and tethered in a sheltered spot for the night. We were then able to eat a water-melon, and were soon sound asleep on our saddle-cloths in the open.

The next day's ride was as bad. The scenery, however, was very wild and beautiful. We breakfasted at the place we ought to have arrived at the previous night, and then we resumed our second bad day in the Kasrawán, the worst desert of Syria. The horses were tired of jumping from ledge to ledge. We passed some Arab tents, and camped for the night.

The following morning we rode to the top of Jebel Sunnin, one of the three highest points in Syria, and we had another six hours of the Kasrawán, which is called by the Syrians "The road of Gehenna." We were terribly thirsty, and at last we found a little khan, which gave us the best *leben* I ever tasted. I was so thirsty that I seemed as if I could never drink enough. I could not help laughing when, after drinking off my third big bowl, the poor woman of the khan, in spite of Arab courtesies, was obliged to utter a loud "Máshálláh!" We were still surrounded by amphitheatre-shaped mountains, with the points to the Sea of Sidon. The sunset was splendid, and the air was cool and pleasant. We debated whether to camp or to go on; but the place was so tempting that we ended by remaining, and were repaid by a charming evening.

The next day we rode quietly down the mountains. We enjoyed a grand view and a pleasant ride but it was as steep as a railway-bank; and we came at last to another little khan, where we breakfasted. The Anti-Lebanon rose on the opposite side. Miss Ellen Wilson, who had a Protestant mission at Zahleh in this district, asked us to her house, and we accepted her hospitality for the night, instead of remaining in our tents. We stayed at Miss Wilson's for a few days; and we visited and were visited by the Governor of Zahleh, the Bishop, and other dignitaries. Richard was taken with fever. I nursed him all night, and caught the complaint. We both suffered horribly, in spite of every attention on the part of our friends. Richard soon shook off his illness, but I did not; I fancied I could not get well unless I went home to Bludán.

So at sunset on August 11, after we had been at Miss Wilson's rather more than a week, our horses were made ready. I was lifted out of bed and put into a litter. We wound out of Zahleh, descended into the plain, and began to cross it. I was so sorry for the men who had to carry my litter that I begged to be allowed to ride. I told my Arab stallion Salim to be very quiet. We went at foot's pace till 1 o'clock a.m. in bright moonlight across the plain. Then we passed regular defiles, where once or twice the horses missed their footing, and struck fire out of the rocks in their struggles to hold up. At two o'clock in the morning I felt that I was going to drop out of my saddle, and cried for quarter. The tents were hastily half pitched, and we lay down on the rugs till daylight. By that time I had to repair to my litter again, but I felt so happy at coming near home that I thought I was cured.

As we neared Bludán I was carried along in the litter, and I lay so still that everybody thought that my corpse was coming home to be buried. The news spread far and wide, so I had the pleasure of hearing my own praises and the people's lamentations.

We had not long returned to Bludán before a great excitement arose. When we had been home about a fortnight, on August 26, Richard received at night by a mounted messenger two letters, one from Mr. Wright, chief Protestant missionary at Damascus, and one from the chief dragoman at the British Consulate, saying that the Christians at Damascus were in great alarm; most of them had fled from the city, or were flying, and everything pointed to a wholesale massacre. Only ten years before (in 1860) there had been the most awful slaughter of Christians at Damascus; and though it had been put down at last, the embers of hatred were still smouldering, and might at any time burst into a flame. Now it seemed there had been one of those eruptions of ill-feeling which were periodical in Damascus, resulting from so many religions, tongues, and races being mixed up together. The chief hatred was between the Moslems and the Christians, and the Jews were fond of stirring up strife between them, because they reaped the benefit of the riot and anarchy. It appeared that the slaughter day was expected on August 27—on the morrow. It had been so timed All the chief authorities were absent from Damascus, as well as the Consuls, and therefore there would be nobody to interfere and nobody to be made responsible. We only got notice on the night before, the 26th.

Richard and I made our plans and arrangements in ten minutes, and then saddled the horses and cleaned the weapons. Richard would not take me to Damascus, however, because, as he said, he intended to protect Damascus, and he wanted me to protect Bludán and Zebedani. The feeling that I had something to do took away all that remained of my fever. In the night I accompanied Richard down the mountain. He took half the men, and left me half. When we got into the plain, we shook hands like two brothers, and parted, though it might have been that we should never see one another again. There were no tears, nor any display of affection, for emotion might have cost us dear.

Richard rode into Damascus, put up his horse, and got to business. When he stated what he had heard, the local authorities affected to be surprised; but he said to them, "I must telegraph to Constantinople unless measures are taken at once." This had the desired effect, and they said, "What will you have us do?" He said, "I would have you post a guard of soldiers in every street, and order a patrol at night. Issue an order that no Jew or Christian shall leave their houses until all is quiet." These measures were taken at once, and continued for three days; not a drop of blood was shed, and the flock of frightened Christians who had fled to the mountains began to come back. In this way the massacre at Damascus was averted. But I may mention that some of the Christians who had run away in panic to Beyrout, as soon as they were safe, declared that there had been no danger whatever, and they had not been at all frightened. I grieve to say it, but the Eastern Christian is often a poor thing. But all this is to anticipate.

When I had parted from Richard in the plain, I climbed up to my eagle's nest at Bludán, the view from which commanded the country, and I felt that as long as our ammunition lasted we could defend ourselves, unless overpowered by numbers. Night was coming on, and of course I had not the slightest idea of what would happen, but feared the worst. I knew what had happened at the previous massacre of Christians at Damascus; and flying, excited stragglers dropped in, and from what they said one would have supposed that Damascus was already being deluged in blood, and that eventually crowds of Moslems would surge up to Bludán and exterminate us also. I fully expected an attack, so I collected every available weapon and all the ammunition. I had five men in the house; to each one I gave a gun, a revolver, and a bowie-knife. I put one on the roof with a pair of elephant guns carrying four-ounce balls, and a man to each of the four sides of the house, and I commanded the terrace myself. I planted the Union Jack on the flagstaff at the top of the house, and I turned my bull terriers into the garden to give notice of any approach. I locked up a little Syrian girl whom I had taken into my service, and who was terribly frightened, in the safest room; but my English maid, who was as brave as any man, I told off to supply us with provisions and make herself generally useful. I then rode down the hill to the American Mission and begged them to come up and take shelter with me, and then into the village of Bludán to tell the Christians to come up to me on the slightest sign of danger. I gave the same message to the handful of Christians at Zebedani. I rode on to the Shaykhs, and asked them how it would be if the news proved true. They told me that there would be a fight, but they also said, "They shall pass over our dead bodies before they reach you." It was a brave speech and kindly meant; but if anything had happened I should have been to the fore. I did not wish the Shaykhs to think I was afraid, or wanted their protection against their co-religionists.

When all preparations were completed, I returned to the house, and we waited and watched, and we watched and waited for three days. Nobody came, except more flying stragglers with exaggerated news. After having made all my preparations, I can hardly explain my sensations, whether they were of joy or of disappointment. The suspense and inaction were very trying. I was never destined to do anything worthy of my ancestress, Blanche Lady Arundell, who defended Wardour Castle against the Parliamentary forces.

During the three days we were in suspense a monster vulture kept hovering over our house. The people said it was a bad omen, and so I fetched my little gun, though I rather begrudged the cartridge just then; and when it was out of what they call reach, I had the good luck to bring it down. This gave them great comfort, and we hung the vulture on the top of the tallest tree.

At last at midnight on the third day a mounted messenger rode up with a letter from Richard, saying that all was well at Damascus, but that he would not be back for a week.

After this excitement life fell back into its normal course at Bludán, and the only variations were small excursions and my doctoring. *A propos* of the latter, I can tell some amusing anecdotes. Once a girl sent to me saying she had broken her leg. I had a litter constructed, hired men, and went down to see her. When I came near the place where she was, I met her walking. "How can you be walking with a broken leg?" I said. She lifted up her voice and wept; she also lifted up her petticoat and showed me a scratch on her knee that an English baby would not have cried for. Sometimes women would come and ask me for medicine to make them young again, others wished me to improve their complexions, and many wanted me to make them like Sarai of old. I gently reminded them of their ages, and said that I thought that at such a time of life no medicines or doctors could avail. "My age!" screamed one: "why, what age do you take me for?" "Well," I answered politely, "perhaps you might be sixty" (she looked seventy-five). "I am only twenty-five," she said in a very hurt tone of voice. "Well then," I said, "I must congratulate you on your early marriage, for your youngest daughter is seventeen, and she is working in my house. Anyway it is really too late to work a miracle."

On another occasion I received a very equivocal compliment. A woman came to me and begged for medicines, and described her symptoms. The doctor was with me, but she did not know him. He said in

French, "Do not give her anything but a little effervescing magnesia. I won't have anything to do with her; it is too late, and risks reputation." I did as he bade me, simply not to seem unkind. The next day she was dead. Soon afterwards a young man of about twenty came to me and said, "Ya Sitti, will you give me some of that nice white bubbling powder for my grandmother that you gave to Umm Saba the day before yesterday? She is so old, and has been in her bed these three months, and will neither recover nor die." "Oh thou wicked youth!" I answered; "begone from my house! I did but give Umm Saba a powder to calm her sickness, for it was too late to save her, and it was the will of Allah that she should die."

I will here mention again my little Syrian maid, to whom I had taken a fancy at Miss Wilson's Mission, where I first met her, and I took her into my service. She was a thorough child of Nature, quite a little wild thing, and it took me a long time to break her into domestic habits. She was about seventeen years of age, just the time of life when a girl requires careful guiding. When she first came to us, she used to say and do the queerest things. Some of them I really do not think are suited to ears polite; but here are a few.

One day, when we were sitting at work, she startled me by asking:

"Lady, why don't you put your lip out so?" pouting a very long under-lip.

"Why, O Moon?"

"Look, my lip so large. Why, all the men love her so because she pout."

"But, O Moon, my lip is not made like yours; and, besides, I never think of men."

"But do think, Lady. Look, your pretty lip all sucked under."

I know now how to place my lip, and I always remember her when I sit at work.

On another occasion, seeing my boxes full of dresses and pretty trinkets, and noticing that I wore no jewellery, and always dressed in riding-habits and waterproofs for rough excursions, and looked after the stables instead of lying on a divan and sucking a narghíleh, after the manner of Eastern women, she exclaimed:

"O Lady, Ya Sitti, my happiness, why do you not wear this lovely dress?"—a *décolletée* blue ball-dress, trimmed with tulle and roses. "I hate the black. When the Beg will come and see his wife so darling, he will be so jealous and ashamed of himself. I beg of you keep this black till you are an old woman, and instead be joyful in your happy time."

After she had been in the house a fortnight, her ideas grew a little faster; and speaking of an old sedate lady, and hoping she would do something she wished, she startled me by saying, "If she do, she do; and if she don't, go to hell!"

The girl was remarkably pretty, with black plaits of hair confined by a coloured handkerchief, a round baby face, large eyes, long lashes, small nose, and pouting lips, with white teeth, of which she was very proud: a temperament which was all sunshine or

"THE MOON," LADY BURTON'S SYRIAN MAID   [Page 442.

thunder and lightning in ten minutes. She had a nice, plump little figure, encased in a simple, tight-fitting cotton gown, which, however, showed a stomach of size totally disproportionate to her figure. Seeing this, I said gently:

"O Moon, do wear stays! When you get older, you will lose your pretty figure. You are only seventeen, and I am past thirty, and yet I have no stomach. Do let me give you some stays."

She burst into a storm of tears and indignation at being supposed to have a fault of person, which brought on a rumbling of the stomach. She pointed to it, and said:

"Hush! do you hear, Lady? She cry because she is so great."

Our kawwass having picked up a little bad language on board ship from the sailors, was in the habit of saying wicked words when angry, and the Moon imitated him. The Moon, on being told to do something one day by my English maid, rapped out a volley of fearful oaths, and my maid fled to me in horror. I was obliged to speak very seriously to the Moon, and told her that these were bad words used by the little gutter-boys in England when they had bad parents and did not know God.

Our dragoman, I regret to say, once took liberties with her. She complained to me.

"O Lady, all the men want my lip and my breast. Hanna he pulled me, and I told him, 'What you want? I am a girl of seventeen. I have to learn how I shall walk. You know the Arab girl. Not even my brother kiss me without leave. Wait till I run and tell Ya Sitti.'"

This frightened Hanna, a man like a little old walnut, with a wife and children, and he begged her not to do so. But she came and told me, and I replied:

"O Moon, the next time he does it, slap his face and scream, and I will come down and ask him what he takes my house to be. He shall get more than he reckons on."

There was a great deal of ill-feeling simmering between the Moslems and Christians all this summer, and there were many squabbles between them. Sometimes the Christians were to blame, and needlessly offended the susceptibilities of the Moslems. I was always very careful about this, and would not eat pig for fear of offending the Moslems and Jews, though we were often short of meat, and I hungered for a good rasher of bacon. I used to ride down to Zebedani, the next village to Bludán, to hear Mass, attended by only one servant, a boy of twenty. The people loved me, and my chief difficulty was to pass through the crowd that came to kiss my hand or my habit, so I might really have gone alone. I would not mention this but that our enemies misreported the facts home, and it went forth to the world that I behaved like a female tyrant, and flogged and shot the people. How this rumour arose I know not, for I never shot anybody, and the only time I flogged a man was as follows. I do not repent of it, and under similar circumstances should do the same over again.

One day I was riding alone through the village of Zebedani; as usual every one rose up and saluted me, and I was joined by several native Christians. Suddenly Hasan, a youth of about twenty-two, thrust himself before my horse, and said, "What fellows you fellahin are to salute this Christian woman! I will show you the way to treat her." This was an insult. I reined in my horse; the natives dropped on their knees, praying me not to be angry, and kissed my hands, which meant, "For Allah's sake bear it patiently! We are not strong enough to fight for you." By this time quite a crowd had collected, and I was the centre of all eyes. "What is the meaning of this?" I asked Hasan. "It means," he answered, "that I want to raise the devil to-day, and I will pull you off your horse and duck you in the water. I am a Beg, and you are a Beg. Salute me!" Salute him indeed! I did salute him, but hardly in the way he bargained for. I had only an instant to think over what I could do. I knew that to give him the slightest advantage over me would be to bring on a Consular and European row, and a Christian row too, and that if I evinced the smallest cowardice I should never be able to show my face in the village again. I had a strong English hunting-whip, and was wearing a short riding-habit. So I sprang nimbly from my saddle, and seized him by the throat, twisting his necktie tightly, and at the same time showering blows upon his head, face, and shoulders with the butt-end of my whip till he howled for mercy. My servant, who was a little way behind, heard the noise at this moment, and, seeing how I was engaged, thought that I was attacked, and flew to the rescue. Six men flung themselves upon him, and during the struggle his pistol or blunderbuss went off, and the ball whizzed past our heads to lodge in the plaster wall. It might have shot me as well as Hasan, though afterwards this fact was used against me. The native Christians all threw themselves on the ground, as they often do when there is any shooting. The brother of Hasan then dragged him howling away from me. I mounted my horse again, and rode on amid the curses of his brothers. "We will follow you," they shouted, "with sticks and stones and guns, and at night we will come in a party and burn your house, and whenever we meet an English son of a pig we will kill him." "Thank you for your warning," I said; "you may be quite sure I shall be ready for you."

I went home and waited to see if any apology would be offered, but none came. The Shaykhs came up, and the Christians told me if I allowed this insult to pass in silence they would be unable to stay in the village, they were too few. I waited, however, some time, and then wrote an account of the affair and sent it to Damascus to the Wali. The Wali, who at that time was not ill-disposed towards Richard, behaved like a gentleman. He expressed regret at the incident, and sent soldiers up to burn and sack the home of Hasan and his family, but I interceded and got them off with only a few weeks' imprisonment. The father of the youth Hasan, accompanied by about fifty of the principal people, came up to beg my pardon the morning after the insult. I, however, received them coldly, and merely said the affair had passed out of my hands. But I begged them off all the same.

There was a sequel to this story, which I may as well mention here. The following summer, when we were at Bludán, Hasan and I became great friends. One day, after doctoring him for weak eyes, I said, "What made you want to hurt me, O Hasan, last summer?" He replied, "I don't know; the devil entered my heart. I was jealous to see you always with the Shaykhs and never noticing us. But since I have got to know you I could kill myself for it." He had an excellent heart, but was apt to be carried off his head by the troubles of the times. I may mention that I reported the matter to the Consul-General, who had also received the story in another form; to wit, that I had seen a poor Arab beggar sitting at my gate, and because he did not rise and salute me I had drawn a revolver and shot him dead. This is a specimen of Turkish falsehood.

CHAPTER XV

GATHERING CLOUDS

(1870—1871)

> One who never turned his back, but marched breast forward;
> Never doubted clouds would break;
> Never dreamed, though right were worsted, wrong would triumph
> Held, we fall to rise again; are baffled, to fight better;
> Sleep, to wake!
>
> BROWNING.

IN October Richard and I left Bludán to return to our winter quarters at Salahíyyeh, Damascus. But as we were in a mood for excursions, we went by a longer and roundabout route. We had a delightful ride across the Anti-Lebanon, and then we went by way of Shtora across a mountain called Jebel Báruk, and then a long scramble of six hours led us to the village of Báruk, a Druze stronghold in a wild glen on the borders of the Druze territory. We did not find our tents; but it did not signify, as we were among friends and allies, who welcomed us. We went at once to the Shaykh's house. Richard was always friendly with the Druzes; and as they played an important part in our life at Damascus, I think that I had better give some description of them. They are a fine, brave people, very athletic. The men are tall, broad, and stalwart, with splendid black eyes, and limbs of iron. They have proud and dignified manners, and their language is full of poetry. The women are faithful wives and good mothers. They wear a long blue garment and a white veil. The whole face is hidden except one eye. I remember once asking them if it took a long time to decide which was the prettier eye, at which small joke they were much amused.

We remained for the night with the Shaykh, and had breakfast with him in the morning, and then went on to Mukhtára, which is the centre of the Lebanon Druzes. It was a most interesting ride; and whilst we were still in the barren plain a band of horsemen came out to meet us in rich Druze dress, and escorted us through a deep defile, and then up a rocky ascent to a Syrian palace, the house of the Sitt Jumblatt, which is situated in olive groves on the heights. Arrived at the house, we were cordially received by the Sitt Jumblatt—a woman who was the head of the princely family of the Lebanon Druzes—with all the gracious hospitality of the East, and with all the well-bred ease of a European *grande dame*. She took us into the reception-room, when water and scented soap were brought in carved brass ewers and basins, incense was waved before us, and we were sprinkled with rose-water, whilst an embroidered gold canopy was held over our heads to concentrate the perfume. Coffee, sweets, and sherbet were served, and then I was shown to a very luxurious room.

The following morning we spent in visiting the village schools and stables, and in listening to the Sitt's grievances, on which she waxed eloquent. At night we had a great dinner, and after dinner there were dancing and war-songs between the Druzes of the Lebanon and the Druzes of the Haurán. They also performed pantomimes and sang and recited tales of love and war until far into the night.

The next day we started early. I was sorry to leave, for the Sitt Jumblatt and I had formed a great friendship. We rode to B'teddin, the palace of the Governor of the Lebanon, where we were received with open arms. Five hundred soldiers were drawn up in a line to salute us, and the Governor, Franco Pasha, welcomed us with all his family and suite. After our reception we were invited to the divan, where we drank coffee. Whilst so engaged invisible bands struck up "God save the Queen"; it was like an electric shock to hear our national hymn in that remote place—we who had been so long in the silence of the Anti-Lebanon. We sprang to our feet, and I was so overcome that I burst into tears.

In the morning we rode back to Mukhtára, where we went to the house of the principal Druze Shaykh, and were most graciously received. I love the Druzes and their charming, courteous ways. Whilst staying here we made several excursions, and among others we ascended Mount Hermon. The Druze chiefs came from all parts to visit us.

After some days we left. Richard was to go home by a way of his own, and I was to return escorted by a Druze Shaykh. Poor Jiryus, my *sais*, walked by my side for a mile when I started, and after kissing my hand with many blessings, he threw his arms round Salim's neck and kissed his muzzle. Then he sat down on a rock and burst into tears. Richard had dismissed him for disobeying orders. My heart ached for him, and I cried too.

Shaykh Ahmad and I descended the steep mountainside, and then galloped over the plain till we came to water and some Bedawin feeding their flocks. The Shaykh gave one fine fellow a push, and roughly ordered him to hold my horse and milk his goats for me. The man refused. "What," I said very gently, "do you, a Bedawin, refuse a little hospitality to a tired and thirsty woman?" "O Lady," he replied quickly, "I will do anything for you—you speak so softly; but I won't be ordered about by this Druze fellow." I was pleased with his manliness, and he attended to my wants and waited on me hand and foot.

We camped out that night, and the night after. I was always fond of sleeping in the tent, and would never go into the house unless compelled to do so. This time, however, our tents were pitched on low ground close to the river, with burning heat by day and cold dews by night. So I got the fever, and I lay in a kind of stupor all day. The next morning I heard a great row going on outside my tent. It turned out to be the Druze Shaykh and our dragoman quarrelling. Shortly after Shaykh Ahmad came into my tent, and in a very dignified way informed me that he wished to be relieved of his duty and return home. I laughed, and refused to allow him to depart. "What, O Shaykh," said I, "will you leave a poor, lone woman to return with no escort but a dragoman"; and he immediately recanted.

Richard joined me here for a night, and then in the morning went off by another route to explore some district round about. I also did some exploring in another direction.

So we went on from day to day, camping about, or rather gypsying, in the desert among the Bedawin. I got to love it very much. I often think with regret of the strange scenes which became a second nature to me: of those dark, fierce men, in their gaudy, flowing costumes, lying about in various attitudes; of our encampments at night, the fire or the moonlight lighting them up, the divans and the pipes, the narghílehs and coffee; of their wild, mournful songs; of their war-dances; of their story-telling of love and war, which are the only themes. I got to know the Bedawin very well during that time, both men and women; and the more I knew them the better I liked them.

I remember one night, when Richard and I were in our tent, we lay down on our respective rugs, and I put out the light. Suddenly Richard called to me, "Come quick! I am stung by a scorpion." I struck a match and ran over to his rug, and looked at the place he pointed to; but there was a mere speck of blue, and I was convinced it was only a big black ant. He did not mind that, so I lay down again. Hardly had I done so when he called out, "Quick, quick, again! I know it is a scorpion." I again struck a light, ran over, plunged my hand inside his shirt near the throat, and drew it out again quickly with a scorpion hanging by its crablike claws to my finger. I shook it off and killed it; but it did not sting me, being, I suppose, unable to manage a third time. I rubbed some strong smelling salts into Richard's wounds, and I found some *raki*, which I made him drink, to keep the poison away from his heart. He then slept, and in the morning was well.

While we were gypsying about in this way we received an invitation to a Druze wedding at Arneh, near Mount Hermon. Richard went to it one way and I another. Whenever we separated, the object was to get information of both routes to our meeting-place, and thus save time and learn more. On meeting, we used to join our notes together.

The wedding was a very pretty one. The bridegroom was a boy of fifteen; and the bride, a Shaykh's daughter, was about the same age. There was a great deal of singing and dancing, and they were all dressed in their best costumes and jewellery. I was invited to the harím of the bride's house, where we had a merry time of it. Whilst we were enjoying our fun the girls blew out all our lights, and we were left in the darkness. The bride ran and threw her arms round me, for protection perhaps, and then commenced such a romping and screaming and pinching and pulling that I hardly knew where I was. It was evidently considered a great frolic. After a few minutes they lit the candles again. At last the bride, robed in an izár and veiled, mounted a horse astraddle, and went round to pay her last visit to her neighbours as a maiden. Coming back, the bride and the bridegroom met in the street, and then we all adjourned to her father's house, where there were more ceremonies and festivities. At midnight we formed a procession to take the bride to her bridegroom's house, with singing, dancing, snapping of fingers, and loud cries of "Yallah! Yallah!" which lasted till 2 a.m. Then the harím proceeded to undress the bride. We were up all night, watching and joining in different branches of festivities.

The wedding over, we returned home to Salahíyyeh by slow stages. It was a terribly hot road through the desert. I suffered with burning eyeballs and mouth parched with a feverish thirst. I know nothing to equal the delight with which one returns from the burning desert into cool shades with bubbling water. Our house seemed like a palace; and our welcome was warm. So we settled down again at Damascus.

We had a troublesome and unpleasant time during the next few months, owing to a continuation of official rows. There were people at Damascus always trying to damage us with the Government at home, and sending lying reports to the Foreign Office. They were most unscrupulous. One man, for instance, complained to the Foreign Office that I had been heard to say that I had "finished my dispatches," meaning that I had finished the work of copying Richard's. Imagine a man noting down this against a woman, and twisting it the wrong way.

I think that the first shadow on our happy life came in July of this year, 1870, when I was at Bludán. An amateur missionary came to Damascus and attempted to proselytize. Damascus was in a very bad temper just then, and it was necessary to put a stop to these proceedings, because they endangered the safety of the Christian population. Richard was obliged to give him a caution, with the result that he made the missionary an enemy, and gave him a grievance, which was reported home in due course.

Another way in which we made enemies was because Richard found it necessary to inform the Jews that he would not aid and abet them in their endeavours to extort unfair usury from the Syrians. Some of the village Shaykhs and peasantry, ignorant people as they were, were in the habit of making ruinous terms with the Jews, and the extortion was something dreadful. Moreover, certain Jewish usurers were suspected of exciting massacres between the Christians and the Moslems, because, their lives being perfectly safe, they would profit by the horrors to buy property at a nominal price. It was brought to the notice of Richard about this time that two Jewish boys, servants to Jewish masters who were British-protected subjects, had given the well-understood signal by drawing crosses on the walls. It was the signal of the massacre in 1860. He promptly investigated the matter, and took away the British protection of the masters temporarily. Certain Israelite money-lenders, who hated him because he would not wink at their sweating and extortions, saw in this an opportunity to overthrow him; so they reported to some leading Jews in England that he had tortured the boys, whom he had not, in point of fact, punished in any way beyond reproving them. The rich

Jews at home, therefore, were anxious to procure our recall, and spread it about that we were influenced by hatred of the Jews. One of them had even the unfairness to write to the Foreign Office as follows:

"I hear that the lady to whom Captain Burton is married is believed to be a bigoted Roman Catholic, and to be likely to influence him against the Jews."

In spite of woman's rights I was not allowed to answer him publicly. When I heard of it, I could not forbear sending a true statement of the facts of the case to Lord Granville, together with the following letter:

"H.B.M. CONSULATE, DAMASCUS,
"*November* 29, 1870.

"MY LORD,

"I have always understood that it is a rule amongst gentlemen never to drag a lady's name into public affairs, but I accept with pleasure the compliment which Sir —— —— pays me in treating me like a man, and the more so as it enables me to assume the privilege of writing to you an official letter, a copy of which perhaps you will cause to be transmitted to him.

"Sir —— —— has accepted the tissue of untruths forwarded by three persons, the chief money-lenders of Damascus, because they are his co-religionists. He asserts that I am a bigoted Roman Catholic, and must have influenced my husband against them. I am not so bigoted as Sir—— ——; for if three Catholics were to do one-half of what these three Jews have done, I would never rest until I had brought them to justice. I have not a prejudice in the world except against hypocrisy. Perhaps, as Damascus is divided into thirty-two religions, my husband and I are well suited to the place. We never ask anybody's religion, nor make religion our business. My husband would be quite unfitted for public life if he were to allow me to influence him in the manner described, and I should be unworthy to be any good man's wife if I were to attempt it. My religion is God's poor. There is no religious war between us and the Jews, but there is a refusal to use the name of England to aid three rich and influential Jews in acts of injustice to, and persecution of, the poor; to imprison and let them die in gaol in order to extort what they have not power to give; and to prevent foreign and fraudulent money transactions being carried on in the name of Her Majesty's Government. Also it has been necessary once or twice to prevent the Jews exciting the Moslems to slaughter, by which they have never suffered, but by which they gratify their hatred of the Christians, who are the victims. I think nobody has more respect for the Jewish religion than my husband and myself, or of the Jews, as the most ancient and once chosen people of God; but in all races some must be faulty, and these must be punished. There are three mouths from which issue all these complaints and untruths; and what one Jew will say or sign the whole body will follow without asking a question why or wherefore, nor in Damascus would their consent be asked. It is a common saying here that 'everybody says yes to them because they have money.' These three men count on the influence of men like Sir —— ——, and one or two others, and impose upon their credulity and religious zeal to get their misdeeds backed up and hidden. But will such men as these protect a fraudulent usurer because he is a Jew?

"I enclose a true statement of the case, and also some private letters, one from our chief and best missionary, which will show you something of the feeling here in our favour.

"I have the honour to be, my Lord,

"Your most obedient and humble servant,

"ISABEL BURTON.

"To the EARL GRANVILLE, etc., etc.,
"Secretary of State for Foreign Affairs."

To this I can only add : if the Shylocks of Damascus hated me, so much the more to my credit.

There were many temptations to turn us from the path of right, if we had a mind to go. Politics at Damascus were most corrupt, and bribes were freely offered to us both from all sides. They did not seem to understand our refusal of anything of the kind. It had evidently been the custom. Richard had as much as £20,000 offered him at once, and personally I had no end of temptations to accept money when I first came to Damascus. If we had taken gold and ignored wrongs, we might have feathered our nests for ever, and doubtless have retired with much honour and glory. But we would not. In this way I refused several Arab horses which I would have given worlds to accept, for I was passionately fond of Arab horses, and could not afford to buy them; but as we should have been expected to do unjust things in return, or rather to allow unjust things to be done, I refused them. I had more jewels offered me than I should have known what to do with, but refused them all; and I take some credit to myself in this matter, because I might have accepted them as gifts without any conditions, and I like diamonds as much as most women, or rather I like their value.

In November we had quite an event in Damascus— the wedding of the Wali's daughter. It was the most splendid wedding I ever beheld. It lasted five days and nights. The men celebrated it in one house, and the women in another. We mustered several hundred in all. I was among the *intimes*, and was treated *en famille*. By my side throughout was Lady Ellenborough, looking like an oriental queen, and the charming young wife of our Italian Consul, whose dress was fresh from Italy. The dresses were wonderful in richness, diamonds blazing everywhere. But one custom took my fancy: the best women wore simply a plain cashmere robe, and no ornaments, but loaded all their jewels on one or two of their slaves, who followed them, as much as to say, "If you want to see all my fine things, look behind me; it is too great a bore to carry them myself."

On the eve of the wedding there was a long procession of female relatives, and we all sat round in the large hall. Every woman in the procession bore branches of lights; and the bride was in the middle, a beautiful girl of fifteen or sixteen. Her magnificent chestnut hair swept in great tresses below her waist, and was knotted and seeded with pearls. She was dressed in red velvet, and blazed all over with precious stones. Diamond stars were also glued to her cheeks, her chin, and her forehead; and they were rather in the way of our kissing her, for they scratched our faces. She was a determined-looking girl, but she had been crying bitterly, because she did not want to be married. She sat on the divan, and received our congratulations sullenly, looking as though she would rather scream and scratch.

On the marriage morn we were up betimes. The harím had begged of me to wear an English ball-dress, that they might see what it was like. I said, "I will do what you ask, but I know that you will be shocked." "Oh no," they replied; "we are quite sure we shall be delighted." So I wore a white glacé silk skirt, a turquoise blue tunic and corsage, the whole affair looped up and trimmed with blush roses, and the same flowers in my hair. Thus arrayed I appeared before the harím. They turned me round and round, and often asked me if I were not very cold about the shoulders; if it were really true that strange men danced with us and put their arms round our waists, and if we didn't feel dreadfully ashamed, and if we really sat and ate and drank with them. I could not answer all these questions over and over again, so I said I would describe a European ball by interpreter. They hailed the idea with delight. I stood up and delivered as graphic an account as I could of my first ball at Almack's, and they greeted me at intervals with much applause.

The marriage was a simple but most touching ceremony. We were all assembled in the great hall. The Wali entered, accompanied by the women of the family; the bride advanced, weeping bitterly, and knelt and kissed her father's feet. The poor man, with emotion, raised her and clasped a girdle of diamonds round her waist, which was before ungirdled; it was part of her dower. No one could unclasp it but her husband, and this concluded the ceremony. Shortly afterwards the bride was borne in procession to the bridegroom's house, where she received the kisses and congratulations of all the women present. After about half an hour she was conducted to a private room by a female relative, and the bridegroom to the same room by a male relative. The door was shut, and the band played a joyous strain. I asked what was going to happen, and they told me that the bridegroom was allowed to raise her veil, to unclasp her belt, and to speak a few words to her in the presence of their relatives. This was the first time they had really seen one another. What an anxious moment for a Moslem woman!

Shortly after this we went on an expedition to visit the Wuld Ali, a chief who was much dreaded by those of other tribes. Richard and I rode into the encampment alone. When first the tribe saw our two dusky figures galloping across the sand in the evening, they rode out to meet us with their lances couched; but as soon as they were close enough to recognize Richard they lowered their weapons, jumped off their horses and kissed our hands, galloped in with us, and held our stirrups to alight. I need not say that we received all the hospitality of Bedawin life. Richard wanted to patch up a peace between the Wuld Ali and the Mezráb tribe, but in this he did not succeed.

We had a delightful ride when leaving one encampment for another, and several of the Bedawin accompanied us. As we mounted Richard whispered to me, "Let's show those fellows that the English can ride. They think that nobody can ride but themselves, and that nothing can beat their mares." I looked round, and saw their thorough-bred mares with their lean flanks. I did not know how it would be with our half-breds; but they were in first-rate condition, full of corn and mad with spirits. So I gave Richard my usual answer to everything he said: "All right; where you lead I will follow." As soon as the "Yallah!" was uttered for starting, we simply laid our reins on our horses' necks, and neither used spur nor whip nor spoke to them. They went as though we had long odds on our ride. We reached the camp for which we were bound an hour and a half before the Bedawin who were to have come with us. Neither we nor our horses had turned a hair. Their mares were broken down, and the men were not only blown and perspiring, but they complained bitterly that their legs were skinned. "Ya Sitti," said one, "El Shaitan himself could not follow you." "I am sorry," I replied, "but our *kaddishes* would go ; *we* wanted to ride with *you*."

When we returned from this expedition we went to Beyrout, where we spent our Christmas. We ate our Christmas dinner with the Consul-General, and his dragoman told me an astounding story about myself which was news to me, as such stories generally are. He said that, a certain Jewish usurer at Damascus had told him that, when I met his wife at the wedding of the Wali's daughter, I tore her diamonds off her head, flung them on the ground, and stamped on them, saying that they were made out of the blood of the poor. I was amused at this monstrous fabrication, but I was also annoyed. In England there may be much smoke but little fire, but in the East the smoke always tells that the fire is fierce, and one must check a lie before it has time to travel far. Knowing what certain Jews in England had reported about me before, I lost no time in putting matters to rights with the authorities, and dispatched the following letter to the Foreign Office :

"*January* 27, 1871.

" MY LORD,

"I trust you will exempt me from any wish to thrust myself into public affairs, but it is difficult for Captain Burton to notice anything in an official letter concerning his wife, neither can we expect the Damascus Jews to know the habits of gentlemen. They respect their own haríms, yet this is the second time I am mentioned discreditably in their public correspondence. In one sense it may be beneficial, as I can give you a better idea of the people Captain Burton has to deal with than official language allows of, and from which my sex absolves me.

"My offences against the Jews are as follows:

"I once said 'Not at home' to —— —— because I heard that he had written unjust complaints to the Government about my husband. Later on the Wali gave a *fête* to celebrate the marriage of his daughter. I was invited to the harím during the whole feast, which lasted five days and nights. The Wali's harím and the others invited made, I dare say, a party of three hundred and fifty ladies. I need not say that men were not admitted; their festivities were carried on in another house. The —— harím was amongst the invited. As I supposed that they knew nothing of what was going on, I was not desirous of mortifying them by any coldness in public, and accordingly I was as cordial to them as I had always been. On the last day the wife of —— separated herself from her party, and intruded herself into the Consulesses' divan. We were all together; but there was often a gathering of the Consulesses for the sake of talking more freely in European languages, Turkish being the language spoken generally, and Arabic being almost excluded. I received her very warmly, begging her to be seated, and conversed with her; but she would talk of nothing but her husband's business. I said to her, 'Pray do not let us discuss this now; it is not the time and place in public, where all can hear us.' She replied, 'I want to talk of this and nothing else. I came for that only.' I said, 'You are a good woman, and I like you, and do not want to quarrel with you. Why speak of it? We are two women. What do we know of business? Leave it for our husbands.' She replied, 'I know business very well, and so do you. I will speak of it.' I then said, 'If you do, I fear I shall say something unpleasant.' She replied, 'I do not mind that, and I will come and see you.' I said, 'Pray do; I shall be delighted.' And so we shook hands and parted.

"Six weeks after I came to Beyrout, and found that it was popularly reported by the Jews that I had torn Madame ——'s diamonds from her hair on this occasion, thrown them on the ground, and stamped upon them. —— —— arrived soon after me; and hearing from some mutual friends that this report had reached me, he came to see me, and told me that it had been invented by his enemies. I replied that I thought it very likely, and that he need not mind. He then told me that his family, and his wife in particular, were very fond of me, and that she had recounted our interview at the wedding to him just as above, and as a proof of their friendly feelings they were coming to see me to invite me to a *soirée*.

" With many regrets for trespassing so long on your valuable time,

" I am, my Lord,

" Your faithful and obedient servant,

" ISABEL BURTON.

" The EARL GRANVILLE,
    " Secretary of State for Foreign Affairs."

A gentleman, Mr. Kennedy, from the Foreign Office at home, was staying at the Consul-General's at Beyrout, so we thought it right to invite him to Damascus, and he accepted our invitation a few weeks later.

As this was an official visit we made every preparation. I met him at Shtora, the half-way house between Beyrout and Damascus, and travelled with him in the diligence. At the last station we found the Wali's carriage and a troop of soldiers as a guard of honour, and we then journeyed in it to our house. The next morning Mr. Kennedy visited the Consulate, and apparently found everything straightforward and satisfactory, and he paid official calls with Richard. During the next few days I showed him most of the sights of Damascus, and one evening I gave a large *soirée* in his honour. Mr. Kennedy was fain to own that in its way it was unique. He had never seen a party like the one I was able to assemble. We had thirty-six different races and creeds and tongues: grey-bearded Moslems, fierce-looking Druzes, a rough Kurdish chief, a Bedawin shaykh, a few sleek Jewish usurers, every one of the fourteen castes of Christians, the Protestant missionaries, and all the Consuls and their staffs; in fact, everything appertaining to public life and local authority, culminating in the various Church dignitaries, bishops, and patriarchs. The triple-roomed hall, with fountains in the middle, lighted with coloured lamps; the bubbling of the water in the garden; the sad, weird music in the distance; the striking costumes; the hum of the narghílehs; the guttural sound of the conversation; the kawwasses in green, red, blue, and gold, gliding about with trays of sherbet, sweets, and coffee,—all combined to make the quaintest scene.

I should like to mention an anecdote here. In the garden next to ours there was a large wooden door, which swung always on its hinges. It made such a noise that it kept Mr. Kennedy awake at night. The garden belonged to an old woman, and I asked her to have her gate fastened. She sent back an answer that she could not, as it had been broken for years, and she had not the money to spare to mend it. So I took the law into my own hands. The next night Mr. Kennedy slept well. At breakfast he remarked the circumstance, and asked how I had managed about the door. "If you look out of the window," I answered, "you will see it in the courtyard. I sent two kawwasses yesterday to pull it down at sunset." He put on that long official face, with which all who are in the service of Her Majesty's Government are familiar, and said, "Oh, but you must really not treat people like that. Supposing they knew of these things at home?" "Suppose they did!" I said, laughing. I had ordered that, after Mr. Kennedy's departure that day, the gate was to be replaced and mended at my expense. The next time the old woman saw me she ran out exclaiming, "O thou light of my eyes, thou sunbeam, come and sit a little by the brook in my garden, and honour me by drinking coffee; and Allah grant that thou mayest break something else of mine, and live for ever; and may Allah send back the great English Pasha to thy house to bring me more good luck!" However, the " great English Pasha " did not return, for that evening a mounted escort with torches and the Wali's carriage came to convey him and myself to the *gare* of the diligence, and we reached Beyrout that evening.

Nothing of importance happened at Damascus during the next few months. It was a terribly cold winter. We were pleasantly surprised by the arrival of Lord Stafford and Mr. Mitford, to whom we showed the sights. We had a few other visitors; but on the whole it was a sad winter, for there was famine in the land. The Jewish usurers had bought up wheat and corn cheap, and they sold grain very dear; it was practically locked up in the face of the starving, dying multitude. It was terrible to see the crowds hanging round the bakers' shops and yearning for bread. I used to save all the money I could—alas that I could not save more!—and telling a kawwass and man to accompany me with trays, I used to order a couple of sovereigns' worth of bread, and distribute it in the most destitute part of our suburb. I never saw anything like the ravenous, hungry people. They would tear the trays down, and drag the bread from one another's mouths. I have sat by crying because I felt it mockery to bring so little; yet had I sold everything we possessed, I could not have appeased the hunger of our village for a single day. I wondered how those men who literally murdered the poor, who kept the granaries full, and saw unmoved the vitals of the multitude quivering for want, could have borne the sight! Surely it will be more tolerable for the cities of the Plain in the day of judgment than for them.

CHAPTER XVI

JERUSALEM AND THE HOLY LAND

(1871)

> Thy servants take pleasure in her stones, and favour the dust thereof.
> PSALM cii. 14.

IT had long been our desire to visit Palestine and the Holy Land thoroughly, and so in March, 1871, we determined to set out. Richard wished me to go by sea and meet him at Jerusalem, as he was going by land with Mr. Drake, who had now returned from England; so I travelled across to Beyrout, with the intention of going from there by sea to Jaffa at once. But when I reached the harbour of Beyrout there was such a rough sea that I judged it better to wait for another steamer. So I put up at the hotel at Beyrout, where I made my first acquaintance with Cook's tourists. They swarmed like locusts over the town, in number about one hundred and eighty; and the natives said of them, "These are not travellers; these are Cookii." Certainly they were a menagerie of curious human bipeds. I lunched and dined with them every day at the *table d'hôte*, and mingled with them as freely as possible, for they interested me greatly, and I used to try and classify them much as an entomologist would classify his beetles and insects. One lady of forbidding appearance was known as "the Sphinx." When on an expedition, it was the custom to call the "Cookii" at 5 a.m., and strike the tents at six. It appears that her bower falling at the stroke of six disclosed the poor thing in a light toilet, whence issued a serious quarrel. She wore an enormous, brown, mushroom hat, like a little table, decorated all over with bunches of brown ribbon. Then there was a rich vulgarian, who had inveigled a poor gentleman into being his travelling companion, in return for his expenses. And didn't he let us know it! This was his line of conversation at the dinner table: "You want wine, indeed! I dare say. Who brought you out, I should like to know? No end of expense. Who pays for the dinner? Who paid for the ticket? What do I get in return? No end of expense." And so on, and so on. I longed to drop a little caustic into Dives, but I was afraid that poor Lazarus would have had to pay for it afterwards.

I embarked on the next steamer bound for Jaffa. She was the smallest, dirtiest, and most evil smelling I have ever boarded, and that is saying a good deal. We had a horrid night, very rough, and the first-class cabin became so abominable that I joined the deck passengers, and I longed to be a drover and lie with the cattle. My little Syrian maid was with me, and she was very ill. Jaffa was a rough place for landing, but we accomplished it after some little difficulty. It is a pretty, fez-shaped town on the hillside.

We remained twenty-four hours in Jaffa, and then

rode on to Ramleh. The gardens around this town were exceedingly beautiful, groves of orange trees, citrons, and pomegranates. We soon entered the Plain of Sharon. The whole road was green and pretty. The country was a beautiful carpet of wild flowers. We reached Ramleh early, and I went at once to the Franciscan Monastery. The monk who acted as porter received me very stiffly at first, until he knew all about me, and then he became very expansive. They put my Syrian girl and me into a clean bedroom with embroidered muslin curtains and chintz tops. At night the monastery was full, and we were served by the monks. When I saw the company assembled in the refectory at supper, I did not wonder at the porter receiving me with such caution. They snorted and grunted and spat and used their forks for strange purposes. If I had not been so hungry, I could not have eaten a bit, though I am pretty well seasoned through living with all kinds of people.

We started early next morning in delightful weather, and I was highly excited by our near approach to Jerusalem. There were several other travellers along the road, all bound for the Holy City. We occupied seven and a half hours on the journey. We passed two *cafés* on the road, impromptu donkey sheds, where we found good Turkish coffee and narghîlehs; and there were shady orange groves, and fields of marigolds, poppies, and suchlike. At last I reached the crest of the hill, and beheld Jerusalem beneath me. I reined in my horse, and with my face towards the Sepulchre gazed down upon the city of my longing eyes with silent emotion and prayer.

Every Christian bared his head ; every Moslem and Jew saluted. We rode towards the Jaffa Gate, outside of which were stalls of horses and donkeys, and a motley crowd, including lines of hideous-looking lepers. I went to the Damascus Hotel, a comfortable and very quiet hostel, with no tourists or trippers, of which I was glad, for I had come on a devotional pilgrimage. In the evening I was able to sit on the terrace and realize the dream of my life. The sun was setting on the Mount of Olives, where our Saviour's feet last touched the earth ; the Mosque of Omar glittered its rosy farewell ; the Arch of Ecce Homo lay beneath ; the Cross of the Sepulchre caught the ruddy glow ; out beyond were the Mountains of Moab, purple and red in the dying day ; and between me and them, deep down I knew, lay the Dead Sea.

My reverie was awakened by the arrival of Richard with the horses and the *sais* and Habíb. Charles Tyrwhitt-Drake was with him.

The next morning we were out early. First we rode to see the Stone of Colloquy on the road to Bethany, so called because it is believed that, when Martha came to tell Jesus that her brother Lazarus was dead, the Saviour sat upon this stone whilst He conversed with her. It is a little table of rock about a yard long. We then went over a jagged country to Bethany, a short hour's journey from Jerusalem. Bethany is now nothing but a few huts and broken walls in a sheltered spot. We went to see the tomb of Lazarus, which is a small empty rock chamber. About forty yards to the south we were shown the supposed

MOSQUE OF OMAR, JERUSALEM.
[Page 472.

house of Martha and Mary. We passed a little field where Christ withered the tree, marked by an excavation in the rock, where there is always a fig. The way we returned to Jerusalem was that by which Jesus rode upon the ass in triumph upon Palm Sunday, down the Mount of Olives, and in at the Golden Gate of the Temple.

On the south of the American cemetery there is a little spot of desolate land, which is the site of a house where, when all was over, our Blessed Lady lived with St. John. Here she passed her last fifteen years; here she died at the age of sixty-three, and was buried near the Garden of Gethsemane. All that remains of the site of this small dwelling are some large stones, said to be the foundations. We then visited the Cœnaculum, or the room of the Last Supper. An ancient church, which is now converted into a mosque, is built on the site of the Last Supper room. It is a long hall with a groined roof, and some say that it is the actual site, built with other materials. We then visited the house of Caiaphas, and in the afternoon we sat in the English burial-ground on Mount Zion, talking and picking a flower here and there.

Charles Tyrwhitt-Drake was our dear friend and travelling companion. He was a young man full of promise for a brilliant Eastern and scientific career. He was tall, powerful, fair, manly, distinguished for athletic and field sports; his intellectual qualities, and his mastery of languages, Arabic and others, were so great that he made me wonder how at twenty-four years of age a young man could know so much. He was a thorough Englishman, the very soul of honour.

I should weary and not edify if I were to describe all we saw at Jerusalem. I have written of it more fully elsewhere,[1] and I can never hope to convey the remarkably vivid way in which it brought home to me the truth of the Gospel narrative. But I think there are two spots which I ought to describe: one is the Calvary Church, and the other is the Holy Sepulchre.

There are six holy spots on Mount Calvary. In the church itself, about four or five yards on the right hand, at the head of the staircase before you advance up the church, the black-and-white rose in the marble shows where our Saviour was stripped. Three yards farther, before an altar, a slab covers the spot where they nailed Him to the Cross; and a little farther on, at the High Altar, the Sacrifice was consummated. The High Altar is resplendent; but one wishes it were not there, for all one's interest is concentrated upon a large silver star underneath it. On hands and knees I bowed down to kiss it, for it covered the hole in the rock where the Cross, with our dying Lord upon it, was planted. I put my arm into the hole, and touched it for a blessing. On the right hand is the hole of the good thief's cross, and on the left the bad thief's, each marked by a black marble cross. The cleft in the solid rock which opened when "Jesus, crying with a loud voice, gave up the ghost," and "the earth quaked and the rocks were rent," is still visible. You can see it again

---

[1] *The Inner Life of Syria, Palestine, and the Holy Land*, by Isabel Burton, 2 vols.

below, in the deepest part of the church, where lies Adam's tomb. The surface looks as if it were oxidized with blood, and tradition says that this colour has ever remained upon it.

We will now proceed from Calvary to the Holy Sepulchre. Entering the Basilica, the vast church where the Holy Sepulchre is, we find a little chapel enclosing the grave. It stands under the centre of the great dome, which covers the whole Basilica. The Holy Sepulchre itself, all of it cut in one solid rock, consists of a little ante-chamber and an inner chamber containing a place for interment. It is carved out of the stone in the form of a trough, which had a stone slab for a covering, and it is roofed by a small arch, also cut in the rock. When St. Helena prepared for building the Basilica with the Holy Sepulchre and Calvary, she separated the room containing the sacred tomb from the mass of rock, and caused an entrance vestibule to be carved out of the remainder. Would that St. Helena had contented herself with building indestructible walls round the sacred spots and left them to Nature, marking them only with a cross and an inscription! They would thus have better satisfied the love and devotion of Christendom, than the little, ornamented chapels which one shuts one's eyes not to see, trying to realize what had once been. In the ante-chamber are two columns, and in the middle is the stone upon which the angel sat when it was rolled back from the Sepulchre. Christians of every race, tongue, and creed burn gold and silver lamps day and night before the grave, so that the chapel inside is covered with them, and priests of each form of Christian faith officiate here in turn. The exterior of the Sepulchre is also covered with gold and silver lamps, burnt by different Christians. Fifteen lamps of gold hang in a row about the grave itself. The Turks hold the keys. In going in or coming out all kneel three times and kiss the ground. After you cross the vestibule, which is dark, you crouch to pass through the low, rock-cut archway by which you enter the tomb. You kneel by the Sepulchre, which appears like a raised bench of stone; you can put your hands upon it, lean your face upon it, if you will, and think and pray.

I was in Jerusalem all through Holy Week, from Palm Sunday until Easter Day, and I attended all the services that I could attend, and so kept the week of our Lord's Passion in the Holy City. On Good Friday I went to the "Wailing-place of the Jews" by the west wall of the enclosure around the Mosque of Omar, an old remain of the Temple of Solomon, and listened to their lamentations, tears, prayers, and chants. They bewailed their city, their Temple, their departed glory, on the anniversary of the day when their crime was accomplished and Christ was crucified. The scene and the hour made me think deeply. I shall never forget either the scene in the Basilica on Holy Saturday, when the Patriarch undressed to show that he had nothing with him to produce the Greek fire, and bared his head and feet, and then, in a plain surplice, entered the Sepulchre alone. Five minutes later the "Sacred Fire" issued, and a really wonderful scene followed. All the congregation struggled to catch the first fire. They jumped on each other's heads, shoulders, and backs; they hunted each other round the church with screams of joy. They pass it to one another; they rub it over their faces, they press it to their bosoms, they put it in their hair, they pass it through their clothes, and not one of this mad crowd feels himself burnt. The fire looked to me like spirits on tow; but it never went out, and every part of the Basilica is in one minute alight with the blaze. I once believed in this fire, but it is said now to be produced in this manner: In one of the inner walls of the Sepulchre there is a sliding panel, with a place to contain a lamp, which is blessed, and for centuries the Greeks have never allowed this lamp to go out, and from it they take their "Sacred Fire." Richard was assured by educated Greeks that a lucifer box did the whole business, and that is probable; but be that so or not, there was a man-of-war waiting at Jaffa to convey the "Sacred Fire" to St. Petersburg.

It was later on in the day, after we had made an excursion to see the Convent of the Cross, that Richard, Charles Tyrwhitt-Drake, and I went off to explore the Magharat el Kotn, also called the Royal Caverns. They are enormous quarries, the entrance to which looks like a hole in the wall outside Jerusalem, not far from the Gate of Damascus. We crept in, and found ourselves lost in endless artificial caves and galleries. Richard and Mr. Drake were delighted with them; but I soon left the enthusiasts, for the caves did not interest me. I had kept Lent fasting; I had attended all the long ceremonies of Holy Week; and I was therefore very tired on this day, Holy Saturday, the more so because I had not only attended my own Church's ceremonies, but all those of every sect in Jerusalem. So I gave up exploring the caves, and sauntered away to the northernmost point of Mount Bezetha, and saw the Cave of the Prophet Jeremias. It was here that he wrote his Lamentations.

I then climbed up to a large cave somewhat to the left, above that of Jeremias, where I could look down upon Jerusalem. Here, worn out with fatigue, fasting, and over-excitement, I lay down with my head upon the stone, and slept a long sleep of two hours, during which time I dreamed a long, vivid dream. Its details in full would occupy a volume. Byron says: " Dreams in their development have breath and tears and torture and the touch of joy. They leave a weight upon our waking thoughts and look like heralds of eternity. They pass like the spirits of the past; they speak like sibyls of the future." The spirit of Jeremias might have touched the stone upon which I slept, or Baruch might have dwelt there. I dreamed for hours, and then I awoke. A goat-herd had entered the cave, and I half fancy he had shaken me, for he looked scared and said, "Pardon, Ya Sitti; I thought you were dead."

The bells of the Sepulchre were giving out their deep-tongued notes and re-echoing over the hills. I looked at my watch; it was the Ave Maria—sunset. I came back with a rush to reality; all my dream views vanished, and the castles in the air tumbled down like a pack of cards. Nothing remained of my wondrous dream, with its marvellous visions, its stately procession of emperors, kings, queens, pontiffs, and ministers—nothing remained of them all, but only my poor, humble self, private and obscure, still to toil on and pray and suffer. I had to rouse myself at once, and almost to run, so as to pass the gates before I was locked out of the city for the night. No one would have thought of looking for me in that cave. I should certainly have been reported as murdered. When I arrived home it was long past sunset, but Richard and Mr. Tyrwhitt-Drake had not returned from their visit to the Caves of Magharat el Kotn. The gates of Jerusalem were shut, and I felt seriously alarmed, lest they should have met with some accident; so before settling myself to write my dream, I ordered my horse and rode back to the Damascus Gate to propitiate the guard and to post a kawwass at the gate, that I might get into the city again. It was pitch dark; so I went down myself to the caves, which were miles long and deep, with lights and ropes. After a quarter of an hour's exploration I met them coming back, safe. As soon as we got home I locked myself in my room and wrote down the incidents of my dream.

The next morning, Easter Sunday, I was up before dawn, and had the happiness of hearing two Masses and receiving Holy Communion in the Sepulchre. I was the only person present besides the celebrant and the acolyte. During the day we walked round about Jerusalem, and visited many sacred spots.

On Easter Monday in the afternoon we rode over bad country to the Cave of St. John the Baptist, where he led the life of a hermit and prepared for his preaching. It was a small cave, and there is a bench in it cut in the stone, which served the Baptist as a bed. The priests now celebrate Mass on it.

On Easter Tuesday one of Her Majesty's men-of-war arrived at Jaffa, and a number of sailors rode up to Jerusalem in the evening, and kept high festival. It sounded strange in the solemn silence of the Holy City to hear the refrains of "We won't go home till morning" until past midnight. But a truce to sentiment; it did me good to hear their jolly English voices, so I ordered some drink for them, and sent a message to them to sing "Rule Britannia" and "God save the Queen" for me, which they did with a hearty good-will. They made the old walls ring again.

On Wednesday we went to Bethlehem. There is a monastery over the holy places where the Nativity took place. You descend a staircase into the crypt, which must have formed part of the old khan, or inn, where Mary brought forth our Lord. The centre of attraction is a large grotto, with an altar and a silver star under it, and around the star is written, "Hic de Virgine Maria Jesus Christus natus est." The manger where the animals fed is an excavation in the rock.

The next day, having exhausted the objects of interest in and about Bethlehem, we continued our travels. We rode on to Hebron, an ancient town lying in a valley surrounded by hills. The houses are old and ruinous. One cannot go out upon one's roof without all the other roofs being crowded, and cries of "Bakshísh" arise like the cackle of fowls. There is a mosque of some interest, which we explored ; but it was very disappointing that Richard, who had made the pilgrimage to Mecca, and who was considered as having a right to enter where Moslems enter, could not be admitted by the Hebronites to the cave below the mosque, the only part which was not visited by travellers. The answer was, "If we went, you should go too; but even we dare not go now. The two doors have been closed, one for seventy years, and the other for one hundred and fifty years." Speaking generally, we found Hebron a dirty, depressing place, full of lazy, idle people, and a shaykh told us that there was not a Christian in the place, as though that were something to be proud of.

On Low Sunday we left Hebron and rode back to Jerusalem, where I enjoyed several days quietly among the holy sites. While we were there we were invited by the Anglican Bishop Gobat to a *soirée*, which we enjoyed very much indeed, and we met several very interesting people, including Mr. Holman Hunt.

On April 24 we left Jerusalem. Quite a company went with us as far as Bir Ayyúb—Joab's Well. Then our friends rode back to Jerusalem; Richard and Mr. Tyrwhitt-Drake went in another direction ; and I remained alone with servants, horses, and baggage. I sent them on in advance, and turned my horse's head round to take a long, last look at the sacred walls of Jerusalem. I recited the psalm "Super flumina Babylonis illic sedimus," and then after a silent meditation I galloped after my belongings.

After half an hour's riding through orchards and grass I came to a wide defile two or three miles long, winding like a serpent, and the sides full of caves. I climbed up to some to describe them to Richard. The country was truly an abomination of desolation, nothing but naked rockery for miles and miles, with the everlasting fire of the sun raining upon it.

There was a monastery in the defile at the end, a Greek Orthodox monastery. They say that whatever woman enters the monastery dies. I had a great mind to enter it as a boy, for I was very curious to see it. However, I thought better of it, and pulled the ends of my habit out of my big boots and presented myself at the door of the monastery in my own character. The monk who played janitor eyed me sternly, and said, "We do not like women here, my daughter; we are afraid of them." "You do not look afraid, Father," I said. "Well," he answered, laughing, "it is our rule, and any woman who passes this door dies." "Will you let me risk it, Father?" I asked. "No, my daughter, no. Go in peace." And he slammed the door in a hurry, for fear that I should try. So I strolled off and perched myself on an airy crag, from which I could look down upon the monastery, and I thought that at any rate the monks liked to look at that forbidden article, woman, for about sixty of them came out to stare at me. When Richard and Charles Tyrwhitt-Drake arrived, they were admitted to the monastery, and shown over everything, which I thought very hard, and I was not greatly reconciled by being told that there was really nothing to see. We camped here for the night. The sun was still tinting the stone-coloured hills, the dark blue range of Moab, when a gong sounded through the rocks, and I saw flocks of jackals clamber up to the monastery to be fed, followed by flights of birds. The monks tame all the wild animals.

Next day we went off to the Dead Sea. We had read in guide-books that the way to it was very difficult, but we did not believe it. I wish we had, for our ride to it across the desert was terrible. The earth was reeking with heat, and was salt, sulphurous, and stony. We were nearly all day crossing the Desert of Judah, and at last our descent became so rugged and bad that our baggage mules stuck fast in the rocks and sand. We had to cut away traps and cords, and sacrifice boxes to release them. We could see the bright blue Dead Sea long before we reached it, but we had to crawl and scramble down on foot as best we could under the broiling sun. It reminded me more of a bleak and desolate Lake of Geneva than anything else. While we were waiting for the mules and baggage we tried to hide from the sun, and tied the horses to bits of rocks. Then we plunged into the sea, and had a glorious swim. You cannot sink. You make very little way in the water, and tire yourself if you try to swim fast. If a drop of the water happens to get into your eye, nose, or mouth, it is agonizing; it is so salt, hard, and bitter. Next day I felt very ill from the effects of my bath. In the first place, I was too hot to have plunged into the cold water at once; and, in the second place, I stopped in too long, because, being the only woman, and the place of disrobing being somewhat public, the others kept out of sight until I was well in the water, and when the bath was ended I had to stay in the water until Richard and Charles Tyrwhitt Drake had gone out and dressed, all the time keeping my head of course discreetly turned in the other direction, so that by the time they had finished I had been nearly an hour in the Dead Sea, and the result was I suffered from it. After bathing we dined on the borders of the sea. The colours of the water were beautiful, like the opal; and the Mountains of Moab were gorgeous in the dying light.

The next day we rode over very desolate country to Neby Musa, the so-called tomb of Moses, and we camped for the night on the banks of the Jordan. I was very feverish, weak, and ill. All the others bathed in the sacred river, but I only dipped my head in and filled three bottles to bring home for baptisms. I was most anxious to bathe in Jordan, and I cried with vexation at not being able to do so in consequence of my fever. In the cool of the following afternoon we rode to Jericho, which consists of a few huts and tents; a small part of it is surrounded by pleasant orchards. It was hard to imagine this poor patch of huts was ever a royal city of palaces, where cruel Herod ruled and luxurious Cleopatra revelled.

Next morning we rode out of the valley of the Jordan, which, fringed with verdure, winds like a green serpent through the burning plain of the desert. We encamped for the night at Bethel, where Jacob dreamed of his ladder. I felt so ill—all that Dead Sea again—

THE DEAD SEA. [Page 48.

that it was proposed that we should ride on to Náblus next day, about ten hours distant, and that we should encamp there for four or five days to let me recover.

We rode over endless stony hills, relieved by fruitful valleys. I felt very ill, and could scarcely go on; but at last we arrived at our camping ground. It was by a stream amidst olive groves and gardens outside Náblus. As this was the boundary between the Damascus and the Jerusalem consular jurisdiction, we now considered ourselves once more upon our own ground. We stayed at Náblus four days, and visited all the places of interest in it and around it, which I have not time to dwell upon now.

We left Náblus in the early morning, and after a delightful ride through groves and streams we entered Samaria, where, however, we did no more than halt for a space, but rode on to Jennin, where we camped for the night. There were several other camps at Jennin besides our own—two of Englishmen, and likewise an American and a German camp—five camps in all. We had quite a foregathering in the evening; and a glorious evening it was, with a May moon. The little white village with its mosque peeped out of the foliage of palm trees and mulberry groves.

We left early next morning, and rode to Scythopolis, where we camped.

The next morning Richard and Mr. Drake went on ahead to take some observations; I jogged on more leisurely behind, and our camp was sent on to Nazareth. Everywhere the earth was beautifully green, and carpeted with wild flowers. The air was fresh and balmy, and laden with the scents of spring. I passed the black tents of some Arabs, who gave me milk to drink. We also passed one well, where we watered the horses. It was a perfect day, but I was alone. We rode on until we came to Nain, and thence to Endor. Here we reposed under some fig trees for an hour, and were twice insulted for so doing. The district around Nazareth was very turbulent. First came some "bigwig" with a long name, who, thinking I was only an Englishwoman, told me to "get up," and said he "didn't care for consuls, nor English, nor kawwasses." A poor woman standing by begged me to go out again into the sun, and not shade myself under the figs, and thus displease this great man. You see, when I was sitting down, he thought that by my voice and face I was a woman, and as long as my servants only addressed me in coarse Arabic he bounced accordingly. But when I arose in my outraged dignity, and he saw my riding-habit tucked into my boots, he thought that I was a boy, or rather a youth; and I flourished my whip and cried, "You may not, O Shaykh, care for consuls, nor English, nor kawwasses, but I am going to make you care for something." Thereupon he jumped up as nimble as a monkey, and ran for his life. Then the villagers, thinking me the better man of the two, brought me milk for driving him away. He was soon succeeded by a fellah with half a shirt, who came out of his way to insult a stranger, and asked me by what right we sat under the shady figs; but the *sais* gave him a knock with his knobbed stick, and after that we were left in peace. Endor consists of about twenty wretched huts on the side of a hill, and the women look like descendants of the original witch. I went to a big fountain where crones were drawing water, dreadful old women, who accused me of having the Evil Eye, which made my servant very nervous. Blue eyes are always considered to be dangerous in the East. I said, "You are quite right, O ye women of Endor ; I was born with the Evil Eye" ; whereupon they became very civil, that I might not hurt them. We then descended into the plain between Endor and Nazareth, and it was so hot and close that I fell asleep on my horse for fully an hour. At last we reached the Vale of Nazareth. I was glad to ride into the camp, where I found all our former travellers. They were very hospitable, and gave me shelter until our tents were pitched. The camps were all pitched in a small plain without the town. Our camp was near the Greek Orthodox Church, and hidden from the others by a slight eminence.

At sunrise next morning a Copt wanted to enter my tent, either for stealing or some other purpose. I was still in bed, half awake, and I heard the servants tell him to go. He refused, and was very insolent. He took up stones, and threw them, and struck the men. The noise awoke me thoroughly. I got up, and watched the proceedings through the top of my tent wall. I called out to my servants to leave him alone ; but by this time they were angry, and began to beat the Copt. A little affair of this sort among the people would hardly be noticed in the usual way ; but as ill-luck would have it, the Greeks, whom it didn't concern, were coming out of church, and seeing a quarrel they joined in it and sided with the Copt. Our servants were only six, and the Greeks were one hundred and fifty. Richard and Mr. Tyrwhitt-Drake, hearing the noise, ran out of their tents half dressed to see what was the matter, and said and did everything to calm the people. They were received with a hailstorm of stones, each the size of a melon, which seemed to darken the air for several minutes. A rich and respectable Greek called out, " Kill them all ; I'll pay the blood money." Our Druze muleteer called out, "Shame ! This is the English Consul of Damascus on his own ground." Another Greek shouted, "So much the worse for him." I put on some clothes while the fighting was going on, and watched Richard. As an old soldier accustomed to fire, he stood perfectly calm, though the stones hit him right and left. Most men under such pain and provocation would have fired, but he contented himself with marking out the ringleaders, to take them afterwards. I ran out to give him two six-shot revolvers, but before I got within stone's reach he waved me back ; so I kept near enough to carry him off if he were badly wounded, and put the revolvers in my belt, meaning to have twelve lives for his if he were killed. Seeing that he could not appease the Greeks, and three of the servants were badly hurt, and one lay for dead on the ground, Richard pulled a pistol out of Habíb's belt and fired a shot into the air. I understood the signal, and flew round to the other camps and called all the English and Americans with their guns. When they saw a reinforcement of ten armed English and Americans running down to them, the cowardly crew of one hundred and fifty Greeks turned and fled. But for this timely assistance, we none of us should have been left alive. The whole affair did not last ten minutes.

We found out afterwards that the cause of the Greek ill-feeling originated with the Greek Orthodox Bishop of Nazareth, who had snatched away a synagogue and cemetery from British-protected Jews, against which arbitrary proceeding Richard had strongly protested. Richard went later in the day to report what had happened to the Turkish official, the Káim-makám, and to ask for redress, but he was unable to do anything. He had only twelve zaptíyeh (policemen), armed with canes! So we had to wait at Nazareth five days, until Richard sent to St. Jean d'Acre for soldiers. The Greeks were at first very insolent; but when they found that Richard was in earnest about having the offenders punished, they came in a body to beg pardon. The Bishop also sent to say that he deeply regretted the part he had taken. But whilst the Greeks were so occupied in our presence, they were manufacturing the most untruthful and scandalous report of the affair, which they sent to Damascus and Beyrout, to St. Jean d'Acre and to Constantinople, which was signed and sealed by the Bishop and endorsed by the Wali of Syria, who never waited or asked for one word of explanation from Richard.

The Greeks said, in their report, that we began the quarrel, and many other things absolutely false. For instance, they stated that Richard fired upon them several times when they were playing at games; that he entered the church armed to profane it, tore down the pictures, broke the lamps, and shot a priest; and that I also went forth in my nightgown, and, sword in hand, tore everything down, and jumped and shrieked upon the *débris*, and did many other unwomanly things. This report was actually signed and sealed by the Bishop and by the Wali, and forwarded, unknown to us, to Constantinople and London. Naturally Richard's few enemies at home tried to make capital out of the accident.

The whole day after the brutal attack upon us we had to do all the work of our tents and the cooking and attend to our horses ourselves. Even if we had wished to move away from Nazareth we could not have done so with four of our servants disabled and helpless. Dr. Varden and myself were entirely occupied with the suffering men. Richard and Mr. Tyrwhitt-Drake took charge of the tents and horses, and the doctor sent me a woman to help to cook, as it was necessary to prepare soup and invalid food for the wounded, who, in consequence of their injuries, suffered from fever. Richard's sword arm was injured by stones, and the sprained muscles were not thoroughly cured for two years afterwards. Besides this, we had to be prepared for a night attack of revenge. And what with the whispering of the Turkish soldiers, who had come from St. Jean d'Acre, the evident excitement prevailing in the town, and the barking of dogs, the nights were not peaceful enough to admit of sleep.

On May 10 we left Nazareth, and every one came out to see our departure. Our exit was over a steep country composed of slabs of slippery rock, but we soon got into a better district, over flowery plains, now and then varied by difficult passes and tracks. We camped for the night by the Lake of Tiberias, the Sea of Galilee. Next day we hired a boat and went round the lake. Towards night there was a glare behind the mountains, as if some town in the neighbourhood was on fire. We could not sleep in consequence of the stifling heat, and flies and mosquitoes were numerous. The day after I went off to the hot baths of Hamath, or Emmaus. They were salt and sulphuric. In the middle of the bath-house was a large marble basin, through which the water passed, with little rooms around. Here people bathed for bone-aches. The women advised me to enter cautiously. I laughed; and by way of showing them that Englishwomen were accustomed to water and were not afraid, I plunged in for a swim. But I soon repented. I felt as if I had jumped into boiling water. My skin was all burnt red, and I began to be faint. However, on leaving the bath I felt much invigorated, and lost all the fever and illness resulting from my swim in the Dead Sea.

The next morning we galloped round the northern end of the Sea of Galilee. In the afternoon we rode to Safed, where we camped for the night. Safed is a town of considerable size, and surrounded by beautiful gardens. There is a large Jewish quarter, and from the hour of our coming the Jews were all hospitality and flocked to our tents to greet us. It was very hot at Safed in the daytime; and when we left the next day we had a most trying ride across a country burnt black with the recent prairie fire. We encamped for the night in a lonely spot, which turned out to be a perfect paradise for mosquitoes, spiders, scorpions, and other pests, but a perfect hell for us. We could do nothing but wrap ourselves up completely in sheets, and walk up and down all night long by the camp-fires, while the jackals howled outside. When the morning light came, we were able to laugh at one another's faces, all swollen with bites and stings. Mine was like the face one sees in a spoon.

I need not dwell upon the next three days, because they were all exactly alike. We rode all day and camped at night until the morning of May 19 dawned. In the cool light we entered the Plain of Damascus. We halted for breakfast under a favourite fig tree, where were shade, water, and grass. We then ambled for three and a half hours over the barren plain, until at last we arrived on the borders of the green groves around Damascus. We entered our own oasis. Oh how grateful were the shade, the cool water, and the aromatic smells! One hour more and we entered our own little paradise again, and met with a cordial greeting from all. It was a happy day. I did not know it then, but our happy days at Damascus were numbered.

CHAPTER XVII

THE RECALL

(1871)

> I call to mind the parting day
> That rent our lives in twain.
> ALF LAYLAH WA LAYLAH
> (*Burton's "Arabian Nights"*).

ON returning to Damascus, Richard made the necessary explanations concerning the riot at Nazareth to the authorities, and he concluded that the "village row" was ended. I also wrote a full and accurate account of the affair to Sir Henry Elliot, our Ambassador at Constantinople (who had kindly expressed his willingness to hear from me when I had anything special to communicate), to supplement Richard's report. Sir Henry had telegraphed to know what it all meant.

As Richard had still a fortnight's leave on hand, he thought he would use it by going to return the visit of the Druzes, who had paid us many friendly visits during our two years' sojourn at Damascus, and had asked Richard to come and see them in the Haurán. He called upon the Wali before his departure, and told him of his projected visit. The Wali expressed his gladness, and said, "Go soon, or there will be no water." He also wrote to the Consul-General at Beyrout to acquaint him of his intention, and started with Mr. Tyrwhitt-Drake.

I was left behind. A few days after Richard had gone, the Wali, with whom I had always been on friendly terms, wrote me an extraordinary letter. He accused Richard of having made a political meeting with the Druze chiefs in the Haurán, and of having done great harm to the Turkish Government. I knew that he had done nothing of the kind, and so I wrote to the Wali and told him that he had been deceived, and asked him to wait until Richard came home. I pointed out to him how fond people were of inventing and circulating falsehoods to make mischief between him and the Consuls. He pretended to be satisfied. But a Turkish plot had been laid on foot of which I knew nothing. A disturbance had been purposely created between the Bedawin and the Druzes, which enabled the Turkish Government to attack the Druzes in the Haurán. The Wali let Richard go in order to accuse him of meddling. The fact was, the Wali had intended a little campaign against the Druzes, and was endeavouring, by means known only to the unspeakable Turk, to stir up sedition among them, in order to have an excuse for slaughtering them; but Richard had, unknowingly, spoiled the whole plan by counselling the Druzes to submit. It was that which made the Wali so angry, for it spoilt his plot; and he reported that Richard meddled with Turkish affairs, and agitated for his recall. I wrote again to Sir Henry Elliot, stating the true facts of the case. For, as I told our Ambassador, I heard that the "Home Government is actually contemplating pleasing a handful of bad people, headed by this Wali, by probably removing my husband from the very place for which his natural gifts and knowledge fit him," and I asked him, who knew the East, to acquaint Lord Granville how matters stood.

One day while Richard was still away, a European, who was a favourite of the Wali, asked me what day Richard would return to Damascus, and by what road. I asked why he wanted to know. "Because," he said, "my child is to be baptized, and I want him to be present." I found out the next day that the christening was fixed for the day before Richard's return, and I was asked; so that the man had not given me the true reason for wanting to know when Richard was coming back. I scented danger, and by a trusty messenger I instantly dispatched a warning to Richard to "look out for tricks." By God's blessing it was in time. Richard changed his road, and from a concealed shelter he watched the progress of a Ghazu, or armed band, beating the country, looking for some one. By whom they were sent, whom they were looking for, and for what fell purpose may be imagined.

My heart was torn with anxiety. Nevertheless I went to the christening, and kept a calm exterior. I felt a qualm when a certain Greek said to me, with a meaning, unpleasant smile, "There is a telegram or something important arrived for you." "Oh, is there?" I said coolly ; "well, I dare say I shall get it when I go home." Presently a kawwass came in, and saluted and said, "The Consul is returned, Sitti, and wants you." Making my excuses, I retired from the festivities ; and jumping on my horse, I galloped home, where I found Richard safe and sound. The telegram, which was quite unimportant, did not arrive until several hours later. Had the Ghazu fallen in with Richard, the verdict would have been, "Fallen a prey to his wild and wandering habits in the desert." But it was not God's will that he should be removed in this way.

About this time the trouble with the Shazlis also came to a head. The Shazlis were Sufis, or mystics, esoterics of El Islam, who tried to spiritualize its material portions. Richard was most interested in them, and he used to study them and their history. The mystic side of their faith especially appealed to him. He thought he saw in it a connexion between Sufiism in its highest form and Catholicism; and indeed it was so. He followed it up unofficially, disguised as a Shazli, and unknown to any mortal except myself. He used to mix with them, and passed much of his time in the Maydán at Damascus with them. Many of the Shazlis were secretly converted to Christianity in the spring of 1870. It was only natural that it should be so, for there was a link between the highest form of Sufiism and the true Catholic Church. Before long the news of these conversions leaked out, and the Wali determined to crush conversion, because it would add to European influence, of which he was already jealous, and he persecuted and imprisoned the converts. Richard endeavoured to protect them, and thus brought himself into conflict with the Wali.

Richard thought very seriously of this revival of Christianity in Syria, and wrote to the Protestant missionaries about it. He also wrote to Sir Henry Elliot and to Lord Granville on the subject, so impressed was he with its vigour and vitality. And indeed there was a remarkable revival going on below the surface. The persecutions to which the Shazlis had been subjected had caused the movement to grow with redoubled force, and the number of converts increased from day to day. Many were secretly baptized, and many more were yearning for baptism. Richard knew all this, and sympathized with the converted Shazlis heart and soul. Indeed I think he was never nearer a public profession of Catholicity than at that time. What he might have done for them, if he had had the chance, I know not; but the chance was denied him.

The next week or two went by without anything important happening. On June 25 we went by the Wali's invitation to a grand review at El Haneh, the first ever seen in Syria. Nothing could exceed the kindness and courtesy of the Wali. Indeed every one was very kind to me, the only woman present. We had fireworks and dinner, and then wild native dances, and after a pleasant drive home to Damascus in Abd el Kadir's carriage.

About this time the heat was very great; not a breath of air was stirring, night or day. We felt like the curled-up leaves of a book. Food or sleep was impossible to us. Every one who could fled from Damascus. I refused to go to summer quarters because Richard could not go too, and I would not shirk anything he had to bear. At last, however, I fell ill of fever, and Richard sent me away to Bludán.

One night, when I was sitting alone, I heard a great noise against the door. I seized the only thing handy, a big stick, and ran out. A large serpent had been attracted by a bowl of milk put on the terrace for my large white Persian cat, who was valiantly defending her milk against the snake. It raised up its long neck and hissed at me; but I hit it with my stick a foot away from its tail, which is the proper place to paralyze a snake. It tried to make away, but was unable, and then I killed it. It was two yards and a half long, and as thick as a child's arm. It had a flat head, and was of a bluish silver colour. Another night, when I went up to the housetop, a large wolf sprang over my head. I ran in for my gun, but though I was not gone an instant the wolf was out of my reach. After a few weeks Richard came up and joined me at Bludán with Charles Tyrwhitt-Drake.

During this summer we made many excursions to pleasant spots around Bludán, and we used to invite the Shaykhs and principal people to meet us. We would choose a spot near water, or near Bedawin tents, or a melon plantation; and arriving at the appointed place, we would eat and drink, make a fire, roast and prepare our coffee, and have a siesta. These impromptu picnics were very pleasant, and we always found the Bedawin charming. Those days were very pleasant ones; our lives were peaceful, useful, and happy. But suddenly there came a bolt from the blue. On August 16, 1871, the blow fell.

That morning at Bludán the horses were saddled at the door, and we were going for a ride, when a ragged messenger on foot stopped to drink at the spring, and then came up to me with a note. I saw it was for Richard, and took it into the house to him, never thinking what it contained. It was a curt letter from the Vice-Consul of Beyrout, informing Richard that, by the orders of his Consul-General, he had arrived at Damascus the previous day, and had taken charge of the Consulate.

Richard and Charles Tyrwhitt-Drake were in the saddle in five minutes, and galloped into Damascus without drawing rein. Richard would not let me go with him. A few hours later a mounted messenger came back to Bludán with these few written words: "Do not be frightened. I am recalled. Pay, pack, and follow at convenience." I was not frightened; but I shall never forget what my feelings were when I received that note. Perhaps it is best not to try to remember them.

The rest of the day I went about trying to realize what it all meant. When I went to bed that night, my mind was full of Richard, and I had one of my dreams, a terribly vivid dream. I dreamed that Something pulled me by the arm. I sat up in bed, and I could still see and feel it, and it said in a loud whisper, "Why do you lie there? Your husband wants you. Get up and go to him."

I lay down again, and tried to sleep; but again it happened, and yet again—three successive times; and big drops of sweat were on my forehead. My English maid, who slept in the room, said, "Are you walking about and talking, madam?" "No," I said; "but somebody is. Are you?" "No," she answered, "I have not stirred; but you've been talking in your sleep."

I could bear it no longer, for I believed that the Presence was real. I sprang out of bed, dressed, went to the stable, saddled my horse, and though everybody said I was mad, and wanted to thrust me back to bed again, I galloped out into the night.

I rode for five hours across country, as though it were a matter of life and death, over rock and through swamps, making for Shtora, the diligence station. I shall never forget that night's ride. Those who know the ground well will understand what it meant to tear over slippery boulders and black swamps in the darkness of the night. My little horse did it all, for I scarcely knew where I was going half the time. But no one will ever persuade me that in that ride I was alone. Another Presence was with me and beside me, and guarded my ways, lest I dashed my foot against a stone.

Three or four of my servants were frightened, and followed me afar off, but I did not know it then. At last I came in sight of Shtora, the diligence station. The half-hour's rest had expired, the travellers had taken their places, and the diligence was just about to start. But God was good to me.

Just as the coachman was about to raise his whip, he turned his head in the direction whence I was galloping. I was hot, torn, and covered with mud and dust from head to foot; but he knew me. I was too exhausted to shout, but I dropped the reins on my horse's neck, and held up both my arms as they do to stop a train. The coachman saw the signal, he pulled in his horses and took me into the diligence, and told the ostler to lead my dead-beat horse to the stable.

The diligence rumbled over the Lebanon, and reached Beyrout twenty-four hours before the steamer sailed—the steamer by which Richard was going back to England. For when once he had received his recall, he never looked behind him, nor packed up anything, but went straight away from Damascus, though it was the place where he had spent two of the happiest years of his life. As the diligence turned into Beyrout I caught sight of him, walking alone about the streets, and looking sad and serious. Not even a kawwass was sent to attend him, though this is always the usual courtesy paid a Consul in the East, nor was there any show of honour or respect. The jackals are always ready to slight the dead lion. But *I* was there, thank God; and he was so surprised and rejoiced when he greeted me that his whole face was illuminated. But he only said, "Thank you. Bon sang ne peut mentir." We had twenty-four hours to take comfort and counsel together. It was well that I was with him. Everybody called, and everybody regretted, except our Consul-General, who cut us. The French Consul-

General made us take up our abode with him for those twenty-four hours. I do not know whether Richard felt the neglect or not. I only know that I felt it terribly. Any Consul with one atom of good feeling would at least have paid his fallen colleague proper respect until he had quitted Eastern ground; but the disgrace was to himself, not to Richard.

At four o'clock the following day I went on board the steamer with Richard, and wished him good-bye, and saw the steamer off to England. On returning to the quay, I found his faithful servant Habíb, who had also followed Richard all the way, but had arrived just ten minutes too late, only in time to see the steamer go out. He flung himself down on the quay in a passion of tears.

I took the night diligence back to Damascus. In spite of the August weather it was a cold, hard, seven hours' drive over the Lebanon. I had brought nothing with me; my clothes were dry and stiff, and I was dead tired. On the road I passed our honorary dragoman. From sheer habit I called out to him, but he quickly reminded me that I had no official position now, for he turned his head the other way, and passed me by. I sent a peasant after him, but he shook his head and rode on. It was one of my reminders that "Le roi est mort." I suppose the rule extends everywhere, but perhaps the king's widow feels it most. It was not all like this though, for I shall never forget the kindness which was showered upon me by many during my last days in Syria.

In due time I arrived at the khan, or diligence

station, where I had left my horse two days previously. I slept there for two hours. Early next morning I rode to see a friend, who kindly insisted on my staying a day with her. Here Charles Tyrwhitt-Drake, a kawwass, and servant and horse met me, and escorted me back to Bludán. I arrived home ill, tired, and harassed. I was thankful to find there a woman friend who had come over to keep me company. She was as much grieved as I was myself, and we wept together.

After the insults and neglect which had been meted out to us at Beyrout, I expected in Damascus, where official position is everything, and where women are of no account, that I should be, figuratively speaking, trampled underfoot. I was mistaken. I can never describe the gratitude, affection, and respect which were showered upon me during my last days in Syria. The news of our recall spread like wildfire. All the surrounding villagers poured in. The house and gardens at Bludán were always full of people—my poor of course, but others too. Moslems flung themselves on the ground, shedding bitter tears, and tearing their beards with grief for the loss of the man whose life the Wali had the audacity to report they wished to take. They kept asking, " What have we done that your Government should take him away from us?" "Let some of us go over to your land, and kneel at the feet of your Queen, and pray that he may be sent back to us again." This thing went on for days and days, and I received from nearly all the country round little deputations of Shaykhs, who bore letters of affection or condolence or praise. I loved Syria so dearly it broke my heart to leave it, and always with me was the gnawing thought: How shall I tear the East out of my heart, and adapt myself again to the bustling, struggling, everyday life of Europe?

I lost no time in settling our affairs at Bludán. I paid all the bills, packed Richard's boxes and sent them to England, broke up our establishment at Bludán, and had all that was to accompany me transferred to Damascus.

Two nights before I left Bludán I had another dream. Again Something came to me in the night, and pulled me and whispered, "Go and look after that Bedawi boy, whose grandmother took him away when you were treating him for rheumatic fever." I was tired and miserable, and tried to sleep. I was pulled again. I remonstrated. A third time I was pulled by the wrist. "Go, go, go!" said the voice. "I will go," I answered. At dawn I rode out in the direction where I knew his tribe was encamped. After three hours I saw some black tents in the distance, but before I got to them I met an old crone with a burden covered with sacking on her back. "Is that the boy?" I asked. "Yes," she said; "he is very bad, and wanted to be taken to you, so I was bringing him." I got down from my horse, and assisted her to lay the boy on the sand. I saw that death was near; he looked so wistfully at me with his big black eyes. "Is it too late?" he whispered. "Yes, my boy, it is," I said, taking hold of his cold hand. "Would you like to see Allah?" "Yes," he said, "I should. Can I?" "Are you very sorry for the times you have been naughty and said bad words?" "Yes," he said; "if I get well, I will be better and kinder to grandmother." I parted his thick, matted hair, and, kneeling, I baptized him from the flask of water I always carried about at my side. "What is that?" asked the old woman, after a minute's silence. "It is a blessing," I answered, "and may do him good." I remained with him until he seemed to become insensible. I could not wait longer, as night was coming on; so I rode back, for I could do no good. I felt sure he would not see the sun rise.

When all my sad preparations were finished at Bludán, I bade adieu to the Anti-Lebanon with a heavy heart, and for the last time, choking with emotion, I rode down the mountain and through the Plain of Zebedani, with a very large train of followers. I had a sorrowful ride into Damascus. Just outside the city gates I met the Wali, driving in state with all his suite. He looked radiant, and saluted me with much *empressement*. I did not return his salute. However, the next time we met I had the laugh of him, for he looked very much less radiant a few days later, when the news of his own recall reached him. He fought hard to stay; and I do not wonder, for he had a splendid position. But none of Richard's enemies have ever flourished.

At Damascus I had to go through the same sad scenes, on a much larger scale, that I had gone through at Bludán. Many kind friends, native and European, came to stay about me till the last; in fact, my farewells threatened to assume the character of a demonstration. This I was most anxious to avoid. My one anxiety now was to get away as quietly as possible. I made my preparations for departure from Damascus in the same way as I had done at Bludán. I arranged to sell everything, pay all debts, and pack and dispatch to England our personal effects. I made innumerable adieux, and tried to make provision and find a happy home for every single being, man or beast, that had been dependent upon us.

Two Moslems came to me, and offered to shoot down certain official enemies of mine from behind a rock as they passed in their carriage. A Jew also came to me, and offered to put poison in their coffee. I declined both offers, which they did not seem to understand; and they said that I was threatened and in danger, but I slept in perfect security, with all the windows and doors open. My last act was to go into our little chapel, and dress it with all the pious things in my possession. When the day of the sale of our goods arrived, I could not bear to sit in the house; so I went up to the mountain behind, and gazed down on my Salahíyyeh in its sea of green, and my pearl-like Damascus and the desert sand, and watched the sunset on the mountains for the last time.

My preparations for departure necessarily took some time. But Richard having gone, I had no place, no business, at Damascus, and I felt that it would be much better taste to leave. I began to perceive that the demonstrations in our favour were growing, and threatened to become embarrassing. The Moslems were assembling in cliques at night, and were having prayers in the mosques for Richard's return. They continually thronged up to the house with tears and letters begging him to return, and I saw that my presence and my distress excited them the more.

Unfortunately I did not complete everything until September 12, which obliged me to brave the unlucky 13th. As half the town wanted to accompany me part of the road, and I was afraid that a demonstration might result, I determined to slip away quietly by night. Abd el Kadir and Lady Ellenborough were in the secret, and they accompanied me as far as the city gates, where I bade them an affectionate farewell. The parting with Lady Ellenborough affected me greatly. I was the poor thing's only woman friend. As she wrung my hand these were her last words: "Do not forget your promise if I die and we never meet again."[1] I replied, "Inshallah, I shall soon return." She rode a black thorough-bred Arab mare; and as far as I could see anything in the moonlight, her large sorrowful blue eyes, glistening with tears, haunted me.

It was thus, accompanied on my journey by Mr. Drake and two faithful dragomans, who had never deserted me, and who put themselves and all they possessed at my disposal, that I stole away from Damascus an hour before dawn.

I shall never forget that last ride across the desert. I felt my heart sink as I jogged along for weary miles, wishing mental good-byes to every dearly loved object. I had felt fever coming on for some days, but I had

[1] Lady Ellenborough referred to her biography, which she had dictated to Lady Burton—the true story of her life, which Lady Burton had promised to publish for her, to clear away misrepresentations. In consequence of difficulties which subsequently arose Lady Burton did not publish it.

determined not to be ill at Damascus. Now that I had left it, however, a reaction set in. When I reached that part of the Lebanon looking down upon the sea far above Beyrout, my fever had increased to such an extent that I became delirious, and I had to be set down on the roadside. Half an hour farther on the road was the village of my little Syrian girl, who was accompanying me back to England. I was carried to her father's house, and lay there for ten days very ill, and was nursed by her and my English maid. It was a trying time; but the whole family showed me every kindness and attention, and I had every comfort that the place could afford. Many friends, both English and native, came to visit me from Beyrout and from the villages round about. From here I wrote a long letter to Lord Derby, who had appointed us to Damascus, stating the true facts of the case, and exposing the falsehoods, so far as I knew them, which had led Lord Granville to weakly consent to our recall. I never rested till that cloud was lifted.

I went down to Beyrout as soon as I was well enough to move, and embarked in the Russian ship *Ceres*; the same ship, strange to say, that had brought me from Alexandria to Beyrout, when I first turned my face towards Damascus. As we were about to steam out an English vice-consul in the Levant gaily waved his hand to me, and cried out, "Good-bye, Mrs. Burton; I have been sixteen years in the service, and I have known twenty scoundrels go unpunished, but I never saw a consul recalled except for something disgraceful —certainly never for an Eastern pasha. You will find it is all right when you get home; they would hardly do such a thing to a man like Burton."

We arrived at Alexandria, and I went to a hotel. I dislike Alexandria very much, and was glad to get away on board of a P. & O., the *Candia*, to Southampton. It was all right as far as Malta, but after that we had some very rough weather. At last our ship sighted the lights of Portland Bill, and I knew that I was at home again. These lights at night look like two great eyes, and there is always excitement when they are first seen. All the English on board rushed on deck and cheered Hurrah! It is odd how we exiles love our country, our home, and our friends; it is curious how little they think about us.

On October 14, 1871, I landed again in Old England.

CHAPTER XVIII

THE TRUE REASONS OF BURTON'S RECALL

> No might nor greatness in mortality
> Can censure 'scape: back-wounding calumny
> The whitest virtue strikes. What king so strong,
> Can tie the gall up in the slanderous tongue?
>
> SHAKSPEARE.

AT this point of the narrative it is necessary to turn aside to deal with Miss Stisted's impeachment of Lady Burton, in the matter of her husband's recall from Damascus.

Miss Stisted asserts that the true cause of Burton's recall was Isabel his wife, who had espoused with more zeal than discretion the cause of the Shazli converts to Christianity. She adds: "And while her husband, continually absent exploring or attending to the duties of his Consulate, knew nothing, or next to nothing, about her dangerous proceedings, she impressed upon the people that she acted with his full permission and approval."[1] It was (according to Miss Stisted) Isabel's "imprudence and passion for proselytizing" which so enraged the Moslems and the Turkish authorities

---

[1] Miss Stisted's Life of Sir Richard Burton, p. 360. This book was published December, 1896, eight months after Lady Burton's death.

against Burton that they clamoured for his recall. Thus it is argued that "the true cause of the terrible crash in 1871" was Isabel, and Isabel alone.

This, in brief, is the sum and substance of Miss Stisted's indictment of Lady Burton on this point. She makes her accusation without adducing a scrap or shred of evidence in support of it, and she makes it in the teeth of the most positive evidence on the other side. Let us examine her charges in the light of facts.

Fortunately, in searching for the true reasons of Burton's recall from Damascus, I am not dependent, like Miss Stisted, on a mere opinion of my own, nor am I dependent on the testimony of Lady Burton, which, though correct in every detail, might be refused acceptance, on the plea that it was biassed. The true reasons are to be found in an official Blue Book,[1] which contains a review of the whole case. This book publishes the complete correspondence, official and otherwise, for and against Burton, and comprises a review of his Consulship at Damascus from the time he was appointed, in November, 1868, to the day of his recall, in August, 1871.

It is impossible to read this correspondence dispassionately without wondering how it was that Burton was not removed from his post at Damascus before. In the brief space of two years he seems to have managed to set against himself almost every creed, nationality, and interest in Damascus. From the time

[1] *The Case of Captain Burton, late H.B.M. Consul at Damascus.* Clayton & Co., Parliamentary Printing Works, 1872.

he went there to the day he was recalled it was little but one long strife. Complaints to his Consul-General at Beyrout, to his Ambassador at Constantinople, to his Chief at the Foreign Office, were incessant; and as they came not from one part of the community of Damascus only, but from several, it is a marvel that the authorities at the Foreign Office, who love nothing better than that things should run, or seem to run, smoothly at the embassies and consulates, were so patient and long-suffering. That they were so forbearing was, I think, largely due to his wife—this same Isabel who, according to Miss Stisted, was responsible for her husband's recall and the consequent ruin of his official career. It was Isabel who fought Burton's battles on every charge against him, and she defended him against every attack. Her letters to Lord Granville, to Sir Henry Elliot, Ambassador at Constantinople, to the Consul-General at Beyrout, to Lord Derby and other influential friends in England, and to the permanent officials at the Foreign Office, explaining and defending her husband's action in every particular, are marvels of special pleading. They are not published, because they would fill volumes; but they can be produced, if necessary.

My contention is, that Isabel had nothing to do with her husband's recall from Damascus. On the contrary, had it not been for her, he would have been recalled long before. I also submit that she had very little to do in the matter of the Shazlis, and that little she did with her husband's full consent and approval. Burton alone was responsible for his recall in that he managed to offend nearly every part of the community at Damascus, and so gave the Turkish authorities, who disliked him from the first, an excuse for demanding his recall. I do not say that he was wrong in every instance—far from it; he was often in the right; only it is possible to do the right thing in the wrong way, and this Burton generally did.

And now for the proofs. It is necessary to begin at the beginning. From the first Burton took up his work at Damascus with "pinioned arms," to use his own phrase. In other words, he started with a prejudice against him. Lord Derby (then Lord Stanley), as we know, gave him the appointment; but before it was confirmed Lord Clarnedon succeeded Lord Stanley at the Foreign Office, and in the interval Burton's enemies, chiefly Protestant missionaries, who feared he was anti-missionary, took steps to work upon Lord Clarendon to prevent his appointment going forward. So strong and influential was this opposition that Lord Clarendon sent for Burton specially, and had a long conversation with him. He told him that "very serious objections" to his appointment at Damascus had reached the Foreign Office, and, although he allowed the appointment to go forward, on receiving from Burton assurances that the objections were unfounded, he warned him that, if the feeling stated to exist against him on the part of the authorities and people at Damascus should prevent the proper performance of his Consular duties, it would be the duty of the Government immediately to recall him.

In a subsequent letter Lord Clarendon directed his Secretary to repeat to Burton what he had already told him verbally.[1]

To this letter Burton replied: "I once more undertake to act with unusual prudence, and under all circumstances to hold myself, and myself only, answerable for the consequences."[2]

Whether or not he acted with "unusual prudence" the following will show:

1. *His difference with the English missionaries.*—The first unpleasantness occurred in June and July, 1870, with the Superintendent of the British Syrian School at Beyrout. This gentleman, who was a Protestant missionary, came to Damascus to proselytize, and to distribute tracts among the Moslems, and doubtless acted with little discretion. Burton reprimanded him, and reported him to the Foreign Office. In this no doubt he was right; but his manner of doing it apparently inflamed many against him, especially the wife of the missionary aforesaid, who vigorously espoused her husband's cause, and in this was supported officially by the Consul-General at Beyrout. The matter blew over for a time, but the attack was renewed again in 1871, and there was constant friction going on the whole time of Burton's sojourn at Damascus between himself and the missionary and his wife and their friends, who were very influential persons in Syria.

---

[1] *Vide* Letter from Foreign Office to Captain Burton, June 19, 1869 (Blue Book, p. 2).

[2] Letter of Captain Burton to Foreign Office, June 21, 1869 (Blue Book, p. 2).

2. *His squabble with the Druzes.*—This occurred in 1870. Here we find Burton protecting the missionaries against certain Druzes, who had plundered and maltreated two English missionaries travelling amongst them. Burton's method of punishing the Druzes was summary. He wished to impose a fine upon them. This the Consul-General at Beyrout refused to impose, and again Burton came into conflict with his Consul-General. It was obvious that, whether the Druzes deserved to be fined or not, the man to impose the fine was not the British Consul, but the Turkish Governor-General, as they were Turkish subjects. In this matter therefore, although Burton acted with the best intentions, he exceeded his jurisdiction.

3. *His dispute with the Jews.*—This was one of the most serious affairs in which Burton was engaged; and here again, though there is no doubt that he was perfectly right in what he did, his manner of doing it gave dire offence. He curbed the rapacity of some Jewish money-lenders, under British protection, who wished to "sweat" the native peasantry for the payment of their unjust debts, and desired the British Consul to help them in their extortions. This Burton rightly refused to do. And a little later he arrested two Jewish boys, servants of British-protected Jews, for drawing crosses on the walls—the usual sign for an outbreak of Christian persecution at Damascus—and took away temporarily the British protection from their masters. This gave the usurers the opportunity they had been waiting for, and they wrote to the

Foreign Office an untrue and unjust report, saying that the Consul was full of hatred against the Jews, and demanding his recall. Lord Granville sent a special letter, requesting to know the truth of these charges, which he described as "most serious." Fortunately Burton was able to satisfy him, and the storm blew over. But the Jews neither forgot it nor forgave him.

4. *The Greeks stone him at Nazareth.*—Lady Burton has already given a long account of this incident, and there is no reason to doubt the correctness of her description. Here we find that the Greek Bishop and his people disliked Burton because he had exposed a fraudulent transaction of theirs with the Jews. But whatever was the cause, there was no doubt that they were opposed to him; and the riot, which arose from an apparently accidental cause, was really an outbreak of bitterly hostile feeling against the British Consul. The Greek Bishop of Nazareth at once drew up a grossly exaggerated report of the proceedings, which was endorsed by the Wali of Syria, and forwarded to the authorities at home. Will it be believed that Burton never sent home any report of the affair until some weeks afterwards, when he returned to Damascus, and found a telegram awaiting him from the British Ambassador at Constantinople, asking what it all meant? His silence in this matter, though not intentional, created the very worst impression among the authorities at home. Sir Henry Elliot wrote to Isabel subsequently:

"I received versions of the affair from different quarters, without having a word of explanation from

Captain Burton, from whom I got letters of a date much subsequent to the occurrence."[1]

Considering how very fond Burton was of referring all sorts of questions on the internal government of Syria, with which he had nothing to do, to his Ambassador at Constantinople, his silence on this occasion, in a matter with which he had all to do, was, to say the least, somewhat unfortunate.

5. *His dispute with the Wali.*—The Wali (the Turkish Governor-General of Syria) was, from the first, exceedingly jealous of Burton, because of his knowledge of Eastern affairs, and his habit of interfering with the internal government of the country, with which he had no concern. Corrupt though Turkish rule undoubtedly was, and is, it was no part of the British Consul's duty to be perpetually meddling in disputes between the Wali and his subjects. Sir Henry Elliot wrote to Isabel, in reply to a letter of hers excusing her husband:

"I should not be frank if I allowed you to suppose that your letters had satisfied me that there were not grounds for the complaints which have been made of Captain Burton going beyond the proper attributions of a Consul, who ought to be very careful to avoid encroaching upon the domain of the legitimate authorities, who are responsible for the administration of their district, which he is not. He can be of great service as long as there is a proper understanding with the Government, but a very dangerous state of things is created if he makes himself a rival authority

[1] Letter from Sir Henry Elliot to Lady Burton, July 12, 1871.

to whom the disaffected think that they can look for redress."[1]

This (there is no doubt about it) Burton was always doing; and his knowledge of oriental affairs and methods made him all the more formidable to the Wali. Matters came to a head when Burton went to visit the Druzes in the Haurán, a month or two before his recall. By some means or other he spoiled the Wali's game in that quarter; and this incensed the Governor so much against him that he tried first to have him assassinated in the desert, and that failing, demanded his recall. Of this incident Burton himself says:

"I was not aware that the Wali (Governor-General) had a political move in the Haurán which he did not wish me to see, or that, seeing, it was the signal for him to try and obtain my recall."[2]

If this matter had stood alone, perhaps it would not have been sufficient ground for his recall; but coming as it did on the top of all the others, it was, I think, the most potent factor.

There was another little annoyance too about this time—that is, just before Burton's recall. It had reference to the case of one Hasan, a Moslem converted to Christianity, whom the Wali wanted to punish, but whom Burton protected against him. Burton's action in this matter was chivalrous and generous no doubt, but it did not tend to make him any better friends with the Wali at a time when the irritation between them was already at its

[1] Letter from Sir Henry Elliot to Lady Burton, July 12, 1871.
[2] Blue Book, p. 75.

height. With regard to what followed, I think that I had better give Burton's own words, as they will show very distinctly what were the culminating causes of his recall :

"He (the Wali) actually succeeded in causing the Foreign Office to confine me to Damascus at a time when the climate was peculiarly hot and unwholesome —mid-July. I was suffering from fever, and the little English colony was all in summer quarters. He affected to look upon a trip to the Haurán as an event pregnant with evil to his administration, and actually composed a circular from me to the Druzes. I was compelled, in return, to make known Rashid Pasha's maladministration of Syria, his prostitution of rank, his filling every post with his own sycophants, who are removed only when they have made money enough to pay for being restored; his fatuous elevation of a Kurdish party; his perjuries against the Druzes; his persistent persecution of Moslem converts to Christianity in the teeth of treaties and firmans; his own sympathy with the Greeks, and through them with Russia; and, finally, his preparations for an insurrection in Syria, should Egypt find an opportunity of declaring her independence. I meanwhile continued to push my demand for the six million piastres claimed by British subjects in Syria. My list shows a grand total of eleven, and of these five are important cases. On July 4, 1871, I wrote to the Foreign Office and to the Ambassador, urging that a Commission be directed to inquire into the subject and to settle the items found valid. I expressed a hope that I might be permitted personally to superintend the settlement of these debts, with whose every item the study of twenty-one months had made me familiar, and another six months would have seen Syria swept clean and set in order. On August 16, 1871, I was recalled suddenly, on the ground that the Moslems were fanatical enough to want my life. I have proved that to be like all the rest of Rashid Pasha's reports—utterly false."[1]

With regard to the reasons given by Lord Granville for Burton's recall, I may say that, in a letter which he sent under Flying Seal, dated July 22, 1871, and which reached Burton on the day of his recall, he recapitulated the dispatch written to Burton by Lord Clarendon on his appointment to Damascus, reminding him of the conditions under which he was appointed to the post, and saying that the complaints which he had received from the Turkish Government in regard to his recent conduct and proceedings rendered it impossible that he should allow him to continue to perform any Consular functions in Syria, and requesting him to make his preparations for returning to England with as little delay as possible.[2]

I think that the foregoing statements will fully explain the true reasons which led to the recall of Burton from Damascus. It will be seen that in the above charges against Burton the question of the Shazlis does not enter; and in the face of all this

[1] Blue Book, pp. 140, 141.
[2] *Vide* Letter from Lord Granville to Captain Burton, under Flying Seal, care of Consul-General Eldridge, July 22, 1871 (Blue Book, .p 109).

evidence, how is it possible to maintain that Isabel was the true cause of her husband's recall? The converted Shazlis, whose cause she is supposed to have espoused with fanatical zeal, hardly entered into the matter at all. Indeed, in the whole of the Blue Book from which I have quoted, there is only one reference to the Shazlis, and that is in a letter which Burton addressed to Sir Henry Elliot on the revival of Christianity among them. Miss Stisted says that Burton was as likely to assist in increasing the number of the Syrian Christians, " of whom he had the lowest opinion," " as to join in a Shakers' dance." Yet in this letter to his official chief Burton dwells at length on the revival of Christianity in Syria, and calls attention to the persecution and increasing number of the converted Shazlis, and asks for instructions as to what he is to do. "The revival," he says, "is progressing," and "this persecution," and he regards it in the "gravest light."[1] Also in a special letter to the Protestant missionaries Burton writes:

"Meanwhile I take the liberty of recommending to your prudent consideration the present critical state of affairs in Syria. A movement which cannot but be characterized as a revival of Christianity in the land of its birth seems to have resulted from the measures adopted by the authorities and from the spirit of inquiry which your missions have awakened in the breasts of the people. The new converts are now numbered by thousands: men of rank are enrolling

---

[1] *Vide* Letter of Captain Burton to Sir Henry Elliot, July 14, 1871 (Blue Book, pp. 95, 96).

themselves on the lists, and proselytizing has extended even to the Turkish soldiery."[1]

All this bears out Isabel's statement that her husband was interested in the Shazlis; but, all the same, it does not enter into the question of his recall. Even if it did, so far from acting without her husband's consent in this matter (and she really did very little), she did nothing without his approval, for he actively sympathized in the case of the Shazlis. His letters to the missionaries and to Sir Henry Elliot form proof of this; and in face of this documentary evidence the "Shakers' dance" theory does not hold good. Miss Stisted, however, makes her assertion without any evidence, and says that Lord Granville evaded the main question when sounded on the subject of Burton's recall. How she became aware of the inner mind of Lord Granville is not apparent, and under the circumstances dispassionate readers will prefer the testimony of the Blue Book to her cool assumption of superior knowledge. Something more than mere assertion is needed to support a charge like this.

Equally baseless too is the insinuation against Isabel contained in the following passage:

"Significant enough it is to any unprejudiced reader that the next appointment [*i.e.* of Burton's] was to a Roman Catholic country."[2]

The "unprejudiced reader" would probably see the

---

[1] Letter from Captain Burton to the Rev. E. B. Frankel, Rev. J. Orr Scott, Miss James, Rev. W. Wright, and Rev. John Crawford, Bludán, July 19, 1871 (Blue Book, p. 92).
[2] Miss Stisted's Life of Burton, p. 361.

significance in another light—the significance of refusing to appoint Burton again to a Mohammedan country, and of repeatedly refusing him the post he coveted at Morocco.

None of these accusations or innuendoes against Isabel can be entertained when confronted with sober facts; they are in short nothing but the outcome of a jealous imagination. Isabel the cause of her husband's recall, the ruin of his career! She through whose interest Burton had obtained the coveted post at Damascus; she who fought his battles for him all round; she who shielded him from the official displeasure; she who obeyed his lightest wish, and whose only thought from morning to night was her husband's welfare and advancement; she who would have died for him,—this same woman, according to Miss Stisted, deliberately behind her husband's back ran counter to his wishes, fanned the flame of fanaticism, and brought about the crash which ruined his career! Was there ever a more improbable charge? But the accusation has overshot the mark, and, like the boomerang, it returns and injures no one but its author.

CHAPTER XIX

THE PASSING OF THE CLOUD

(1871—1872)

> Tell whoso hath sorrow
> Grief shall never last:
> E'en as joy hath no morrow,
> So woe shall go past.
> ALF LAYLAH WA LAYLAH
> (*Burton's " Arabian Nights"*).

THE recall from Damascus was the hardest blow that ever befell the Burtons. They felt it acutely; and when time had softened the shock, a lasting sense of the injury that had been done to them remained. Isabel felt it perhaps even more keenly than her husband. The East had been the dream of her girlhood, the land of her longing from the day when she and her lover first plighted their troth in the Botanical Gardens, and the reality of her maturer years. But the reality had been all too short. To the end of her life she never ceased to regret Damascus; and even when in her widowed loneliness she returned to England twenty years after the recall, with her life's work well-nigh done, and waiting, as she used to say, for the "tinkling of his camel's bell," her eyes would glow and her voice take a deeper note if she spoke of those two years at Damascus. It was easy to see that they were the crowning years of her life—the years in which her nature had full play, when in the truest sense of the term she may be said to have lived. From the time they left Damascus, though there were many years of happiness and usefulness in store for her husband and herself, things were never quite the same again. The recall seems to mark a turning-point in her life. Many of the dreams and enthusiasms of her youth were gone, though her life's unfinished work and stern reality remained. To use her own words, "Our career was broken."

Isabel felt the slur on her husband which the recall involved more acutely than he. Burton, though stung to the quick at the treatment the Foreign Office meted out to him for doing what he conceived to be his duty (and certainly the manner of his recall was ungracious almost to the point of brutality), was not a man given to show his feelings to the world, and he possessed a philosophy which enabled him to present a calm and unmoved front to the reverses of fortune. With his wife it was different. She was not of a nature to suffer in silence, nor to sit down quietly under a wrong. As she put it, "Since Richard would not fight his own battles, I fought them for him," and she never ceased fighting till she had cleared away as much as possible of the cloud that shadowed her husband's official career.

On arriving in London, she set to work with characteristic energy. It was a very different home-coming to the one she had anticipated. Two years before she had set out in the best of health and spirits, with every prospect of a long and prosperous career at Damascus for her husband and herself. Now, almost without warning, they had come home with their prospects shattered and their career broken. Nevertheless these untoward circumstances served in no way to weaken her energies; on the contrary, they seemed to lend her strength.

She found her husband occupying one room in an obscure hotel off Manchester Square, engaged as usual with his writings, and apparently absorbed in them. He seemed to have forgotten that such a place as Damascus existed. She found that he had accepted his recall literally. He had made no defence to the Foreign Office, nor sought for any explanation. He had treated the affair *de haut en bas*, and had left things to take their course. He in fact expressed himself to her as "sick of the whole thing," and he took the darkest view of the future. "Are you not afraid?" he asked her, referring to their gloomy prospects. "Afraid?" she echoed. "What, when I have you?" This was the day she came back. He did not refer to the subject again, but returned to his manuscripts, and apparently wanted nothing but to be left alone.

But his wife knew him better; she knew that deep down under his seeming indifference there was a rankling sense of injustice. Her first step was to arouse him to a sense of the position. To discuss verbally matters of this kind with him, she had learnt by experience, was not easy; so she wrote to him to the following effect, and put the note between the leaves of a book he was reading:

"You tell me you have no wish to re-enter official life. Putting my own interests quite out of the question, when there are so few able men, and still fewer gentlemen, left in England, and one cannot help foreseeing very bad times coming, it makes one anxious and nervous to think that the one man whom I and others regard as a born leader of men should retire into private life just when he is most wanted. Now you are not going to be angry with me; you must be scolded. You have fairly earned the right to five or six months of domestic happiness and retirement, but not the right to be selfish. When the struggle comes on, instead of remaining, as you think, you will come to the fore and nobly take your right place. Remember I have prophesied three times for you, and this is the fourth. You are smarting under a sense of injustice now, and you talk accordingly. If I know anything of men in general, and you in particular, you will grow dissatisfied with yourself, if your present state of inaction lasts long."

What the immediate result of this remonstrance was it is not possible to say; but Isabel's next move was to go down to the Foreign Office, where she was already well known as one with whom the usual official evasions were of no avail. She always called herself "a child of the Foreign Office," and she had many friends there among the permanent officials. She brought every influence she could think of to bear. She went to the Foreign

Office day after day, refusing to take "No" for an answer, until at last she simply forced Lord Granville to see her; and when he saw her, she forced him to hear what she had to say. The interview resulted in his saying "that he would be happy to consider anything she might lay before him on the subject of Captain Burton's recall from Damascus." He could hardly have said less, and he could not well have said more. However, she took him very promptly at his word. She occupied herself for three months in getting up her husband's case, and in inducing him to consent to its being put clearly before Lord Granville. By way of going to the root of the matter she insisted on knowing from the Foreign Office the true reasons of his recall. They gave her a long list—the list set forth in the previous chapter. She answered them point by point. Burton of course helped, and the thing was done in his name. The whole matter was subsequently published in the form of a Blue Book—the book before referred to.

The controversy between Isabel and the Foreign Office, if it can so be called, ended in January, 1872, three months after her return to England; and it terminated in a dialectical triumph for her, and the offer of several small posts for her husband, which he indignantly refused. Among others, Burton was offered Para, but would not take it. "Too small a place for me after Damascus," he said.

The Burtons went into inexpensive lodgings, and waited for the brighter days which were slow in dawning. With characteristic pride and independence they kept their difficulties to themselves, and none knew how hard their struggle was at this time. The Burtons received a good deal of kindness in the way of hospitality. There was a general impression that they had been unfairly treated by the Government, and their friends were anxious to make it up to them. They paid many pleasant visits; among others, to one of their kindest friends, Lady Marian Alford. At her house they met Lord Beaconsfield; and at one of her parties, when the Prince of Wales and the Duke of Edinburgh were present, by request of the hostess Burton dressed as a Bedawin shaykh, and Isabel as a Moslem woman of Damascus. She was supposed to have brought the Shaykh over to introduce him to English society; and though many of those present knew Burton quite well, none of them recognized him in his Arab dress until he revealed himself. The Burtons also attended a banquet at the Mansion House, which interested them more than a little; and when they wanted to make remarks—and they were in the habit of expressing themselves very freely—they spoke Arabic, thinking no one would understand it. Suddenly a man next them interrupted their criticisms by saying also in Arabic, "You are quite right; I was just thinking the same thing": the which shows how careful one should be at public dinners.

Early in June, 1872, Burton sailed for Iceland at the request of a certain capitalist, who wished to obtain reports of some sulphur mines there, and who promised him a liberal remuneration, which eventually he did not pay. He, however, paid for Burton's passage and travelling expenses; but as he did not pay for two Isabel was unable to accompany her husband, and during his absence she took up her abode with her father and mother. Afterwards she was very glad that she had done this. For some time past the health of Mrs. Arundell had given cause for anxiety. She had been a confirmed invalid since her stroke of paralysis ten years before, but she had borne up marvellously until the last few months, when it was visible to every one that she was failing. The end came very suddenly. Her dearly loved daughter Isabel was with her at the last. The loss of her mother, to whom she was devotedly attached, was a severe blow to Isabel. Mrs. Arundell was a woman of strength of character, ability, and piety, and possessed rare qualities of head and heart. It is scarcely necessary to say that the little cloud which had arisen between mother and daughter on the occasion of Isabel's marriage had long since passed away; indeed it was of the briefest duration, and Mrs. Arundell came to love Burton as a son, and was very proud of him.

At the end of June, about ten months after the date of the recall from Damascus, official favour smiled upon the Burtons again. Lord Granville wrote and asked Isabel if her husband would accept the Consulate of Trieste, just vacant by the death of Charles Lever, the novelist.

Isabel was praying by her mother's coffin that their troubles might pass away when the letter arrived, and it came to her like an answer to prayer, for their prospects were just then at their gloomiest. She at once wrote to her husband in Iceland, and was able soon after to send his acceptance of the post to Lord Granville.

Trieste, a small commercial consulate, with £600 a year salary and £100 office allowance, was a sad drop after Damascus, at £1,000 a year and work of a diplomatic order. But the Burtons could not afford to refuse the offer, for their needs were pressing, and they took it in the hope of better things, which never came. Burton had a great desire to become Consul at Morocco, and he thought Trieste might lead thither. Alas ! it did not; and the man who had great talents, a knowledge of more than a score of languages, and an unrivalled experience in the ways of Eastern life and oriental methods, was allowed to drag out eighteen years in the obscurity of a second-rate seaport town, where his unique qualifications were simply thrown away. He had had his chance, and had lost it. He was not a "safe man"; and England, or rather the Government, generally reserves—and wisely—the pick of the places in the public service for "safe men." Officialdom distrusts genius—perhaps rightly; and Burton was a wayward genius indeed. However, at Trieste he could hardly get into hot water. The post was a purely commercial one; there was no work which called for any collision with the local authorities. Austria, the land of red tape, was very different to Syria. There was no Wali to quarrel with; there were no missionaries to offend, no Druzes or Greeks to squabble with; and though there were plenty of Jews, their money-lending proclivities did not come within the purview of the British Consul, and the Austrian authorities would have resented in a moment the slightest meddling with their jurisdiction. But if Burton could do no harm, he could also do little good; and his energies were cribbed, cabined, and confined. On the other hand, he was following at Trieste a distinguished man in Charles Lever, and one who, like himself, had literary tastes. It is impossible to deny that Lord Granville showed discrimination in appointing him there at the time. Trieste was virtually a sinecure; the duties were light, and every liberty was given to Burton. He was absent half his time, and he paid a vice-consul to do most of his work, thus leaving himself ample leisure for travel and his literary labours. If his lot had been thrown in a more active sphere, his great masterpiece, *Alf Laylah wa Laylah* (*The Arabian Nights*), might never have seen the light.

Isabel and her husband lost no time in making preparations for their departure. In the month of September Burton returned from Iceland, and the third week in October he left England for Trieste by sea. His wife was to adhere to her usual plan of "pay, pack, and follow"—to purchase in London the usual stock of necessary things, and follow as soon as might be by land.

In November Isabel crossed the Channel, and ran straight through to Cologne. At Cologne she saw the sights, and then proceeded by easy stages down the Rhine to Mayence, and thence to Frankfort. From

Frankfort she went to Wurzburg, where she called on the famous Dr. Döllinger. Thence to Innsbruck, and so on to Venice. It was fourteen years since she had visited Venice. The last occasion was during the tour which she had taken with her sister and brother-in-law before her marriage. She says: "It was like a dream to come back again. It was all there as I left it, even to the artificial flowers at the *table d'hôte*: it was just the same, only less gay and brilliant. It had lost the Austrians and Henry V. Court. It was older, and all the friends I knew were dispersed." Her first act was to send a telegram to Trieste announcing her arrival, and the next to gondola all over Venice. Towards evening she thought it would be civil to call on the British Consul, Sir William Perry. The old gentleman, who was very deaf, and apparently short-sighted, greeted her kindly, and mumbled something about "Captain Burton." Isabel said, "Oh, he is at Trieste; I am just going to join him." "No," said Sir William, "he has just left me." Thinking he was rather senile, she concluded that he did not understand, and bawled into his ear for the third time, "I am Mrs. Burton, not Captain Burton, just arrived from London, and am on my way to join my husband at Trieste." "I know all that," he said impatiently. "You had better come with me in my gondola; I am just going to the *Morocco* now, a ship that will sail for Trieste." Isabel said, "Certainly"; and much puzzled, got into the gondola, and went on board. As soon as she got down to the ship's saloon, lo! there was her husband writing at a table. "Halloo!" he said; "what the devil are you doing here?" "Halloo!" she said; "what are *you* doing here?" And then they began to explain. It turned out that neither of them had received the other's telegrams or letters.

A few days later they crossed over to Trieste. The Vice-Consul and the Consular Chaplain came on board to greet them, but otherwise they arrived at Trieste without any ceremony; in fact, so unconventional was their method of arrival, that it was rumoured in the select circles of the town that "Captain Burton, the new Consul, and Mrs. Burton took up their quarters at the Hôtel de la Ville, he walking along with his gamecock under his arm, and she with her bull-terrier under hers." It was felt that they must be a very odd couple, and they were looked at rather askance. This distrust was probably reciprocated, for at first both Isabel and her husband felt like fish out of water, and did not like Trieste at all.

CHAPTER XX

EARLY YEARS AT TRIESTE
(1872—1875)

> Turn thee from grief nor care a jot,
> Commit thy needs to fate and lot,
> Enjoy the present passing well,
> And let the past be clean forgot.
> For what so haply seemeth worse
> Shall work thy weal as Allah wot;
> Allah shall do whate'er he will,
> And in his will oppose him not.
>   ALF LAYLAH WA LAYLAH
>   (*Burton's "Arabian Nights"*).

ISABEL soon began to like Trieste; the place grew upon her, and later she always spoke of it as "my beloved Trieste." She has left on record in her journal her early impressions:

"Trieste is a town of threes. It has three quarters: the oldest, Citta Vecchia, is filthy and antiquated in the extreme. It has three winds: the *bora*, the winter wind, cold, dry, highly electrical, very exciting, and so violent that sometimes the quays are roped, and some of the walls have iron rails let in, to prevent people being blown into the sea; the *sirocco*, the summer wind, straight from Africa, wet, warm, and debilitating ; and the *contraste*, which means the two blowing at once and against each other, with all the disadvantages of both. It has three races: Italians, Austrians, and Slavs. They are all ready to cut each other's throats, especially the Italians and the Austrians ; and the result is that Trieste, wealthy though she is, wants all modern improvements, simply because the two rival parties act like the two bundles of hay in the fable, and between them the ass starves. North of Ponte Rosso is Germania, or the Austrian colony, composed of the authorities, the *employés*, and a few wealthy merchants, who have a crazy idea of Germanizing their little world, an impossible dream, for there are twelve thousand Italians in Trieste, who speak a sort of corrupted Venetian. One thousand of these are very rich, the others very poor. However, whether rich or poor, the *Italianissimi* hate their Austrian rulers like poison ; and in this hatred they are joined by the mass of the wealthy Israelites, who divide the commerce with the Greeks. The wealthy *Italianissimi* subscribe handsomely to every Italian charity and movement, and periodically and anonymously memorialize the King of Italy. The poor take a delight in throwing large squibs, called by courtesy 'torpedoes,' amongst the unpatriotic petticoats who dare to throng the Austrian balls ; for though Trieste is Austrian nominally, it is Italian at heart. The feud between the Italians and the Austrians goes to spoil society in Trieste ; they will not intermingle. The Slavs also form a distinct party.

"I found these discordant elements a little difficult to harmonize at first. But Richard desired me to form a neutral house, as at Damascus, where politics and religion should never be mentioned, and where all might meet on a common ground. I did so, with the result that we had friends in all camps. There was an abundance of society of all kinds: Austrian, Italian, and what Ouida has called the *haute Juiverie*. We were in touch with them all, and they were all good-natured and amiable. Society in Trieste did not care whether you were rich or poor, whether you received or did not receive; it only asked you to be nice, and it opened its arms to you. I dare say my visiting list, private and consular, comprised three hundred families; but we had our own little *clique intime*, which was quite charming, and included some sixty or seventy persons.

"We women had what Richard used to call 'hen parties' (*Kaffee gesellschaft*), which is really five o'clock tea, where we would dance together, play, sing, recite, and have refreshments; but a man, except the master of the house, was never seen at these gatherings. *En revanche*, we had plenty of evening entertainments for both sexes.

"Some curious little local customs still lingered at Trieste. One of them was, when two friends or relations met in society, after embracing affectionately, they were wont to drop one another an elaborate curtsey. The visiting hours were from twelve till two, an impossible time; and men were expected to call in white cravats, kid gloves and evening dress.

When I first came to Trieste, I was often invited *en intime* to afternoon tea, and was told to come 'just as you are, my dear.' I took the invitation literally of course; and when I arrived, I used to find the other ladies *décolletées*, and blazing with diamonds. I remember feeling very awkward at appearing in an ordinary costume, but my hostess said to me, 'You know, my dear, we are so fond of our jewels; it gives us pleasure to dress even for one another; but do not do it if it bores you.' However, later I always took care to do it, on the principle that when one is at Rome one should do as Rome does. Apart from these little social peculiarities Trieste was the most hospitable and open-hearted town, and people entertained there, if they entertained at all, on a lavish scale and right royally.

"The population of Trieste was very interesting, though a strange medley. To the east of the town the Wallachian *cici*, or charcoal-dealers, wore the dress of the old Danubian homes whence they came. Then there was the Friulano, with his velvet jacket and green corduroys (the most estimable race in Trieste). He was often a roaster of chestnuts at the corners of the street, and his wife was the best *balie* (wet nurse). She was often more bravely attired than her mistress. The Slav market-women were also very interesting. I loved to go down and talk with them in the market-place. They drove in from neighbouring villages with their produce for sale in a kind of drosky, the *carretella* as it was called, with its single pony harnessed to the near side of the pole. Some of the girls, especially those of Servola, were quite beautiful, with a Greek profile, and a general delicacy of form and colour which one would hardly expect to find amongst the peasantry. But their eyes were colourless; and their blonde hair was like tow—it lacked the golden ray. The dresses were picturesque: a white triangular head-kerchief, with embroidered ends hanging down the back; a bodice either of white flannel picked out with splashes of colour, or of a black glazed and plaited stuff; a skirt of lively hue, edged with a broad belt of even livelier green, blue, pink, or yellow; white stockings; and short, stout shoes. The ornaments on high days and holidays were gold necklaces and crosses, a profusion of rings and pendants. This of course was the *contadina*, or peasant girl. Opposed to her was the *sartorella*, or little tailoress, which may be said to be synonymous with the French *grisette*. I always called Trieste *Il Paradiso delle Sartorelle*, because the *sartorella* was a prominent figure in Trieste, and Fortune's favourite. She was wont to fill the streets and promenades, especially on *festa* days, dressed *à quatre épingles*, powdered and rouged and *coiffée* as for a ball, and with or without a veil. She was often pretty, and generally had a good figure; but she did not always look 'nice'; and her manners, to put it mildly, were very *dégagées*. There were four thousand of these girls in Trieste, and they filled the lower-class balls and theatres. There was a *sartorella* in every house, off and on. For example, a family in Trieste always had a dress to make or a petticoat, and the *sartorella* came for a florin a day and her food, and she worked for twelve hours, leaving off work at six, when she began her 'evening out.' I am fain to add the *sartorella* was often a sort of whited sepulchre. She was gorgeously clad without, but as a rule had not a rag, not even a chemise, underneath, unless she were 'in luck.' 'In luck,' I grieve to say, meant that every boy, youth, and man in Trieste, beginning at twelve and up to twenty-five and twenty-eight, had an *affaire* with a *sartorella*; and I may safely assert, without being malicious, that she was not wont to give her heart—if we may call it so—gratis. She was rather a nuisance in a house; though after I had been in Trieste a little while I discovered that she was an indispensable nuisance, because there was always some mending or sewing to be done. She generally turned the servants' heads by telling them that she was going to be married to a real *graf* (count) as soon as he was independent of his parents—a sort of King Cophetua and the Beggar Maid over again, I suppose.

"Trieste was a beautiful place, especially the view round our bay. The hills were covered with woodland and verdure; the deep blue Adriatic was in the foreground, dotted with lateen sails; and the town filled the valley and straggled up the slopes. The sky was softly blue on a balmy day; the bees and birds, the hum of insects, the flowers and fresh air, and the pretty, animated peasants, combined to form a picture which made one feel glad to live.

"The charm of Trieste is that one can live exactly as one pleases. Richard and I drew out a line for ourselves when we first went to Trieste, and we always

TRIESTE.

[*Page 540.*

kept to it as closely as we could. We rose at 3 or 4 a.m. in summer, and at 5 a.m. in winter. He read, wrote, and studied all day out of consular hours, and took occasional trips for his health; and I learned Italian, German, and singing, and attended to my other duties. We took our daily exercise in the shape of an hour's swimming in the sea, or fencing at the school, according to the weather. What with reading, writing, looking after the poor, working for the Church or for the Society for the Prevention of Cruelty to Animals, my day was all too short.

"The prettiest thing in Trieste was the swimming school. It was moored out at the entrance to the harbour. We used to reach it in a boat, and get hold of Tonina, the old woman who provided us with the *camerino*, or little stall to undress in, and who would grin from ear to ear at our chaff and the thought of her *bakshish*. The women's costumes were short trousers, with bodice or belt of blue serge or white alpaca trimmed with red. We plunged into the great *vasca*, or basin, an acre of sea, bottomless, but enclosed on all sides with a loaded net, to keep out the sharks. There were twelve soldiers to teach beginners. They used to begin with a pole and rope, like a fishing-rod and line, and at the end of the rope was a broad belt, which went round the waist of the beginner, and you heard the incessant 'Eins, zwei, drei' of the drill. Next they would lead the beginners round the edge of the basin with a rope, like pet dogs. But we adepts in swimming plunged in head first from a sort of trapeze, or from the roofs of the dressing-rooms, making a somersault on the way.

The swimmers did the prettiest tricks in the water. Young married women met in the middle to shake hands and hold long conversations. Scores of young girls used to romp about, ducking each other under and climbing on each other's backs for support, and children of three or four used to swim about like whitebait, in and out, among us all. One stout old lady used to sit lazily in the water, like a blubber fish, knitting, occasionally moving her feet. We used to call her 'the buoy,' and hold on to her when we were tired."

It was the custom of Isabel and her husband, whenever they went to a new place, to look out for a sort of sanatorium, to which they might repair when they wanted a change or were seedy or out of sorts. Thus, when Burton was sent to Santos, they chose São Paulo; when they were at Damascus, they pitched on Bludán; and as soon as they arrived at Trieste, they lighted upon Opçina. Opçina was a Slav village high above Trieste, and about an hour's drive from it. This height showed Trieste and the Adriatic spread out like a map below, with hill and valley and dale waning faintly blue in the distance, and far away the Carnian Alps topped with snow. There was an old inn called Daneu's, close to an obelisk. They took partly furnished rooms, and brought up some of their own furniture to make up deficiencies and give the place a homelike air. It was their wont to come up to Opçina from Saturday to Monday, and get away from Trieste and worries. They always kept some literary work on hand there; and sometimes, if they were in the mood for it, they would stay at Opçina for six weeks on end. The climate was very bracing.

Isabel always looked back on these few first years at Trieste as pleasant ones. After the storm and stress of Damascus, and the anxiety and depression consequent upon their recall, she found Trieste a veritable "restful harbour." They varied their life by many journeys and excursions. Their happy hunting-ground was Venice. Whenever they could they would cross over there, order a gondola, and float lazily about the canals. She says of this time: "We lived absolutely the jolly life of two bachelors, as it might be an elder or a younger brother. When we wanted to go away, we just turned the key and left."

It was not until they had been at Trieste six months that they settled down in a house, or rather in a flat at the top of a large building close to the sea. They began their housekeeping with very modest ideas; in fact, they had only six rooms. But Burton and his wife were fond of enlarging their boundaries, and in course of time these six rooms grew until they ran round the whole of the large block of the building. Here they lived for ten years, and then they moved to the most beautiful house in Trieste, a palazzo a little way out of the town.

One of their first expeditions was to Loretto. Thence they went to Rome, where they made the acquaintance of the English Ambassador to the Austrian Court and his wife, Sir Augustus and Lady Paget, with whom they remained great friends all the time they were at Trieste. Isabel also met Cardinal Howard, who was a cousin of hers. He was one of her favourite partners in the palmy days of Almack's, when he was an officer in the Guards and she was a girl. Now the whirligig of time had transformed him into a cardinal and her into the wife of the British Consul at Trieste. As a devout Catholic Isabel delighted in Rome and its churches, though the places which she most enjoyed visiting were the Catacombs and the Baths of Caracalla. At Rome she got blood-poisoning and fever, which she took on with her to Florence, where they stayed for some little time. At Florence they saw a good deal of Ouida, whom they had known for some years. From Florence they went to Venice, crossed over to Trieste just to change their baggage, and then proceeded to Vienna. There was a great Exhibition going on at Vienna, and Burton went as the reporter to some newspaper. They were at Vienna three weeks, and were delighted with everything Viennese except the prices at the hotel, which were stupendous. They enjoyed themselves greatly, and were well received in what is perhaps the most exclusive society in Europe. Among other things they went to Court. Isabel attended as an Austrian countess, and took place and precedence accordingly, for the name Arundell of Wardour is inscribed in the Austrian official lists of the Counts of the Empire. There was a difficulty raised about Burton, because consuls are not admissible at the Court of Vienna. Isabel was not a woman to go to places where her husband was not admitted, and she insisted upon having the matter brought before the notice of the Emperor, though the British Embassy clearly told her the thing was impossible—Burton could not be admitted. When the Emperor heard of the difficulty through the Court officials, he at once solved it by saying that Burton might attend as an officer of the English army. The incident is a trifling one, but it is one more illustration of the untiring devotion of Isabel to her husband, and her sleepless vigilance that nothing should be done which would seem to cast a slur upon his position.[1]

[1] Lady Burton thus describes her visit to the Austrian Court: "I was very much dazzled by the Court. I thought everything was beautifully done, so arranged as to give every one pleasure, and somehow it was the graciousness that was in itself a welcome. I shall never forget the first night that I saw the Empress—a vision of beauty, clothed in silver, crowned with water-lilies, with large rows of diamonds and emeralds round her small head and her beautiful hair, and descending all down her dress in festoons. The throne-room is immense, with marble columns down each side—all the men arranged on one side and all the women on the other, and the new presentations with their ambassadors and ambassadresses nearest the throne. When the Emperor and Empress came in, they walked up the middle, the Empress curtseying most gracefully and smiling a general gracious greeting. They then ascended the throne, and presently the Empress turned to our side. The presentations first took place, and she spoke to each one in her own language, and on her own particular subject. I was quite entranced with her beauty, her cleverness, and her conversation. She passed down the ladies' side, and then came up that of the men, the Emperor doing exactly the same as she had done. He also spoke to us. Then some few of us whose families the Empress knew about were asked to sit down, and refreshments were handed to us—the present Georgina Lady Dudley sitting by the Empress. It was a thing never to be forgotten to have seen those two beautiful women sitting side by side. The Empress Frederick of Germany—Crown Princess she was then—was also there, and sent for some of us on another day, which was in many ways another memorable event, and her husband also came in" (*Life of Sir Richard Burton*, by Isabel his wife, vol. ii., pp. 24, 25).

When the Burtons returned to Trieste, Charles Tyrwhitt-Drake, who had been with them much at Damascus, and had accompanied them on their tour in the Holy Land and many other journeys in the Syrian Desert, arrived. The visit of their friend and fellow-traveller seemed to revive their old love of exploration as far as the limits of Trieste would admit, and among other excursions they went to see a great *fête* at the Adelsberg Caves. These caves were stalactite caverns and grottoes not far from Trieste, and on the day of the *fête* they were lighted by a million candles. One of the caverns was a large hall like a domed ball-room, and Austrian bands and musicians repaired thither, and the peasants flocked down from the surrounding villages in their costumes, and made high revelry. Burton maintained that these caves were the eighth wonder of the world, but the description of them here would occupy too much space. Suffice it to say, in the words of Isabel, "When God Almighty had finished making the earth, He threw all the superfluous rocks together there." From these caves they went to Fiume, and explored the Colosseum there, which, though not so famous as that of Rome, almost rivals it in its ruins and its interest. Another excursion was to Lipizza, the Emperor of Austria's stud farm. It was about two hours from Trieste, and the stables and park were full of herds of thorough-bred mares, chiefly Hungarians and Croats. Lipizza was always a favourite drive of the Burtons.

"Charley's" visit revived many memories of Damascus, and he was the bearer of news from many friends there. He seemed to bring with him "a breath from the desert," and they were loath to let him go. They accompanied him to Venice, where he took his leave of them; and they never saw him again. He died the following year at Jerusalem, at the age of twenty-eight. He was buried in the English burial-ground on Mount Zion, the place where they had all three sat and talked together and picked flowers one afternoon three years before. It was largely at his suggestion that Isabel determined to write her *Inner Life of Syria*, and she unearthed her note-books and began to write the book soon after he left. He was a great friend, almost a son to them, and they both felt his loss bitterly.

About this time Maria Theresa, Contessa de Montelin, ex-Queen of Spain, when she was on her death-bed, sent for Isabel, and charged her to keep up, maintain, and promote certain pious societies which she had started in Trieste. One of these was "The Apostleship of Prayer," whose members, women, were to be active in doing good works, corporally and spiritually, in Trieste. This guild was one of two good works to which Isabel chiefly devoted herself during her life at Trieste. The other was a branch of the Society for the Prevention of Cruelty to Animals and the care of animals generally, a subject always very near her heart. "The Apostleship of Prayer," the legacy of the ex-Queen of Spain, so grew under Isabel's hand that the members increased to fifteen thousand. They elected her president, and she soon got the guild into thorough working order, dividing the members into bands in various quarters of the city of Trieste.

There is not much to relate concerning Isabel's life at Trieste for the first few years. It was uneventful and fairly happy: it would have been quite happy, were it not for the regret of Damascus, where they were then hoping to return, and the desire for a wider sphere of action. Both she and her husband managed to keep in touch with the world in a wonderful way, and did not let themselves drop out of sight or out of mind. One of the reliefs to the monotony of their existence was that, whenever an English ship came into port with a captain whom they knew, they would dine on board and have the delight of seeing English people, and they generally invited the captain and officers and the best passengers back again. The Burtons had a good many visitors from England, most of them well-known personages, who, when they stopped at Trieste, a favourite resting-place for birds of passage, always made a point of calling upon them. Among others was Lord Llandaff, then Mr. Henry Matthews, who had many things in common with Isabel. Owing to their lives being cast on different lines, they only saw one another at intervals, but they always entertained a feeling of mutual friendship. From the many letters he wrote to her I am permitted to publish this one:

"TEMPLE, *December* 28, 1875.

"DEAR MRS. BURTON,

"Of course I have not forgotten you. I never forget. Was it last week, or sixteen years ago, that you were standing in this room with the chequered sunlight shining through the Venetian blind upon you, as you discoursed about Heaven and Grace and an attorney in the City who was not one of the elect?

"I never knew you were in Venice this autumn, and, as it happened, it was fortunate I did not go to Trieste to see you, since you were away. I grieve very much to hear of your bad health. It seems to me you do too much. The long list of occupations which you call 'repose' is enough to wear out any constitution, even one which is so admirably knit as yours. Don't be like the lady in Pope's satire, and 'die of nothing but a rage to live.' There is one part of your labours, however, for which I, with all the rest of the world, shall be thankful; and that is your new book. I shall look for it with impatience, and feel sure of its success.

"I wish you were not going to Arabia; but I know how you understand and fulfil the part of wife to a knight-errant of discovery. Be as prudent and sparing of yourself as you can.

"Yours ever,
"HENRY MATTHEWS."

After they had been at Trieste two years, at the end of 1874 Burton proposed that his wife should go to England and transact some business for him, and bring out certain books which he had written. He would join her later on. Isabel was exceedingly unwilling to go; but "whenever he put his foot down I had to do it, whether I would or no." So she went, and arrived in London in December, after an uneventful journey.

Isabel found her work cut out for her in London. Her husband had given her several pages of directions, and she tried to carry them out as literally as possible. She had to see a number of publishers for one thing, and to work up an interest in a sulphur mine for another. She says: "I got so wrapped up in my work at this time that sometimes I worked for thirteen hours a day, and would forget to eat. I can remember once, after working for thirteen hours, feeling my head whirling, and being quite alarmed. Then I suddenly remembered that I had forgotten to eat all day." She had also the proof-sheets to correct of her own book, which was going through the press. She was in London without her husband for four months, and during that time she had a great shock. A paragraph appeared in *The Scotsman* announcing Burton's death, and speaking of her as his widow. She telegraphed to Trieste at once, and packed up. Just as she was starting she got a telegram from him saying, "I am eating a very good dinner at *table d'hôte*."

Early in May Burton joined her on a lengthy leave of absence, and they did a great deal of visiting, and enjoyed themselves generally. Isabel's *Inner Life of Syria* was published at this time, and she was very anxious about it. It had taken sixteen months to write. The evening of the day on which it made its appearance she went to a party, and the first person she saw whom she knew was a well-known editor, who greeted her with warm congratulations on her book. She says, "It made me as happy as if somebody had given me a fortune."

The favourable reception which was accorded to *The Inner Life of Syria*, which was largely devoted to a

[From the portrait by the late Lord Leighton.

Richard F. Burton

[Page 550.

defence of her husband's action when Consul at Damascus, encouraged Isabel to proceed further on his behalf. So she wrote to, or interviewed, every influential friend she knew, with a view of inducing the Government to make Burton K.C.B., and she prepared a paper setting forth his claims and labours in the public service, which was signed by thirty or forty of the most influential personages of the day. She also induced them to ask that Burton should either return to Damascus, or be promoted to Morocco, Cairo, Tunis, or Teheran. Unfortunately her efforts met with no success, though she renewed them again through another source three years later. In one sense, however, she succeeded; for though she could not convert the Government to her view, the press unanimously took up the cause of Burton, and complained that the Government did not give him his proper place in official life, and called him the "neglected Englishman." As for Burton himself, he took no part in this agitation, except to thank his friends and the press generally for their exertions on his behalf.

They went down to Oxford at Commemoration to visit Professor Jowett and others. At Oxford they met with an ovation. In London they passed a very pleasant season, for private personages seemed anxious to make up for official neglect. This year Frederick Leighton's famous picture of Burton was exhibited in the Royal Academy. Among other celebrated people whom they met was Mr. Gladstone, at Lord Houghton's. Of Burton's meeting with Mr. Gladstone Isabel relates the following: "Very late in the evening Mrs. Gladstone said to me, 'I don't know what it is; I cannot get Mr. Gladstone away this evening'; and I said to her, 'I think I know what it is; he has got hold of my husband, Richard Burton, and they are both so interested in one another, and have so many points of interest to talk over, that I hope you will not take him away.'"

The season over, Burton started on another trip to Iceland; and Isabel was left alone, during which time she paid some visits to the Duke and Duchess of Somerset at Bulstrode, always kind friends of hers, and to Madame von Bülow at Reigate. Madame von Bülow was the wife of the Danish Minister in London, and one of Isabel's most intimate friends—a friendship which lasted all her life.

When Burton returned from Iceland, he went off to Vichy for a cure, and rejoined his wife in London in the autumn; and they went out a great deal, chiefly in scientific, literary, and artistic circles. This year was in some respects one of the pleasantest of Isabel's life. Her book had come out, and was a great success; she had been *fêted* by all her friends and relations; and though her efforts to obtain promotion for her husband had not met with the success which they deserved, yet the kind encouragement which she received from influential friends, who, though not members of the Government, were yet near the rose, made her hope that better days were soon to come.

In December Burton, finding that he had still six months' leave, asked his wife where she would like to go best. She answered, "India." It had long been her desire to go there with her husband, and get him to show her all the familiar spots which he had described to her as having visited or lived at during his nineteen years' service in India. Burton was delighted with the idea. So they got a map, cut India down the middle lengthways from Cashmere to Cape Comorin, and planned out how much they could manage to see on the western side, intending to leave the eastern side for another time, as the season was already too far advanced for them to be able to see the whole of India.

CHAPTER XXI[1]

THE JOURNEY TO BOMBAY

(1875—1876)

> As we meet and touch each day
> The many travellers on the way,
> Let every such brief contact be
> A glorious helpful ministry—
> The contact of the soil and seed,
> Each giving to the other's need,
> Each helping on the other's best,
> And blessing each, as well as blest.

ON December 4, 1875, we left London for Trieste, *en route* for India. It was not a cheerful day for saying good-bye to Old England and dear friends. There was a fog as black as midnight, thick snow was lying about the streets, and a dull red gloom only rendered the darkness visible and horrible. The great city was wrapped in the sullen splendours of a London fog. "It looks," said Richard, "as if the city were in mourning for some great national crime." "No," I said, "rather let us think that our fatherland

---

[1] This and the next chapter are compiled from the original notes from which Lady Burton wrote her *A. E. I.* and sundry letters and diaries. By so doing I am able to give the Indian tour in her own words.

wears mourning for our departure into exile once more." I felt as if I could never rise and face the day that morning. However, we *had* to go, so there was nothing to do but put our shoulders to the wheel. We lunched with my father and family by lamplight at one o'clock in the day. We prolonged the "festive" meal as much as we could, and then set out, a large family party, by the 4.45 train to Folkestone. We all had supper together at Folkestone, and enjoyed ourselves immensely. The next day my relations wished me good-bye—always a hard word to say. One parting in particular wrung my heart: I little thought then I should meet no more my brother Rudolph, the last of my four dear brothers, all of whom died young by untoward accidents. It was strange I was always bidding good-bye to them every three or four years. One ought to have been steeled to parting by now. Nevertheless every time the wrench was as keen as ever.

We stopped in Folkestone until Tuesday, and then Richard and I got into a sleigh, which took us over the snow from the hotel to the boat. We had a very cold crossing, but not a rough one; and as we neared Boulogne we even saw a square inch or so of pale blue sky, a sight which, after London, made us rejoice.

The old port at Boulogne stretched out its two long lean arms to our cockle-shell of a steamer, as though anxious to embrace it. I thought, as we came into the harbour, how much this quaint old town had been bound up with my life. I could never see it without recalling the two years which I had spent in Boulogne years ago, and going over again in my mind the time when I first saw Richard—the day of my life which will always be marked with a great white stone. He was a young lieutenant then on furlough from India, just beginning to spring into fame, and I a mere girl, who had seen nothing of life but one hurried London season.

We stayed at Boulogne two days, and we wandered about all over the place together, calling back to our memory the scenes of our bygone youth. We walked on the old Ramparts where we first made acquaintance, where Richard used to follow my sister Blanche and myself when we were sent out to learn our lessons *al fresco*. We even saw the wall where he chalked up, "May I speak to you?" and I chalked back, "No; mother will be angry." I hunted out my little brother's grave too, and planted it with fresh rose trees; and I visited my old friend Carolina, the Queen of the Poissardes. She was still a beautiful creature, magnificent in her costume. She reminded me of a promise I had made her in the old days, that if ever I went to Jerusalem I would bring her a rosary. I little dreamt then that I should marry Richard Burton, or that he would be Consul at Damascus, or that I should go to Jerusalem. Yet all these things had come to pass. And so I was able to fulfil my promise, to her great delight.

From Boulogne we went to Paris, which I found terribly changed since the Franco-German War. The marks of the terrible Siege were still burnt upon its face; and this applied not only to the city itself, but to the people. The radical changes of the last five years, and the war and the Commune, had made a new world of Paris. The light, joyous character of the French was no doubt still below the surface, but the upper crust was then (at least so it struck me) one of sulkiness, silence, and economy run mad, a rage for lucre, and a lust *pour la revanche*. Even the women seemed to have given up their pretty dresses, though of course there were some to be seen. Yet things were very different now to what they had been under the splendours of the Second Empire, that Empire which went "like a dream of the night." The women seemed to have become careless, an unusual thing in Parisiennes: they even painted badly; and it is a sin to paint—badly. I am afraid that I am one of the very few women who do not like Paris. I never liked it, even in its palmy days; and now at this time I liked it less than ever. I was so glad to leave at the end of the week, and to move out of the raw, white fog sunwards. We had a most uncomfortable journey from Paris to Modane, and the officials at the Customs seemed to delight in irritating and insulting one. When I was passing into the custom-pen, I was gruffly addressed, "On ne passe pas!" I said, "On ne passe pas? Comment on ne passe pas?" The only thing wanting, it seemed, was a visiting-card; but the opportunity of being safely insolent was too tempting to the Jack-in-office for him to pass it over. I could not help feeling glad these *braves* had never reached Berlin; they would have made Europe uninhabitable. France was charming as an empire or as a monarchy, but as a brand-new republic it was simply detestable.

We went on to Turin, where we stayed for a day or two; and while here I sent a copy of my *Inner Life of Syria* to the Princess Margherita of Savoy, now Queen of Italy, who was pleased to receive the same very graciously. From Turin we went to Milan, where we lapsed into the regular routine of Italian society, so remarkable for the exquisite amenity of its old civilization (as far as manners are concerned), and for the stiffness and mediæval semi-barbarism of its surroundings. As an instance of this we had occasion to call on a personage to whom we had letters of introduction. We sent in our letters with a visiting-card by the porter, asking when we should call. The reply was, "Va bene," which was pleasant, but vague. We took heart of grace, and asked at the door, "Is the Signor Conte visible?" The janitor replied, "His Excellency receives at 8 o'clock p.m." We replied, "At that time we shall be on the railway." The domestic, with leisurely movement, left us in the hall, and dawdled upstairs to report the remarkable case of the importunate English. By-and-by he returned, and showed us into the saloon, a huge, bare, fireless room, with a few grotesque photographs and French prints on the walls, and a stiff green sofa and chairs. The Signor Conte kept us waiting twenty minutes, whilst he shaved and exchanged his dressing-gown for the suit of sables which is the correct raiment of the Latin race. Nothing could be more polished than his manners. He received us with a cordiality which at once won our hearts. But we were introduced to him by a bosom friend; our pursuits and tastes were the same. Why then could not he ask us up to his cosy study to give us coffee and a cigarette? "Sarebbe proprio indecente" ("It would really be too rude"), was the reply, although both he and we would have liked it extremely. So for want of time to crack this hard nutshell we never got at the kernel.

From Milan we went to Venice, which we found enveloped in a white fog, with a network of lagoons meandering through streets of the foulest mud. Venice is pre-eminently a hot-weather city. In winter, with her cold canals and wet alleys, deep rains and dense mists, her huge, unwarmed palaces, and her bare, draughty hotels, she is a veritable wet place of punishment. We stayed in Venice for some days, and made several pleasant acquaintances. I had with me a German maid, who had never seen Venice. She went in a gondola for the first time, and was at the highest pitch of excitement at finding that all was water. She marvelled at the absence of cabs and dust, and exclaimed perpetually, "Nothing but water, water everywhere"; which we naturally capped with, "But not a drop to drink," until I believe she fancied that drink was the only thing we English ever thought of.

On December 23 we went across to Trieste by the midnight boat, and next morning I was at Trieste again, my much-loved home of four years and a half. I found it all to a hair as I had left it just a year ago, for I had been absent twelve months in England. Christmas Night, however, was a little sad. We had accepted an invitation for a Christmas dinner, and had given the servants leave to go out to see their friends;

but Richard was unfortunately taken ill, and could not dine out, and he went to bed. Of course I stayed with him; but we had nobody to cook for us, nor anything to eat in the house except bread and olives. I went to the pantry and foraged, and with this simple fare ate my Christmas dinner by his bedside.

We stopped in Trieste eight days, just to pack up and complete arrangements for our tour; and on the last day of the old year we left for Jeddah. We were aware that we were starting for India two or three months too late, and would have to encounter the heat and fatal season to accomplish it; but as Richard said, "Consuls, like beggars, can't be choosers," and we were only too glad to be able to go at all. Everybody was most kind to us, and a lot of friends came to a parting midday dinner, and accompanied us to our ship to see us off. The Government boat, containing the *Capitaine du Port* and the sailors, in uniform, took us to our ship, an honour seldom accorded to any but high Austrian officials; and the Duke of Würtemberg, Commander-in-chief at Trieste, and several others came to wish us "God-speed." I shall never forget their kindness, for I appreciated the honour which they did to Richard. It is strange how much more willing those in authority abroad were to do him justice than the Government at home.

The run from Trieste to Port Said occupied six days and six nights. Our ship was the *Calypso* (Austrian Lloyd's), a good old tub, originally built for a cattle-boat. We were the only passengers, and, with the captain and his officers, we made a family party, and I was never more comfortable on board ship in my life. The voyage to Port Said has been so often described that I need not dwell upon it again. We had fair weather for the first five days, and then there was a decided storm, which, however, did not last long. One gets so knocked about in a steamer that baths are impossible; one can only make a hasty toilet at the most, being obliged to hold on to something, or be knocked the while from one end of the cabin to the other; one dines, so to speak, on the balance, with the food ever sliding into one's lap. Our boat danced about throughout the voyage in a most extraordinary manner, which made me think that she had but little cargo. I spent most of the time on deck, "between blue sea and azure air," and I did a good deal of reading. I read Moore's *Veiled Prophet of Khorassán* and other books, including *Lalla Rookh* and *The Light of the Harím*; also Smollett's *Memoirs of a Lady of Quality*, which I found coarse, but interesting. Some one told me that a course of Smollett was more or less necessary to form one for novel-writing, so I took that and *The Adventures of Roderick Random* on board to study, in case I should ever write a novel. I felt rather displeased when Smollett's Lady of Quality married her second husband, and quite *bouleversée* long before I arrived at her fifteenth lover.

Port Said shows itself upon the southern horizon in two dark lines, like long piles or logs of wood lying upon the sea, one large and one small. These are the white town and the black town, apparently broken by an inlet of sea, and based upon a strip of yellow sand.

The sea is most unwholesome and stagnant. The houses of Port Said looked like painted wooden toys. The streets were broad, but the shops were full of nothing but rubbish, and were surrounded by dogs and half-naked, dark-brown gutter-boys. There is a circular garden in the centre of the European part, with faded flowers, and a kiosk for the band to play in. The most picturesque and the dirtiest part is the Arab town, with its tumble-down houses and bazar. The people wear gaudy prints and dirty mantles bespangled with gold. There were a great many low-class music-halls and gambling- and dancing-saloons. Port Said is in fact a sort of Egyptian Wapping, and I am told the less one knows about its morals the better.

While we were strolling about the Arab part, my German maid, who was in an Eastern place for the first time, came upon a man filling a goat-skin with water. She saw a pipe and the skin distending, and heard the sound. She had often heard me say how cruel the Easterns were to animals; and knowing my tenderness on that point, she ran after me in a great state of excitement, and pulled my arm, crying out, "*O Euer Gnaden!* The black man is filling the poor sow with gas! Do come back and stop him!"

The next morning early we began to steam slowly up the long ditch called the Canal, and at last to the far east we caught a gladdening glimpse of the desert—the wild, waterless Wilderness of Sur, with its waves and pyramids of sand catching the morning rays, with its shadows of mauve, rose pink, and lightest blue, with its plains and rain-sinks, bearing brown dots, which

PORT SAID.

[Page 562.

were tamarisks (manna trees). The sky was heavenly blue, the water a deep band of the clearest green, the air balmy and fresh. The golden sands stretched far away ; an occasional troop of Bedawin with their camels and goats passed, and reminded me of those dear, dead days at Damascus. It all came back to me with a rush. Once more I was in the East. I had not enjoyed myself so much with Nature for four years and a half. With the smell of the desert air in our nostrils, with Eastern pictures before our eyes, we were even grateful for the slowness of the pace at which we travelled. They were the pleasantest two days imaginable, like a river picnic. We reached Suez, with its air of faded glory, at length ; and there we shipped a pious pilot, who said his prayers regularly, and carefully avoided touching my dog. Of course he was from Mecca ; but, unhappily for his reputation, the first night spent at Jeddah gave him a broken nose, the result of a scrimmage in some low coffee-house.

At last we neared Jeddah, the port of Mecca. The approach was extraordinary. For twenty miles it is protected by Nature's breakwaters, lines of low, flat reefs, barely covered, and not visible until you are close upon them. There was no mark or lighthouse save two little white posts, which might easily be mistaken for a couple of gulls. In and out of these reefs the ship went like a serpent. There was barely passage for it between them ; but of course no pilot would attempt it save in broad daylight. At length we reached the inner reef. We found the open roadstead full of ships, with hardly room to swing, and a strong north-west wind, so that we could not get a place. We ran right into the first at anchor, the *Standard*, a trading-ship of Shields, built of iron. Richard and I were standing on the bridge, and he touched my arm and said:

"By Jove! We're going right into that ship."

"Oh no," I answered; "with the captain and the pilot on the bridge, and all the crew in the forecastle, it can only be a beautiful bit of steering. We shall just shave her."

The words were scarcely out of my mouth when smash went our bulwarks like brown paper, and our yardarms crumpled up like umbrellas. I had jokingly threatened them with the "thirteenth" the day before, but they had laughed at me.

"Il tredici!" shouted the second officer, as he flew by us.

The crews of both ships behaved splendidly, and the cry on board our ship was, "Where is the English captain? I do not see him."

"No," we answered, "you do not see him, but we can hear him." And sure enough there he was all right, and swearing quite like himself. There is nothing like an Englishman for a good decisive order; and who can blame him if he adds at such times a little powder to drive the shot home?

We were about three hours disentangling ourselves.

I was delighted with my first view of Jeddah. It is the most *bizarre* and fascinating town. It looks as if it were an ancient model carved in old ivory, so white and fanciful are the houses, with here and there a minaret. It was doubly interesting to me, because

Richard came here by land from his famous pilgrimage to Mecca. Mecca lies in a valley between two distant ranges of mountains. My impression of Jeddah will always be that of an ivory town embedded in golden sand.

We anchored at Jeddah for eight days, which time we spent at the British Consulate on a visit. The Consulate was the best house in all Jeddah, close to the sea, with a staircase so steep that it was like ascending the Pyramids. I called it the Eagle's Nest, because of the good air and view. It was a sort of bachelors' establishment; for in addition to the Consul and Vice-Consul and others, there were five bachelors who resided in the building, whom I used to call the "Wreckers," because they were always looking out for ships with a telescope. They kept a pack of bull-terriers, donkeys, ponies, gazelles, rabbits, pigeons; in fact a regular menagerie. They combined Eastern and European comfort, and had the usual establishment of dragomans, kawwasses, and servants of all sizes, shapes, and colour. I was the only lady in the house, but we were nevertheless a very jolly party.

Our first excursion was to Eve's Tomb, as it is called, a large curious building in a spacious enclosure. Two or three holy people are buried here, and the place commands a lovely view of the distant mountains, beyond which lies Mecca.

The inhabitants of Jeddah are very interesting in many ways. There are some two hundred nautch-girls there; but they are forbidden to dance before men, though I have heard that the law can be evaded on occasions. In the plains there are two different types of Arabs : the Bedawin, and the "settled men." The latter are a fine, strong, healthy race, though very wild and savage. We used frequently to ride out into the desert and make excursions. I would have given anything to have gone to Mecca. It was hard to be so near, and yet to have to turn round and come back. There was a rumour that two Englishmen had gone up to Mecca for a lark, and had been killed. This was not true. But all the same Mecca was not safe for a European woman, and it was not the time to show my blue eyes and broken Arabic on holy ground. I therefore used to console myself by returning from our expeditions in the desert through the Mecca Gate of Jeddah, and then riding through the bazars, half dark and half lit, to see the pilgrims' camels. The bazars literally swarmed with a picturesque and variegated mob, hailing from all lands, and of every race and tongue. We were not interfered with in any way; though had it been 1853, the year when Richard went to Mecca, to have taken these rides in the desert, and to have walked through the Mecca Gate, would most certainly have cost us our lives. I also saw the khan where Richard lived as one of these pilgrims in 1853, and the minaret which he sketched in his book on Mecca. While we were at Jeddah the Governor and all those who knew the story of his pilgrimage to Mecca called on us, and were very civil.

Our days at Jeddah were very pleasant ones. In the evening we used to sit outside the Consulate, and

ARAB CAMEL-DRIVERS. [*Page* 566.

have some sherry and a cigarette, and play with the dogs. One evening Richard came in and discovered me anxiously nursing what I thought was a dying negro. He was very angry, for he found him to be only drunk, and there was a great shout of merriment among all our colony in the Consulate—" my boys," as I used to call them—when the truth came out. These terrible boys teased the negro by putting snuff up his nose. They were awful boys, but such fun. They were always up to all sorts of tricks. When the food was bad, they used to call the cook in, and make him eat it. "What's this?" they would say. "No! no! Massa; me lose caste." "Hold your tongue, you damned scoundrel! Eat it directly." One day it was seven big *smoked* onions which the cook had to consume. I am bound to say that it had a good effect upon him, for the table was certainly excellent after this. I wish we could follow some such plan in England with our cooks. Even more did I wish we could do so at Trieste. I thought the dogs were worse than the boys. There were about ten bull-dogs in the house. They used to worry everything they saw, and sent every pariah flying out of the bazars. Since I left Jeddah I heard that the natives had poisoned all these dogs, which I really think served the boys right, but not the dogs. I remember too, on one or two occasions, when we were riding out Meccawards, my horse was so thin and the girths were so large that my saddle came round with me, and I had a spill on the sand, which greatly delighted the boys, but did not hurt me.

I was so sorry to part with them all; we were good friends together. But after eight exceedingly pleasant days at Jeddah we received notice to embark, and we had to say good-bye and go on board the *Calypso*. The sea was very rough, and I sat on a chair lashed to the deck. The *Calypso* was bound for Bombay, and had taken on board at Jeddah and stowed away some eight hundred pilgrims, who were returning to India from Mecca. They were packed like cattle, and as the weather was very rough the poor pilgrims suffered terribly. The waves were higher than the ship. I crawled about as well as I could, and tried to help the pilgrims a little. The second day one of them died, and was buried at sunset. I shall never forget that funeral at sea. They washed the body, and then put a strip of white stuff round the loins, and a bit of money to show that he is not destitute when he arrives in the next world. Then they tied him up in a sheet, and with his head and feet tied he looked just like a big white cracker. He was then laid upon a shutter with a five-pound bar of iron bound to his feet, and after a short Arabic prayer they took him to the side and hurled him over. There was no mourning or wailing among the pilgrims. On the contrary, they all seemed most cheerful over this function; and of course, according to their way of thinking, a man would be glad to die, as he went straight to heaven. But I am bound to say that it had a most depressing effect upon me, for we had twenty-three funerals in twelve days. They seemed to take it very much as a matter of course; but I kept saying to myself, "That poor Indian and I might both be lying dead to-day. There would be a little more ceremony over me, and (not of course including my husband) my death would cast a gloom over the dinner-table possibly a couple of days. Once we were shunted down the ship's side, the sharks would eat us both, and perhaps like me a little the better, as I am fat and well fed, and do not smell of cocoa-nut oil; and then we would both stand before the throne of God to be judged—he with his poverty, hardships, sufferings, pilgrimage, and harmless life, and I with all my faults, my happy life, my luxuries, and the little wee bit of good I have ever done or ever thought, to obtain mercy with; only equal that our Saviour died for us both."

I can hardly express what I suffered during that fortnight's voyage on board the pilgrim-ship. It was an experience which I would never repeat again. Imagine eight hundred Moslems, ranging in point of colour through every shade from lemon or *café au lait* to black as ebony; races from every part of the world, covering every square inch of deck, and every part of the hold fore and aft, packed like sardines, men, women, and babies, reeking of cocoa-nut oil. It was a voyage of horror. I shall never forget their unwashed bodies, their sea-sickness, their sores, the dead and the dying, their rags, and last, but not least, their cookery. Except to cook or fetch water or kneel in prayer, none of them moved out of the small space or position which they assumed at the beginning of the voyage. Those who died did not die of disease so much as of privation and fatigue, hunger, thirst, and opium. They died of vermin and misery. I shall never forget the expression of dumb, mute, patient pain which most of them wore. I cannot eat my dinner if I see a dog looking wistfully at it. I therefore spent the whole day staggering about our rolling ship with sherbet and food and medicines, treating dysentery and fever. During my short snatches of sleep I dreamt of these horrors too. But it was terribly disheartening work, owing to their fanaticism. Many of them listened to me with more faith about food and medicines because I knew something of the Korán, and could recite their Bismíllah and their call to prayer.

At last we arrived at Aden, where a troop of Somali lads came on board, with their bawling voices and their necklaces and their mop-heads of mutton wool, now and then plastered with lime. They sell water, firewood, fowls, eggs, and so forth. We landed at Aden for a few hours. It is a wild, desolate spot; the dark basalt mountains give it a sombre look. Richard and I spent some hours with the wife of the Governor, or Station Commandant, at her house. It was terribly hot. I think it was Aden where the sailors reappeared who had died and gone to certain fiery place; and on being asked why they came back, they replied that they had caught cold, and had got leave to come and fetch their blankets!

We returned at half-past four in the afternoon to our ship and the pilgrims. The weather that night became very rough, and during the night a Bengali fell overboard. His companion, who witnessed the accident, said nothing; and on being asked later where he was, replied casually, "I saw him fall overboard about three hours ago." Such are the ways of these peculiar pilgrims. They have no more sympathy for one another than cattle. None would give a draught of water to the dying; and as for praying over the corpses before throwing them overboard, if they could help it they would scarcely take the trouble. It was too rough all the next day for reading or writing; and to add to our discomfort two Russian passengers got drunk, and fought at the table, and called each other " liar and coward," " snob and thief," " spy and menial," and other choice epithets. However, their bark was worse than their bite, for they cooled down after they had succeeded in upsetting us all.

I staggered about on deck for the next few days as much as possible, and again did what I could for the pilgrims; but it was weary work. I doctored several of them; but our Russian passengers aforesaid brought me word later that when those who must in any case have expired, died, the others said it was I who poisoned them; and that was all the thanks I got for my pains. If it were so, I wonder why did the whole ship run after me for help? One old man said, " Come, O bountiful one, and sit a little amongst us and examine my wife, who has the itch, and give her something to cure it." But I got wary, and I said, " If I were to give her any medicine, she will presently die of weakness, and I shall be blamed for her death." However, I did what I could. In some of the cases I asked my maid to come and help me; but she turned away in disgust, and said, " No thank you; I have the nose of a princess, and cannot do such work." And really it was horrible, for many came to me daily to wash, clean, anoint, and tie up their feet, which were covered with sores and worms.

On January 30 a north-east wind set in with violence. Every one was dreadfully sick. The ship danced like a cricket-ball, and the pilgrims howled with fright, and six died. The next day the weather cleared up, and it lasted fine until we reached Bombay. We had a delightful evening, with balmy air, crescent moon, and stars, and the Dalmatian sailors sang glees. That day another pilgrim died, and was robbed. His body was rifled of his bit of money as he lay dying, and they fought like cats before his eyes for the money he had been too avaricious to buy food with and keep himself alive.

At last, betimes, on February 2, the thirty-third day after leaving Trieste, a haze of hills arose from the eastward horizon, and we knew it to be India. Then the blue water waxed green, greenish, and brown, like to liquid mud. The gulls became tamer and more numerous, and jetsam and flotsam drifted past us. We sighted land very early. As we were running in the pilot came alongside, and called up to the captain, "Have you any sickness on board?" The answer was, "Yes." "Then," said the pilot, "run up the yellow flag. I will keep alongside in a boat, and you make for Butcher's Island" (a horrible quarantine station). I was standing on the bridge, and, seeing the yellow flag hoisted, and hearing the orders, felt convinced that there was a mistake. So I made a trumpet with my hands, and holloaed down to the pilot, "Why have you run up that flag? We have got no disease." "Oh yes you have; either cholera or small-pox or yellow jack." "We have nothing of the sort," I answered. "Then why did the captain answer 'Yes'?" he replied. "Because it is the only English word he knows," I cried. Then he asked me for particulars, and said he would go off for the doctor, and we were to stand at a reasonable distance from Bombay. This took place in a spacious bay, surrounded by mountains, a poor imitation of the Bay of Rio. Presently the doctor arrived. Richard explained, and we were allowed to land. I shall never forget the thankfulness of the pilgrims, or the rush they made for the shore. They swarmed like rats down the ropes, hardly waiting for the boats. They gave Richard and me a sort of cheer, as they attributed their escape from quarantine to our intervention. Indeed, if we had been herded together a few more days, some disease must have broken out.

And thus we set foot in India.

CHAPTER XXII

INDIA

(1876)

> Where'er I roam, whatever realms to see,
> My heart, untravelled, fondly turns to thee.
>
> GOLDSMITH.

ON arriving at **Bombay**, we housed ourselves at Watson's Esplanade Hotel, a very large building. We went to see the sights of the town, and I was very much interested in all that I saw, though the populace struck me as being stupid and uninteresting, not like the Arabs at all. As I was new to India I was much struck by the cows with humps; by brown men with patches of mud on their foreheads, a stamp showing their Brahmin caste; by children, and big children too, with no garments except a string of silver bells; and by men lying in their palanquins, so like our hospital litters that I said, "Dear me! The small-pox must be very bad, for I see some one being carried to the hospital every minute." The picturesque trees, the coloured temples, and the Parsee palaces, garnished for weddings, also impressed themselves upon my mind.

The next day we made an excursion to see the Caves

THE CAVES OF ELEPHANTA.

(*Page* 574.)

of Elephanta. These caves are on an island about an hour's steaming from Bombay. They are very wonderful, and are natural temples, or chapels, to Shiva in his triune form, Brahma, Vishnu, and Shiva, and other gods, and are carved or hewn out of the solid rock. The entrance to the caves is clothed with luxuriant verdure.

The day following a friend drove us with his own team out to Bandora, about twelve miles from Bombay, where he had a charming bungalow in a wild spot close to the sea. We drove through the Máhim Woods—a grand, wild, straggling forest of palms of all kinds, acacias, and banyan trees. The bungalow was rural, solitary, and refreshing, something after the fashion of the Eagle's Nest we had made for ourselves at Bludán in the old days in Syria. Towards sunset the Duke of Sutherland (who, when Lord Stafford, had visited us at Damascus) and other friends arrived, and we had a very jolly dinner and evening. It was the eve of a great feast, and young boys dressed like tigers came and performed some native dancing, with gestures of fighting and clawing one another, which was exceedingly graceful.

The feast was the *Talút*, or Mūharram, a Moslem miracle play; and on our return to Bombay I went to see it. I had to go alone, because Richard had seen it before, and none of the other Europeans apparently cared to see it at all. The crowd was so great I had to get a policeman's help. They let me into the playhouse at last. The whole place was a blaze of lamps and mirrors. A brazier filled with wood was flaring up, and there was a large white tank of water. It was an extraordinary sight. The fanaticism, frenzy, and the shrieks of the crowd made a great impression on me. The play was a tragedy, a passion play; and the religious emotion was so intense and so contagious that, although I could not understand a word, I found myself weeping with the rest.

Among other things, during our stay at Bombay, we went to the races at Byculla, a very pretty sight, though not in the least like an English racecourse. The Eastern swells were on the ground and in carriages, and the Europeans in the club stand. There was only one good jockey, and whatever horse he rode won, even when the others were more likely. There was an Arab horse which ought to have beaten everything, but the clumsy black rider sat like a sack and ruined his chances. I saw that at once, and won nine bets one after another.

We went to a great many festivities during our stay at Bombay. Among other things we breakfasted with a Persian Mirza, who knew Richard when he was at Bombay in 1848. After breakfast—quite a Persian feast—I visited his harím, where we women smoked a narghíleh and discussed religious topics, and they tried to convert me to El Islam. I also went to the wedding feast of the daughter of one of the most charming Hindú gentlemen, whose name is so long that I do not quote it, a most brilliant entertainment. I also went to some steeplechases and a garden-party at Parell (Government House). There was a large attendance, and much dressing; it was something like a mild Chiswick party. I amused myself with talking to the Bishop. I also went to the Byculla ball, which was very well done. While at Bombay I saw the mango trick for the first time. It is apt to astonish one at first to see a tree planted and grow before one's eyes without any apparent means to accomplish it. The Indian jugglers are clever, but I have seen better at Cairo. We were tired of the child being killed in the basket, and the mango trick soon became stale.

On February 21 we left Bombay for Mátherán, up in the mountains. We went by train to Narel; but the last stage of the journey, after Narel, had to be performed on horseback, or rather pony-back. We rode through seven miles of splendid mountain scenery, an ascent of two thousand seven hundred feet. Carriages could not come here unless they were carried upon the head like the philanthropist's wheelbarrows by the Africans of Sierra Leone. Our road was very rough, and our ponies stumbled and shied at the dogs. I was badly dressed for the occasion. My small hired saddle cut me; it was loose, and had too long a stirrup; and although we were only two hours ascending, and six hours out, I was tired by the time we arrived at Mátherán.

The next day we were up betimes. I was delighted with the wooded lanes and the wild flowers, the pure atmosphere, and the lights and shadows playing on the big foliage. We looked down on magnificent ravines among buttressed-shaped mountains. The fantastic Ghâts rose up out of the plain before us. On clear days there was a lovely view of Bombay and the sea with the bright sun shining upon it. The scenery

everywhere was grand and bold. We made several
excursions in the neighbourhood, and I found the
natives, or jungle people, very interesting.

On the 23rd we left Mátherán. We started early in
the morning for **Narel**, walked down the steep descent
from Mátherán, then **rode**. We arrived hot and a little
tired at Narel station, and the train came in at 10 a.m.
We mounted the break, and much enjoyed the ascent
of the Highlands, arriving in about three hours at
Lanauli on the Bhore Ghát. At Lanauli we found a
fairly comfortable hotel, though it was terribly hot.
What made the heat worse was that most of the houses
at Lanauli were covered with corrugated-iron roofs,
which were bad for clothes, as they sweated rusty
drops all over the room, which left long stains on one's
linen and dresses. I came away with everything ruined.
The air was delicious, like that of São Paulo or
Damascus in the spring.

The next morning we were up and off at dawn to
the Karla Caves. There was brought to the door at
dawn for Richard a jibbing, backing pony, with vicious
eyes, and for me a mangy horse like a knifeboard,
spavined, with weak legs, and very aged, but nevertheless showing signs of "blood." On top of this poor
beast was a saddle big enough for a girl of ten, and I,
being eleven stone, felt ashamed to mount. However,
there was nothing else to be done. We rode four miles
along the road, and then crossed a river valley of the
mountains. Here we descended, and had to climb a
goatlike path until we came to what looked like a gash
or ridge in the mountain-side, with a belt of trees.

When we got to the top, we sat on the stones, facing one of the most wonderful Buddhist temples in India. It was shaped just like our cathedrals, with a horseshoe roof of teak-wood, which has defied the ravages of time. The Brahmins keep this temple. On either side of the entrances are splendid carved lions, larger than life. A little temple outside is consecrated by the Brahmins to Devi. We were not allowed to go nearer to this goddess than past a triangular ornament covered with big bells; but they lit it for us and let us peep in, and it disclosed a woman's face and figure so horribly ugly as to give one a nightmare—a large, round, red face, with squinting glass eyes, open mouth, hideous teeth, and a gash on her cheek and forehead. She is the Goddess of Destruction, and is purposely made frightful.

It was very hot returning. My poor horse suddenly faltered, giving a wrench to my back, and bringing my heart into my mouth when it almost sat down behind. We passed troops of Brinjari, whose procession lasted for about two miles. This is a very strong, wild race, which only marries among its own tribe. The women were very picturesquely dressed, and glared at me defiantly when I laughed and spoke to them. They carried their babies in baskets on their heads. We got home about 11 a.m., so that we had made our excursion betimes.

After breakfast and bath we went to the station. Soon our train came up, and after a two and a half hours' journey through the Indrauni river valley we arrived at Poonah. The next day we drove all about Poonah, and went to see the Palace of the Peshwas, in the

Indian bazar. It is now used as a library below and a native law courts above. Then we went to Parbat, the Maharatta chief's palace. There are three pagodas in this building, and one small temple particularly struck me. As it was sunset the wild yet mournful sound of tom-tom and kettle and cymbal and reed suddenly struck up. I could have shut my eyes and fancied myself in camp again in the desert, with the wild sword-dances being performed by the Arabs.

The following day at evening we left Poonah for Hyderabad. We travelled all night and next day, and arrived towards evening. Hyderabad lies eighteen hundred feet above sea-level. As most people know, it is by far the largest and most important native city in India, and is ruled over by our faithful ally the Nizam. Richard and I were to be the guests of Major and Mrs. Nevill; and our kind friends met us cordially at the station. In those days Major Nevill was the English officer who commanded the Nizam's troops; and though he ranked as Major, he was really Commander-in-chief, having no one over him except Sir Salar Jung. Mrs. Nevill was the eldest daughter of our talented predecessor in the Consulate at Trieste, Charles Lever, the novelist. She was most charming, and a perfect horsewoman. We had delightful quarters in Major Nevill's "compound." The rooms were divided into sleeping- and bath-rooms, and tents were thrown out from either entrance. The front opened into the garden. Two servants, a man and a woman, were placed at our disposal. In short, nothing was wanting to our comfort. That night we went to a dinner-party and ball at Government House—Sir Richard and Lady Meade's.

Next morning we were up betimes, and out on elephants to see the town. It was my first mount on an elephant, and my sensations were decidedly new. The beasts look very imposing with their gaudy trappings; and as we rode through Hyderabad we were most cordially greeted by all. The houses were flat, something like those of Damascus; and the streets were broad and spanned by high arches, whose bold simplicity was very striking. The Nizam's palace, at least a mile long, was covered with delicate tracery; and many a mosque, like lacework, rose here and there. But the *cachet* of all in Hyderabad was size, boldness, and simplicity.

After inspecting the town we proceeded to the palace of Sir Salar Jung. We found him a noble, chivalrous, large-hearted Arab gentleman, of the very best stamp; and throughout our stay at Hyderabad he was most kind to us. His palace contained about seven courts with fountains, and was perfectly magnificent; but unfortunately, instead of being furnished with oriental luxury, which is so grand and rich, it was full of European things—glass, porcelain, and bad pictures. One room, however, was quite unique: the ceiling and walls were thickly studded with china—cups, saucers, plates, and so forth—which would have aroused the envy of any china-maniac in London. Sir Salar entertained us to a most luxurious breakfast, and when that was over showed us a splendid collection of weapons, consisting of swords, sheaths, and daggers, studded with gorgeous jewels. After that we inspected the stables, which reminded me somewhat of the Burlington Arcade, for they were open at both ends, and the loose boxes, where the shops would be, opened into a passage running down the centre. There were about a hundred thorough-bred Arab and Persian horses. When we left Sir Salar, he presented me with four bottles of attar of roses.

The next few days formed a round of festivity. There were breakfasts, dinner-parties at the Residency and elsewhere, with a little music to follow, and many excursions. Sir Salar Jung lent me a beautiful grey Arab, large, powerful, and showy. He had never before had a side-saddle on, but he did not seem to mind it a bit. Among other places we visited the palace of the Wikar Shums Ool Umárá, one of the three great dignitaries of the Nizam's country, where we were received with great honour by a guard of soldiers and a band of music. The Wikar was a thin, small, well-bred old gentleman, with a yellow silk robe and a necklace of large emeralds. He was attended by a fat, jolly son in a green velvet dressing-gown, and one tall, thin, sallow-faced youth, who looked like a bird with the pip. We had a capital breakfast. The hall was full of retainers and servants, who pressed me to eat as they served the dishes, and "Take mutton cutlet, 'im very good" was whispered in my ear with an excellent English accent. We then visited the jewellery of the palace, a most beautiful collection; and the sacred armour, which surpasses description. At last we saw something very unique—an ostrich race.

The man mounts, sits back, puts his legs under the wings, and locks his feet under the breast. The birds go at a tremendous pace, and kick like a horse.

The next day we witnessed an assault-of-arms. There were about two hundred performers, and three hundred to look on. There were some very good gymnastics, sword exercises, single-stick, and so on. They also showed us some cock-fighting, and indeed all sorts of fighting. They fight every kind of animal, goats, birds, even quails and larks, which are very plucky, and want to fight ; but they pull them off if they want to ill-use one another too much. I did not care to see this, and went away.

The next day we drove to the country palace of the Amir el Kebir. He was the third of the three great men in Hyderabad, who jointly managed the Nizam's affairs. The other two were Sir Salar Jung, Regent and Prime Minister, and the Wikar Shums Ool Umárá. They were all relations of the Nizam. Here again was a beautiful palace in gardens, full of storks, pigeons, and other birds. Besides birds, there were flowers ; and all the gardens and terraces were covered with their beautiful purple Indian honeysuckle. We inspected the town also, each riding on a separate elephant. And when that was over every one went back to breakfast with the Amir ; and a charming breakfast it was, with delicious mangoes. Our host wore a lovely cashmere robe, like a dressing-gown, and gorgeous jewels.

Our last recollections of Hyderabad were brilliant, for Sir Salar Jung gave a magnificent evening *fête*. One of the large courts of the palace was illuminated :

the starlight was above us, the blaze of wax lights and chandeliers lit up every hall around the court, and coloured lamps and flowers were everywhere. There was a nautch, which I thought very stupid, for the girls did nothing but eat sweetmeats, and occasionally ran forward and twirled round for a moment with a half-bold, semi-conscious look; and only one was barely good-looking. Perhaps that is the nautch to dance before ladies; but in Syria, I remember, they danced much better without being "shocking." We had a most delicious dinner afterwards, at which we were waited on by retainers in wild, picturesque costumes. When that was over, the band played. We walked about and conversed, were presented with attar of roses, and went home.

The next morning we went to Secunderabad. It was a prosperous European station, with three regiments, but nothing interesting. We proceeded on elephants to Golconda, a most interesting place; but as no European has ever been permitted to enter it, I can only describe what we were allowed to see without. We viewed the town from outside, and saw a hill covered with buildings. The throne-hall, with arched windows, they say is a mere shell. The King's palace and defences occupy the mound which is in the midst of the town. The town proper is on the flat ground. It is surrounded by walls, battlements, and towers, and reminded me of old Damascus and Jerusalem. In it dwells many an old feudal chief. Past these walls no European or Christian has ever been allowed. The Tombs of the Kings are very ancient, and are situated outside the town. We were admitted to these, and they reminded me of the Tower Tombs of Palmyra. They were enormous domes, set on a square, broad base, the upper section beautifully carved, or covered with Persian tiles, which bore Arabic and Hindústani inscriptions. Abdullah's tomb and that of his mother are the best. The prevailing style in both is a dome standing on an oblong or square, both of grey granite. The predominant colour is white, and in some cases picked out with green. There was also a beautiful garden of palm trees, and a labyrinth of arches. We wandered about this romantic spot, of which we had heard so much, and thought of all the mines and riches of Golconda. It was a balmy night when we were there; fireflies spangled the domed tombs in the palm gardens, lit by a crescent moon. I could not forget that I was in the birthplace of the famed Koh-i-noor.

We returned to Hyderabad, and next morning we rose at four o'clock, and took the train at seven to return to Bombay. Our kind host and hostess, the Nevills, and Sir Richard Meade, the Governor, came to see us off. We had a comfortable carriage, and the railway officials were all most kind and civil; but the heat was so great that they were walking up and down periodically to arouse the passengers, as they have occasionally been found dead, owing to the heat; and two or three cases happened about that time.

When we got down to Bombay, we found it all *en fête* for the departure of the Prince of Wales, who was then doing his celebrated Indian tour. I shall never forget the enthusiasm on that occasion. The Prince was looking strong and well, brown, handsome, and happy, and every inch a Royal Imperial Prince and future Emperor. He went away taking with him the hearts of all his subjects and the golden opinions of all true men and women.

We stayed at Bombay some little time, and among other things we visited the Towers of Silence, or Parsee charnel-house, the burying-place of the "Fire Worshippers," which are situated on a hill-summit outside Bombay. We ascended by a giant staircase, half a mile long, overhung by palms and tropical vegetation. We obtained a splendid view of Bombay from this eminence, which we should have enjoyed had it not been that the palms immediately around us were thick with myriads of large black vultures, gorged with corpses of the small-pox and cholera epidemic, which was then raging in Bombay. The air was so heavy with their breath that (though people say it was impossible) I felt my head affected as long as we remained there. These myriads of birds feed only on corpses, and of necessity they must breathe and exhale what they feed upon. They fattened upon what bare contact with would kill us; they clustered in thousands. This burying-place, or garden, was full of public and private family towers. The great public tower is divided into three circles, with a well in the middle. It has an entrance and four outlets for water. First, there is a place for clothes, and a tank, like a huge metal barrel lying on its side. Here the priests, who are the operators, leave their garments. A large procession of Parsees, having accompanied the body as far as this spot, turn and wait outside the tower. The priests then place the body, if a man, in the first circle; if a woman, in the second circle; if a child, in the third: in the centre there is the door, well covered with a grating. The priests then stay and watch. The vultures descend; they fly round the moment they see a procession coming, and have to be kept at bay until the right moment. The body is picked clean in an hour by these vultures. It is considered very lucky if they pick out the right eye first instead of the left, and the fact is reported by the priests to the sorrowing relatives. When the bones are perfectly clean, a Parsee priest pushes them into the well. When the rain comes, it carries off the ashes and bones; and the water runs through these four outlets, with charcoal at the mouths to purify it, before entering and defiling the earth, which would become putrid and cause fever. The Parsees will not defile the earth by being buried in it, and consider it is an honour to have a *living sepulchre*. The vultures have on an average, when there is no epidemic, about three bodies a day, so that they can never be said to starve. The whole thing struck me as being revolting and disgusting in the extreme, and I was glad to descend from this melancholy height to Bombay.

We had a good deal of gaiety during our stay in Bombay, and every one was most kind. We saw many interesting people, and made many pleasant excursions, which were too numerous to be mentioned in detail here.

I have given a description of the Parsee burial-ground, and I think at the risk of being thought morbid that I must also describe our visit to the Hindú Smáshán, or burning-ground, in the Sonápur quarter, where we saw a funeral, or rather a cremation. The corpse was covered with flowers, the forehead reddened with sandalwood, and the mouth blackened. The bier was carried by several men, and one bore sacred fire in an earthenware pot. The body was then laid upon the pyre; every one walked up and put a little water in the mouth of the corpse, just as we throw dust on the coffin; they then piled more layers of wood on the body, leaving it in the middle of the pile. Then the relatives, beginning with the nearest, took burning brands to apply to the wood, and the corpse was burned. The ashes and bones are thrown into the sea. It was unpleasant, but not nearly so revolting to me as the vultures in the Parsee burying-ground. All the mourners were Hindú except ourselves, and they stayed and watched the corpse burning. Shortly the clothes caught fire, and then the feet. After that we saw no more except a great blaze, and smelt a smell of roasted flesh, which mingles with the sandalwood perfume of Bombay. The Smáshán, or burning-ground, is dotted with these burning-places.

A very interesting visit for me was to the Pinjrapole, or hospital for animals sick, maimed, and incurable. It was in the centre of the native quarter of Bombay, and was founded forty years ago by Sir Jamsetji Jijibhoy, who also left money for its support. I was told that the animals here were neglected and starved; but we took them quite unawares, and were delighted to find the contrary the case. There were old bullocks here that had been tortured and had their tails wrung off, which is the popular way in Bombay of making them go faster. There were orphan goats and calves, starving kittens and dogs. The blind, the maimed, the wounded of the animal creation, here found a home. I confess that I admire the religion that believes in animals having a kind of soul and a future, and permits their having a refuge where at least no one can hurt them, and where they can get food and shelter. God is too just to create things, without any fault of their own, only for slow and constant torture, for death, and utter annihilation.

Turning now to society at Bombay, and indeed Indian society generally, I must say that it is not to be outdone for hospitality. There is a certain amount of formality about precedence in all English stations, and if one could only dispense with it society would be twice as charming and attractive. I do not mean of course the formality of etiquette and good-breeding, but of all those silly little conventions and rules which arise for the most part from unimportant people trying to make themselves of importance. Of course they make a great point about what is called " official rank " in India, and the women squabble terribly over their warrants of precedence : the gradations thereof would puzzle even the chamberlain of some petty German court. The Anglo-Indian ladies of Bombay struck me for the most part as spiritless. They had a faded, washed-out look; and I do not wonder at it, considering the life they lead. They get up about nine, breakfast and pay or receive visits, then tiffen, siesta, a drive to the Apollo Bunder, to hear the band, or to meet their husbands at the Fort, dine and bed—that is the programme of the day. The men are better because they have cricket and polo. I found nobody stiff individually, but society very much so in the mass. The order of precedence seemed to be uppermost in every mind, and as an outsider I thought how tedious " ye manners and customs of ye Anglo-Indians" would be all the year round.

I found the native populace much more interesting. The great mass consists of Konkani Moslems, with dark features and scraggy beards. They were clad in chintz turbans, resembling the Parsee headgear, and in long cotton coats, with shoes turned up at the toes, and short drawers or pyjamas. There were also Persians, with a totally different type of face, and clothed in quite a different way, mainly in white with white turbans. There were Arabs from the Persian Gulf, sitting and lolling in the coffee-houses. There were athletic Afghans, and many other strange tribes. There were conjurers and snake-charmers, vendors of pipes and mangoes, and Hindú women in colours that pale those of Egypt and Syria. There were two sorts of Parsees, one white-turbaned, and the other whose headgear was black, spotted with red. I was much struck with the immense variety of turban on the men, and the *choli* and headgear on the women. Some of the turbans were of the size of a moderate round tea-table. Others fit the head tight. Some are worn straight, and some are cocked

THE BORAH (NATIVE) BAZAR, BOMBAY.

[*Page* 590.

sideways. Some are red and horned. The *choli* is a bodice which is put on the female child, who never knows what stays are. It always supports the bosom, and she is never without it day or night, unless after marriage, and whilst she is growing it is of course changed to her size from time to time. They are of all colours and shapes, according to the race. No Englishwoman could wear one, unless it were made on purpose for her; but I cannot explain why.

Bombay servants are dull and stupid. They always do the wrong thing for preference. They break everything they touch, and then burst into a " Yah, yah, yah!" like a monkey. If you leave half a bottle of sherry, they will fill it up with hock, and say, " Are they not both white wines, Sá'b?" If you call for your tea, the servant will bring you a saucer, and stare at you. If you ask why your tea is not ready, he will run downstairs and bring you a spoon, and so on. As he walks about barefoot you never hear him approach. You think you are alone in the room, when suddenly you are made to jump by seeing a black face close to you, star-gazing. If you have a visitor, you will see the door slowly open, and a black face protruded at least six times in a quarter of an hour. They are intensely curious, but otherwise as stolid as owls.

On April 16 we started for Máhábáleshwar, the favourite of all the sanatoria in India, save the Neilgherries, which are so far off as to be a very expensive journey from Bombay. Máhábáleshwar, in the Western Gháts, is therefore largely visited by Europeans from Bombay. We left Bombay by the

1.15 express train, reaching Poonah in seven hours. The air was like blasts out of a heated furnace. We dined at Poonah at a very comfortable inn. The distance from Poonah to Máhábáleshwar was seventy-five miles by road; so as we were going on the same evening we ordered a trap, and after dinner we set forth.

I cannot say it was a comfortable journey, for the springs of the trap were broken, and projections were sticking through the hard, narrow cushions in all directions into our unhappy bodies. Nevertheless we enjoyed the drive very much. It was a charming night, the moon late, being in the last quarter. We saw a great Moslem *fête* coming out of Poonah at night. The hills were illuminated in patterns and letters. We slept when it was dark, and I remember we drank a great deal of water, for it was a most thirsty night. At 6 a.m. we passed a wayside bungalow at Soorool, where we brought out our basket and tea, and had milk from the cow belonging to the old soldier who kept the bungalow. At the foot of the third steep mountain, Pasarni, we passed through Wye (Wahi), one of the prettiest and most interesting places, with the prettiest women in Western India, besides being a village of temples and holy tanks. The general effect of the temples, which were strewn about in all sizes and shapes, was that of a series of *blancmange* moulds.

At Wahi we alighted from the trap, and our ascent up the steep Pasarni Ghât was performed for us by sixteen coolies. It occupied us about two hours, and was very hot and dusty, and cruelly hard work; but the coolies did it much better than horses could have done. Once we came to a travelling bungalow, and stopped a few minutes to tie up some of our broken springs. After this we were very tired, and the last thirteen miles seemed almost insupportable. At last we entered the verdure of Máhábáleshwar at the summit, 4,780 feet above sea-level; but the inaccessibility of the place is compensated for by its interest when you arrive there, just as Palmyra is more precious than Ba'albak.

When at last we arrived we were thoroughly tired out. We dined, and went to bed. We had been out twenty-five hours, and had had no sleep for forty-one hours. I did not even remember the end of my dinner, and I have no recollection of how I got into bed for very sleepiness. We lodged at the Máhábáleshwar Hotel, which was very cheap, clean, and comfortable.

The next morning we were up at 5 a.m., and drove in a *tonga*, a sort of tea-cart, with small *tattoo* ponies, to Elphinstone Point, and to see the temples. It was a most enjoyable excursion; but it was quite spoiled for me by the brutal way in which the driver beat the poor little "tats" with his thick cowhide whip. It was misery to me. I got quite nervous; I bullied the driver, took his whip away, promised him *bakshísh* if he would not do it, and finally tried to drive myself. Then the foolish ponies stood stock-still directly I took the reins, and would not budge without the whip. At this point Richard cut in, and swore at the driver for being so cruel, and scolded me for spoiling an excursion by my ridiculous sensibilities. Then my fox-terrier put in her oar, and tried to bite the coachman for beating the ponies; and not being allowed, she laid her head on my shoulder and went into hysterics—the tears actually ran down her cheeks. We had a grand view from Elphinstone Point, and the temples also were interesting. We were glad to get back again at 9 a.m., for the sun was very trying. We made several pleasant excursions during our stay, and people were very kind. All the same, I did not greatly care for Máhábáleshwar. There was too much society; one could not ruralize enough. "Sets" are the rule, and priggishness is rampant, even in the primeval forest. Our visit was a brief one, and then we returned to Bombay.

After two days at Bombay Richard and I set sail in the British Indian Steamship Company's *Rajpootna* for distant and deserted Goa, a thirty-six hours' passage. It was a calm, fine evening when we started, but intensely hot. The next day there was a heavy swell, and many were ill. I went to bed thoroughly tired out, expecting to land the next morning. About five o'clock, as the captain told me overnight not to hurry myself, I got up leisurely. Presently a black steward came down, and said:

"Please, ma'am, the agent's here with your boat to convey you ashore. The captain desired me to say that he's going to steam on directly."

I was just at the stage of my toilet which rendered it impossible for me to open the door or come out, so I called through the keyhole:

"Please go with my compliments to the captain, and beg him to give me ten minutes or a quarter of an hour, and tell my husband what is the matter."

"I will go, ma'am," he answered; "but I am afraid the captain can't wait. It is his duty to go on."

"Go!" I shouted; and he went.

In two minutes down came the negro again.

"Captain says it's impossible; in fact the ship's moving now."

Well, as we were tied to time and many other things, and could not afford to miss our landing, I threw on a shawl and a petticoat, as one might in a shipwreck, and rushed out with my hair down, crying to the steward:

"Bundle all my things into the boat as well as you can; and if anything is left, take it back to the hotel at Bombay."

I hurried on deck, and to my surprise found that the steamer was not moving at all. Richard and the captain were quietly chatting together, and when they saw me all excited and dishevelled they asked me the cause of my undress and agitation. When I told them, the captain said:

"I never sent any message of the kind. I told you last night I should steam on at seven, and it is now only five."

I was intensely angry at the idea of a negro servant playing such a practical joke. I was paying £10 for a thirty-six hours' passage; and as I always treated everybody courteously, it was quite uncalled for and unprovoked. I thought it exceedingly impertinent, and told the captain so. Nevertheless he did not trouble to inquire into the matter. The Bishop of Ascalon,

Vicar-Apostolic at Bombay, was on board, and I told him about it, and he said that he had been treated just in the same way a year before on the same spot. The idea that such things should be allowed is a little too outrageous. Suppose that I had been a delicate and nervous passenger with heart complaint, it might have done me a great deal of harm.

A large boat arrived to take us and our baggage ashore. We were cast adrift in the open sea on account of a doubtful shoal. We had eight miles to row before we could reach Goa. Fortunately there was no storm. We rowed a mile and a half of open sea, five miles of bay, and one and a half of winding river, and at last landed on a little stone pier jutting a few yards into the water. We found a total absence of anything at Goa but the barest necessaries of life. There was no inn and no tent. We had either to sleep in our filthy open boat, or take our tents and everything with us. Goa is not healthy enough to sleep out *al fresco*. Fortunately a kind-hearted man, who was the agent of the steamers, and his wife, seeing the plight we were in, conceded us a small room in their house with their only spare single bed. Luckily we had one of those large straw Pondicherry reclining-chairs, which I had just bought from the captain of the steamer, and a rug; so Richard and I took the bed in turns night about, the other in the chair. We did not mind much, for we had come to see Goa, and were used to roughing it; but I confess that I like roughing it better out of doors than inside. There was little to be bought in Goa; but all that the residents had to give they offered with alacrity. It is the worst climate I ever was in, and I have experienced many bad ones. The thermometer was not nearly so high as I have known it in other places, but the depression was fearful. There was not a breath of air in Goa even at night, and the thirst was agonizing; even the water was hot, and the more one drank the more one wanted : it was a sort of purgatory. I cannot think how the people manage to live there : the place was simply *dead*; there is no other word for it. Of all the places I have ever been to, in sandy deserts and primeval forests, Goa was the worst. However, Richard wanted to revisit it, and I wanted to see it also with a particular object, which was to pay my respects to the shrine of the Apostle of India, St. Francis Xavier, which is situated in Old Goa.

We hired the only horse in the country, a poor old screw of a pony, broken down by mange and starvation and sores; and we harnessed him to the only vehicle we could find, a small open thing of wood made in the year 1 B.C., with room for two persons only. The wheels were nearly off, and the spring of one side was broken. The harness was made of old rusty chains and bits of string tied together. Our coachman and footman were two boys in little dirty shirts, with something round the loins kept together with bits of twine, and bare legs peeping out underneath like two sticks of chocolate.

Our first drive was to Cazalem, a place which reminded me of the Barra at Santos, in Brazil. Here several Europeans lived, I mean native Portuguese, mainly officials of the Government. As Richard wrote a book about Goa when he was there some thirty years before, there is not much that I can add to his description of the place.

Our next drive was to Old Goa, where is the tomb of St. Francis Xavier. Nothing is left of Old Goa but churches and monasteries. In the distance, with its glittering steeples and domes, it looks a grand place; but when we entered it, I found it to be a city of the dead—indeed it was the very abomination of desolation. The Bom Jesus is the church dedicated to St. Francis Xavier, my favourite saint, on account of his conversion of so many unbelievers. It is after the same pattern as all other Portuguese churches, a long, whitewashed, barn-shaped building. The object of my devotion, the tomb, is contained in a recess on a side of the altar dedicated to Xavier, and consists of a magnificently carved silver sarcophagus, enriched with *alto relievi*, representing different acts of the Saint's life. Inside is a gold box containing the remains of the Saint, shown to people with a great feast once in a century.

We made many excursions around and about Goa. In consequence of the dreadful climate they had of course to be either very early or very late. I shall never forget the moonlight scenery of the distant bay. The dull grey piles of ruined, desolate habitations, the dark hills clothed with a semi-transparent mist, the little streams glistening like lines of silver over the plain, and the purple surface of the creek—such was our night picture of Goa. We made two boat expeditions together—one to see a coffee plantation, in which is a petrified forest. Each expedition occupied two or three days. We embarked for the first in a filthy

GOA.

boat, full of unmentionable vermin, and started down the river in the evening, with storms of thunder and lightning and wind preluding the monsoon. On arrival we toiled up two miles of steep, rocky paths through cocoa groves. At the bottom of the hill was a little rivulet, and pieces of petrified wood were sticking to the bank. As we ascended the hill again we found the petrifications scattered all over the ground; they were composed chiefly of palms and pines; and most interesting they were. We returned from this expedition with our skins in a state of eruption from the bites of the lice and the stings of the mosquitoes.

Our last day at Goa was a very pleasant one. We had received a telegram saying the steamer would pass outside Goa at midnight, and would pick us up for the return journey to Bombay. These steamers are due once a fortnight, and this one was long past her time. Everybody was sorry that we were leaving, and we had great hospitality. In the morning we were entertained at breakfast by a gentleman who owned the largest and the best house in Goa. We had every variety of native food and fruit in abundance, good cool air and water—the latter produced by hanging the earthen water-bottles in the window, clothed with wet hay or grass. We were, in all, ten at table, native and European. Then the heat came on, and we had to retire. In the evening we were taken for an excursion in a boat to Cazalem. We coasted along for an hour, and sang glees under a fine moon, accompanied by a heavy swell. We were carried ashore on the shoulders of the natives, and were heralded first by the watch-dogs and then by the European inmates, who did not expect us. They were assembled in the verandah playing cards by the light of torches. We passed a merry evening, and returned to Goa by carriage. The seat gave way, and we had to sit on the edges.

On our return the night was dark, but we at once started in a large open boat, with four men to row and one to steer, to reach our steamer bound for Bombay, which, as I have already explained, did not pass nearer Goa than eight miles. We rowed down the river, and then across the bay for three hours, against wind and tide, bow on to heavy rollers, and at last reached the mouth of the bay, where is the Fort. We remained bobbing about in the open sea in the trough of the great waves for a considerable time, and a violent storm of rain, thunder, and lightning came on, so we put back to the Fort to find shelter under some arches. Then we went to sleep, leaving the boat *wálá* to watch for the steamer.

At 1.30 I was awakened by the sound of a gun booming across the water. I sprang up and aroused the others; but we could not see the lights of the steamer, and turned to sleep. An officer passed out of the Fort, and I fancied he said to another man that the ship was in; but he only looked at us and passed on. Presently I felt more fidgety, and making a trumpet of my hands I called out to the Secretary, who answered back that the ship had been laying to three-quarters of an hour, and that we should have gone off when the gun fired. People are so lazy and indolent in this climate that he did not trouble to let us know it before, though he was left there for that purpose. If we had not happened to have the mails and the agent with us in the boat, the ship would have gone on without us, which would have been an appalling disaster. So I stirred them up, and we were soon under way again and out to sea. By-and-by I saw the lights of the steamer, which looked about three miles off. Knowing the independence of these captains and the futility of complaints, I trembled lest the steamer should put farther to sea, and determined that no effort of mine should be spared to prevent it.

Richard slept or pretended to sleep, and so did some of the others; but I managed adroitly to be awkward with the boat-hook, and occasionally to prick their shins. I urged the boat *wálás* on with perpetual promises of *bakshish*. Everybody except myself was behaving with oriental calm, and leaving it to Kismet. It was of no use doing anything to Richard, so I pitched into the Secretary, who really had been most kind.

"Can't you shout 'Mails!'" I cried to him, as we got nearer. "They might hear you. You can shout loud enough when nobody wants to hear you."

At last, after an hour of anxiety, we reached the ship; but heavy seas kept washing us away from the ladder. No one had the energy to hold on to the rope, or hold the boat-hook to keep us close to her, so at last I did it myself, Richard laughing all the while at their supineness, and at my making myself so officious and energetic. But it was absolutely necessary. An English sailor threw me the rope. "Thanks," I cried, as I took advantage of an enormous wave to spring on to the ladder ; " I am the only man in the boat to-night." All came on board with us, and we had a parting stirrup-cup, in which they drank my health as " the only man in the boat." We then said farewell to our friends and to Goa.

We stayed at Bombay no longer than was absolutely necessary, and we embarked on our return journey to Trieste in the Austrian Lloyd's *Minerva*. It was an uneventful voyage, take it altogether. There were a good many passengers on board, who grumbled greatly at the food, as the manner is, and it was certainly a very hot and uncomfortable voyage. We stopped at Aden again, and passed Jeddah. Thence we steamed to Suez, where we anchored.

Here Richard and myself and six others left the ship to have a little run through Egypt, and we were soon surrounded by a number of Richard's old friends of Mecca days. It was a lovely evening when we landed, familiar to all who know Suez, with its blue sea, yellow sands, azure sky, and pink-and-purple mountains. Our visit was to Moses' Wells, about three miles in the Arabian Desert—a most picturesque spot, surrounded by tropical verdure, intermingled with fellah huts. The most romantic spot was a single tiny spring under an isolated palm tree, all alone on a little hillock of sand in the desert, far from all else. I said to Richard, " That tree and that spring have been created for each other, like you and I." We took our *kayf* for some hours with the Arabs, and we had some delicious Arab coffee and narghileh with them.

We remained a fortnight in Egypt, or rather more; and after then we embarked in another Lloyd's, the *Apollo*, for Trieste, where we arrived very quickly. I was glad to get back to the beautiful little city again, to receive the ever-warm greetings of our friends.

CHAPTER XXIII

TRIESTE AGAIN

(1876—1880)

>The busy fingers fly; the eyes may see
>Only the glancing needle that they hold;
>But all my life is blossoming inwardly,
>And every breath is like a litany;
>While through each labour, like a thread of gold,
>Is woven the sweet consciousness of thee.

ON their return from India Isabel and her husband settled down at Trieste, and pursued for the most part a quiet literary life. It was summer, and they swam a good deal by way of recreation, and went frequently to Opçina. They started a habit of not dining at home, and of asking their intimates to meet them at one *café* or another, where they would sup in the open air, and drink the wine of the country and smoke cigarettes. These pleasant evenings were quite a feature of their life at this time. Their house too became the centre of many a *réunion*, and a Mecca to which many a literary pilgrim and social, scientific, and political celebrity turned his steps when travelling by way of Trieste. There is no better description of the

Burtons' life at Trieste at this time than that which appeared in *The World* in 1877, written by Burton's old Oxford friend, Mr. Alfred Bates Richards. Lady Burton has quoted it in full in her Life of her husband; but I think that a small part of it which relates to herself will bear repeating here:

"Captain and Mrs. Burton are well, if airily, lodged in a flat composed of ten rooms, separated by a corridor, with a picture of our Saviour, a statuette of St. Joseph with a lamp, and the Madonna with another lamp burning before it. Thus far the belongings are all of the Cross; but no sooner are we landed in the little drawing-rooms than signs of the Crescent appear. Small, but artistically arranged, the rooms, opening in to one another, are bright with oriental hangings, with trays and dishes of gold and silver, brass trays and goblets, chibouques with great amber mouthpieces, and all kinds of Eastern treasures mingled with family souvenirs. There is no carpet; but a Bedawin rug occupies the middle of the floor, and vies in brilliancy of colour with Persian enamels and bits of good old china. There are no sofas, but plenty of divans covered with Damascus stuffs. Thus far the interior is as Mussulman as the exterior is Christian; but a curious effect is produced among the oriental *mise en scène* by the presence of a pianoforte and a compact library of well-chosen books. There is too another library here, greatly cherished by Mrs. Burton; to wit, a collection of her husband's works in about fifty volumes. On the walls there are many interesting relics, medals, and diplomas of honour, one of which is especially prized by Captain Burton. It is the *brevet de pointe* earned in France for swordsmanship. Near this hangs a picture of the Damascus home of the Burtons, by Frederick Leighton.

"As the guest is inspecting this bright bit of colour, he will be aroused by the full strident tones of a voice skilled in many languages, but never so full and hearty as when bidding a friend welcome. The speaker, Richard Burton, is a living proof that intense work, mental and physical, sojourn in torrid and frozen climes, danger from dagger and from pestilence, 'age' a person of good sound constitution far less than may be supposed. . . .

"Leading the way from the drawing-rooms, or divans, he takes us through bedrooms and dressing-rooms furnished in Spartan simplicity, with the little iron bedsteads covered with bear-skins, and supplied with writing-tables and lamps, beside which repose the Bible, the Shakspeare, the Euclid, and the Breviary, which go with Captain and Mrs. Burton on all their wanderings. His gifted wife, one of the Arundells of Wardour, is, as becomes a scion of an ancient Anglo-Saxon and Norman Catholic house, strongly attached to the Church of Rome ; but religious opinion is never allowed to disturb the peace of the Burton household, the head of which is laughingly accused of Mohammedanism by his friends. The little rooms are completely lined with rough deal shelves, containing perhaps eight thousand or more volumes in every Western language, as well as in Arabic, Persian, and Hindústani. Every odd corner is piled with weapons, guns, pistols, boar-spears, swords of every shape and make, foils and masks, chronometers, barometers, and all kinds of scientific instruments. One cupboard is full of medicines necessary for oriental expeditions or for Mrs. Burton's Trieste poor, and on it is written 'The Pharmacy.' Idols are not wanting, for elephant-nosed Gumpati is there cheek by jowl with Vishnu.

"The most remarkable objects in the room just alluded to are the rough deal tables, which occupy most of the floor space. They are almost like kitchen or ironing tables. There may be eleven of them, each covered with writing materials. At one of them sits Mrs. Burton, in morning *négligé*, a grey *choga*—the long loose Indian dressing-gown of camel's hair—topped by a smoking-cap of the same material. She rises and greets her husband's old friend with the cheeriest voice in the world. 'I see you are looking at our tables; every one does. Dick likes a separate table for every book, and when he is tired of one he goes to another. There are no tables of any size in Trieste, so I had these made as soon as I came. They are so nice. We may upset the ink-bottles as often as we like without anybody being put out of the way. These three little rooms are our "den," where we live, work, and receive our *intimes*; and we leave the doors open, so that we may consult over our work. Look at our view!' From the windows, looking landward, one may see an expanse of country extending over thirty or forty miles, the hills covered with foliage, through which peep trim villas. Beyond the hills higher mountains dotted with villages, a bit of the wild Karso peering from above. On the other side lies spread the Adriatic, with Miramar, poor Maximilian's home and hobby, lying on a rock projecting into the blue water, and on the opposite coast are the Carnian Alps, capped with snow. 'Why we live so high up,' explained Captain Burton, 'is easily explained. To begin with, we are in good condition, and run up and down stairs like squirrels. We live on the fourth storey because there is no fifth. If I had a *campagna*, and gardens and servants, and horses and carriages, I should feel tied, weighed down in fact. With a flat and two or three maid-servants one has only to lock the door and go. It feels like " light marching order," as if we were always ready for an expedition ; and it is a comfortable place to come back to. Look at our land-and-sea-scape : we have air, light, and tranquillity ; no dust, no noise, no street smells. Here my wife receives something like seventy very intimate friends every Friday—an exercise of hospitality to which I have no objection save one, and that is met by the height we live at. There is in every town a lot of old women of both sexes, who sit for hours talking about the weather and the scandal of the place, and this contingent cannot face the stairs.' . . .

"The *ménage Burton* is conducted on the early rising principle. About four or five o'clock our hosts are astir, and already in their 'den,' drinking tea made over a spirit-lamp, and eating bread and fruit, reading and studying languages. By noon the morning's work is got over, including the consumption of a cup of soup, the ablution without which no true believer is happy, and the obligations of a Frankish toilet. Then comes a stroll to the fencing-school, kept by an excellent broadswordsman, an old German trooper. For an hour Captain and Mrs. Burton fence in the school, if the weather be cold; if it be warm, they make for the water, and often swim for a couple of hours.

"Then comes a spell of work at the Consulate. 'I have my Consulate,' the chief explains, 'in the heart of the town. I do not want my Jack Tar in my sanctum; and when he wants me he has generally been on the spree, and got into trouble.' While the husband is engaged in his official duties, the wife is abroad promoting a Society for the Prevention of Cruelty to Animals, a necessary institution in southern countries, where, on the purely gratuitous hypothesis that the so-called lower animals have no souls, the utmost brutality is shown in the treatment of them. 'You see,' remarks our host, 'that my wife and I are like an elder and younger brother living *en garçon*. We divide the work. I take all the hard and the scientific part, and make her do all the rest. When we have worked all day, and have said all we have to say to each other, we want relaxation. To that end we have formed a little "Mess" with fifteen friends at the *table d'hôte* of the Hôtel de la Ville, where we get a good dinner and a pint of the country wine made on the hillside for a florin and a half. By this plan we escape the bore of housekeeping, and are relieved from the curse of domesticity, which we both hate. At dinner we hear the news if any, take our coffee, cigarettes, and *kirsch* outside the hotel, then go home and read ourselves to sleep, and to-morrow *da capo.*'"

This summer, while at Gorizia, Isabel saw again the Comte de Chambord (Henri V. of France) and the Comtesse. She had been received by them at Venice before her marriage, and they remembered her and sent for her. They were staying at Gorizia with a small Court. Isabel had an audience of them twice, and they desired that she should dine with them. She had to explain that she had nothing but a travelling-dress; but they waived that objection, and allowed her to "come as she was." This incident will seem a small thing to many; but it was a great thing to Isabel, for like many members of old English Catholic families, she was a strong Legitimist, and she appreciated the kindness which was shown to her by this king and queen *de jure* with their shadowy Court and handful of faithful followers, more than if they had come into their own and received her royally at the Tuileries.

A little later Burton took it into his head to make an expedition to Midian in Arabia. Many years before, in his Arab days, Burton had come upon this golden land (though at that time he thought little of gold and much of reputation); and a quarter of a century later, seeing Egypt suffering from lack of the precious metal, and knowing that Midian belonged to Egypt, he asked leave of the Foreign Office to go to Cairo, where he imparted his views on the subject of the wealth of the Mines of Midian to Khedive Ismail. His Highness was so much impressed that he equipped an expedition in a few days, and sent Burton to explore the land. His report of the possibilities of the Mines of Midian was so promising that the Khedive engaged him to come back the following winter, and himself applied to the English Foreign Office for the loan of Burton's services. Burton accordingly went again to Midian, and discovered the region of gold and silver and precious stones. He sketched the whole country, planned an expedition, and brought back various metals for analysis. The Khedive was delighted with the prospect of wealth untold, and he made contracts with Burton which, had they been carried out, would have placed him and his wife in luxury for their lives. It used to be a joke with the Burtons at this time that they would die "Duke and Duchess of Midian." Unfortunately Ismail Khedive abdicated just when the third expedition was about to come off, and the new Khedive, Tewfik, did not consider himself bound by any act of his father. The English Government would not stir in the matter, and so Burton not only lost his chance of realizing a large fortune, but also the money which he and his wife had got together for paying expenses in connexion with the expedition, and which they thought would surely have been refunded. The only gain was that Burton wrote some interesting books on the Land of Midian, its history, and its inhabitants. Until the day of her death Lady Burton never ceased to believe in the vast wealth which was lying waste in the Mines of Midian, and used to wax quite enthusiastic about it.

Isabel was anxious to accompany her husband on his first expedition to Midian ; but as there was not enough money for both of them, she had to make the usual sacrifice and stay at home. During her husband's absence she spent most of her time at Opçina and up in the mountains, as she was busily engaged in correcting the proofs of one of his books.

When Burton started on his second expedition to Midian, it was arranged between him and his wife that, as Ismail Khedive was in such a very good humour, Isabel should make her way out to Cairo, and induce the Khedive to send her after her husband to Midian. She was eager and impatient to start, and as soon as she could possibly complete her arrangements she went on board an Austrian Lloyd's and made the voyage from Trieste to Alexandria. When she arrived at the latter place, she found a letter from her husband saying, "You are not to attempt to join me unless you can do so in proper order." This rather upset her plans, as she did not know what "proper order" meant. She therefore went on at once to Cairo, made her representations in the proper quarter, and then returned to Suez. After remaining there some time in a state of great impatience, she was informed that a ship was going to be sent out, and that she was to have the offer of going in her, though it was intimated to her privately that the Khedive and the Governor, Said Bey, very much hoped that she would refuse. She had no intention of refusing, and the next morning she went down to the ship, which was an Egyptian man-of-war, the *Senaar*. It was to anchor off the coast until the expedition returned from the desert, and then bring them back. The captain, who was astonished at her turning up, received her

SUEZ.

[*Page* 612.

with honour. All hands were piped on deck, and a guard and everything provided for her. Notwithstanding their courtesy, Isabel's woman's instinct told her that she was a most unwelcome guest—far more unwelcome than she had anticipated. She saw at once that the situation was impossible, and prepared to beat a graceful retreat. So, after looking round the quarters prepared for her, she thanked the captain and officers exceedingly for their courtesy, and explained, to their evident relief, that she would not trouble them after all. She returned to the town, took some small rooms at the Suez Hotel, and applied herself to literary work. The reason she gave as an excuse for her change of mind was that her expedition would be too dangerous, as she would have to cross the Red Sea in an open *sambuk* with head-winds blowing, and then to find her way alone across the desert upon a camel to Midian. The danger, however, would hardly have weighed with her, for she was always careless of her own safety. The real reason was that she was afraid of injuring her husband's prospects with the Khedive.

She was at Suez some time. At last, after many weeks, the Governor sent her a slip of paper saying, "The *Senaar* is in sight." It was the ship by which Burton returned. She went on board to welcome him, and found him looking very ill and tired. The Khedive sent a special train to meet him on his return from Midian, and the Burtons went at once to Cairo, where they were received with great *éclat*.

From Cairo the Burtons went back to Trieste, or rather to Opçina, for a brief rest, and then proceeded to London. From London they went to Dublin, where they joined the annual meeting of the British Association. Burton delivered several lectures, and Isabel was busy writing her *A. E. I.* (*Arabia, Egypt, and India*). From Dublin they returned to London, which they made their headquarters for some time, breaking their stay in town by many country visits. The most memorable of these was a visit to Lord and Lady Salisbury at Hatfield, where they again met Lord Beaconsfield, who, strange to say, though he had much in common with the Burtons—notably a love of the East and mysticism, and had a liking for them, and for Isabel especially, with whom he was wont to discuss her favourite *Tancred*, his book—never did anything for them, though he must have known better than most men how Burton was thrown away at a place like Trieste. Perhaps Burton's strong anti-Semitic views had something to do with this neglect.

It was during this stay in London that the Burtons attended a meeting on spiritualism, at which Burton read a paper. On the subject of Lady Burton's attitude towards spiritualism we shall have something to say later; but it is better to interpolate here a speech which she made at this meeting, as it explains her views in her own words:

"It appears to me that spiritualism, as practised in England, is quite a different matter to that practised in the East, as spoken of by Captain Burton. Easterns are organized for such manifestations, especially the Arabs. It causes them no surprise; they take it as a natural thing, as a matter of course; in short, it is no religion to them. Easterns of this organization exhale the force; it seems to be an atmosphere surrounding the individual; and I have frequently in common conversation had so strong a perception of it as to withdraw to a distance on any pretext, allowing a current of air to pass from door or window between them and myself. There is no doubt that some strange force or power is at work, trying to thrust itself up in the world, and is well worthy of attention. When I say 'new,' I mean in our hemisphere. I believe it to be as old as time in Eastern countries. I think we are receiving it wrongly. When handled by science, and when it shall become stronger and clearer, it will rank very high. Hailed in our matter-of-fact England as a new religion by people who are not organized for it, by people who are wildly, earnestly seeking for the truth, when they have it at home—some on their domestic hearth, and others next door waiting for them—it can only act as a decoy to a crowd of sensation-seekers, who yearn to see a ghost as they would go to a pantomime; and this can only weaken and degrade it, and distract attention from its possible true object—science. Used vulgarly, as we have all sometimes seen it used, after misleading and crazing a small portion of sensitive persons, it must fall to the ground."[1]

Early in February, 1879, her book *A. E. I.* came out, and the publisher was so pleased with it that he gave a large party in honour of the authoress. There were seventeen guests, and there were seventeen copies

[1] Speech at the British National Association of Spiritualists, December 13, 1878.

of the book piled in a pyramid in the middle of the table. After supper one was given to each guest. They must have made a merry night of it, for Isabel notes that the gaieties began at 11 p.m. and did not end until 5 a.m. Notwithstanding this auspicious send-off, the book did not reach anything like the success achieved by her first work, *The Inner Life of Syria*.

The longest leave comes to an end, and it was now time to return to Trieste. Burton started ahead as was his wont, leaving his wife to "pay, pack, and follow." She paid and she packed, and when she was leaving the house to follow a beggar woman asked her for charity. She gave her a shilling, and the woman said, " God bless you ! May you reach your home without an accident." She must have had the Evil Eye ; for the day after, when Isabel arrived in Paris, *en route* for Trieste, she tumbled down the hotel stairs from top to bottom, arriving at the bottom unconscious. She was picked up and put to bed. When she came to herself she exclaimed, "Do not send the carriage away ; I must get my work done and go on." But when she attempted to rise, she fainted again. The visible injuries resolved themselves into a bad sprain and twisted ankle. After the fourth day she had herself bound up and conveyed to the train. She travelled straight through to Turin. There she had to be carried to an inn, as she was too ill to go on. The next day she insisted on being packed up again, and travelled to Mestre. The heat was intense, and she had to wait four hours in the wretched station at Mestre, during which she suffered great pain. Then she travelled on by the *post-zug*, a slow train, and arrived at Trieste at half-past eight in the morning, where her eyes were gladdened by seeing her husband waiting to receive her on the platform. She was carried home and promptly put to bed.

This illustrates the literal way in which she used to obey her husband's lightest directions. He told her to follow him "at once," and she followed him, not even resting on account of her accident. In fact it is absolutely true to say that nothing short of death would have prevented her from carrying out his slightest instructions to the letter.

The accident which she met with in Paris turned out to be more serious than she had at first supposed. It was a long time before she could leave her bed. She had injured her back and her ankle very badly, and she underwent a long course of massage and baths; but she never permanently got quite well again. She said herself, "Strength, health, and nerve I had hitherto looked upon as a sort of right of nature, and supposed that everybody had them; I never felt grateful for them as a blessing, but I began to learn what suffering was from this date." Henceforth we see her not as the woman who was ready to share any dare-devil adventure or hair-breadth escape, and who revelled in a free and roving life of travel, but rather as the wife, whose thoughts now turned more than ever to the delights of home, and how to add to her husband's domestic comforts.

Expressions of sympathy and goodwill were called forth by her accident from friends far and wide. Among others, Lady Salisbury wrote:

"Châlet Cecil, Puys, Dieppe, *September* 22.

" Dear Mrs. Burton,

"We were all very sorry to hear of your misfortunes, and I hope that the Viennese doctors and their baths have now cured you and restored you to perfect health. It was indeed most trying to have that accident at Paris just as you were recovering from your illness in London. I suppose you are now thinking of the preparations for your Egyptian trip, unless the new Khedive has stopped it, which he is not at all likely to have done, as its success would redound so much to his own advantage. We have been here for the last two months, and are beginning to think our holiday is over, and that we ought to go back to England again.

"Of course we have all been talking and thinking of nothing but Cabul lately. The Afghans really seem like the Constantinople dogs, quite untamable. I suppose we shall soon hear of the English troops entering Cabul and all the horrors of the punishment, which, as is usual in such cases, is almost sure to fall on the innocent instead of the guilty.

"This country seems very prosperous. People are rich and orderly, and every one seems as busy and happy as possible; the harbour is full of ships, and new houses are being built and new shops opened; and, according to M. Waddington, who was here the other day, this is the same all over France. What is the real truth about Count A———'s resignation? Is it health or weariness, or what is it? We are all puzzled at it here. I suppose Prince Bismarck's visit will lead to some *éclaircissement*.

"We hear occasionally from Lord Beaconsfield, who seems very well. He is at Hughenden. We often think of the pleasant days you spent with us at Hatfield when he was there.

"With kind regards to Captain Burton and yourself from us all,

"Believe me very sincerely yours,
"G. SALISBURY."

In the autumn Isabel went to Venice on a brief visit; but had to return shortly, as Burton had made up his mind to go once more to Egypt to try his luck about the Midian Mines. There was nothing for her to do but to see him off (there was no money for two) and remain behind to spend her Christmas alone at Trieste.

Soon after the new year Isabel began to get ill again. She had not really recovered from her fall in Paris nine months before. The doctors advised her to see a bone-setter. She wrote and told her husband, who was then in Egypt, and he replied by telegram ordering her to go home to London at once. She reached London, and went through a course of medical treatment. She notes during this dreary period a visit from Martin Tupper, who came to see her on the subject of cruelty to animals. (Burton always joked with his wife about "Tupper and the animals.") He presented her with a copy of his *Proverbial Philosophy*, and also wrote her the letter which is reproduced here:

"WEST CROYDON, *January* 17, 1880.

"MY DEAR MADAM,

"I hope you will allow a personal stranger,

though haply on both sides a book friend, to thank you for your very graphic and interesting *A. E. I.* travels; may the volume truly be to you and yours an everlasting possession! But the special reason I have at present for troubling you with my praise is because in to-day's reading of your eleventh chapter I cannot but feel how one we are in pity and hope for the dear and innocent lower animals so cruelly treated by their savage monarch, man, everywhere during this evil æon of the earth. To prove my sympathy as no new feeling, I may refer your kindly curiosity to my Proverbial Chapters on ' The Future of Animals,' to many of my occasional poems, and to the enclosed, which I hope it may please you to accept. You may like to know also, as a kindred spirit (and pray don't think me boastful), that years ago, through a personal communication with Louis Napoleon, I have a happy reason to believe that the undersigned was instrumental in stopping the horrors of Altorf, besides other similar efforts for poor animals in America and elsewhere. I believe, with you, that they have a good future in prospect (perhaps in what is called the millennial era of our world), that they understand us and our language, especially as to oaths, and that those humble friends will be met and known by us in our happier state to come.

"But I must not weary you with what might be expanded into a treatise; I am confident we agree; and I know in my own experiences (as doubtless you do in yours) that the poor horses and dogs we have pitied and helped, love and appreciate and may hereafter be found capable of rewarding—in some small way

—those who are good to them in this our mutual stage of trial.

"With my best regards then, and due thanks, allow me to subscribe myself
"Your very sincere servant,
"MARTIN F. TUPPER."

Isabel was anxious about her husband, as things in Egypt were in a very unsettled condition. Ismail Khedive had now abdicated, and Tewfik had succeeded him. This, as we know, upset all Burton's plans; he got no farther than Egypt on his way to Midian, and remained at Alexandria eating out his heart in despair at his bad luck. One night on coming home from dinner he was attacked by a band of roughs, who hit him over the head from behind with a sharp instrument. It was supposed to be foul play with a motive, as the only thing they stole was his divining-rod for gold, which he carried about with him, and they did not take his money. He kept the loss a secret, in order that it should be no hindrance to him if he had the chance to go back to work the Mines of Midian. But that chance never came. He returned to Trieste, and did not let his wife know of the assault until she joined him there on her return from London.

In the meantime she had not been idle. Despite her ill-health when in London she had been agitating for her husband's promotion, and had built high hopes on the kind interest of Lord Beaconsfield and Lord Salisbury. Unfortunately for her Lord Beaconsfield's last Administration collapsed in April with a crash, and her hopes were buried in the ruins. Lord Granville, who had recalled Burton from Damascus, succeeded Lord Salisbury at the Foreign Office, and she knew that she could not hope for much from Lord Granville. When she saw the turn the General Election of 1880 had taken, she made a last despairing effort to induce the out-going Government to do something for her husband before the Ministers gave up their seals. She received the following kind letter from Lady Salisbury:

"HATFIELD HOUSE, HATFIELD, HERTS, *April* 18.

"MY DEAR MRS. BURTON,

"I received your note here yesterday, and fear it is too late to do anything, as the lists went in yesterday, and Lord Beaconsfield is with the Queen to-day. So we must bear our misfortunes as best we can, and hope for better days. I cannot help feeling that this change is too violent to last long. But who can say? It is altogether so astonishing. As regards Captain Burton, I hope you will not lose anything. So valuable a public servant will, I hope, be sure of recognition whatever Government may be in office.

"With our united kind regards to him and to you,

"Yours very sincerely,

"G. SALISBURY."

It was a sad home-coming for Isabel; for not only were her hopes, so near fruition, dashed to the ground, but she found her husband very ill from the effects of his accident and from gout. The first thing she did was to send for a doctor, and take him off to Opçina.

It is sad to note that from this time we find in their letters and diaries frequent complaints of sickness and suffering. They, who had rarely known what illness meant, now had it with them as an almost constant companion. From Opçina they went to Oberammergau to see the Passion Play, which impressed them both very much, though in different ways. Isabel wrote a long description of this play, which has never been published. Burton also wrote an account, which has seen the light. When they returned to Trieste, they had a good many visitors, among others the late Mr. W. H. Smith and his family. He was always a kind friend to Isabel, as indeed he was to every one he liked. And that (like Lord Beaconsfield, Lord Salisbury, Lord Clarendon, Lord Derby, and many other leading statesmen) he had a high opinion of her abilities is, I think, evident from the following letter. Men do not write in this way to stupid women:

"3, GROSVENOR PLACE, S.W., *March* 1, 1881.

"DEAR MRS. BURTON,

"Your kind letters have reached us since our arrival here. We were earlier in our return than we had at first intended, as Parliament was called together so soon; but our house was not ready, and my family had to stay in the country for some little time. It is very good of you to send me the *Lusiads*. I am keeping them for those delightful days of quiet and enjoyment which are to be had sometimes in the country, but not in these stormy days in London. Are we to have peace and quiet? Ireland will be sullenly quiet now under coercion, after having been stimulated by oratory almost to madness. South Africa is a very serious matter indeed. I am told the Dutch colonists within the Cape will remain loyal; but our reputation as an invincible race suffers with all the natives. And then the European East, nothing at present can look blacker, and all because of passionate words and hatred. I am afraid too we are low in the estimation of the people of the West, and likely to remain so.

"Your good Christmas wishes reached us long after the New Year; but we had a very pleasant Christmas at Malta with many of our old naval friends, and we spent our New Year's Day at a little port in Elba. What a charming island it is! Small, no doubt; but not a bad prison for an Emperor if he had books and papers and some powers of self-control. Coming up to Nice we had very heavy weather; but the yacht behaved well, and it was certainly pleasanter at sea with a strong easterly wind than on shore.

"There is to be a great Candahar debate in the Lords to-night. Lord Lytton speaks remarkably well —as an old debater would—and great interest is felt in the event. All the same Candahar will be given up; and some time hence, if we have soldiers left, we shall probably have to fight our way back again to it.

"Pray give our united kind regards to Captain Burton. I shall be so glad to hear any news if anything transpires at Trieste.

"Yours very sincerely,
"W. H. SMITH."

CHAPTER XXIV

THE SHADOWS LENGTHEN

(1881—1885)

O tired heart!
  God knows,
Not you nor I.

THE next four or five years were comparatively uneventful. There was little hope of promotion from the new Government, so the Burtons resigned themselves to Trieste with what grace they might; and though they were constantly agitating for promotion and change, neither the promotion nor the change came. Burton hated Trieste; he chafed at the restricted field for his energies which it afforded him; and had it not been for frequent expeditions of a more or less hazardous nature, and his literary labours, life at the Austrian seaport would have been intolerable to him. With Isabel it was different. As the years went on she grew to love the place and the people, and to form many ties and interests which it would have been hard for her to break. Notwithstanding this she warmly seconded her husband's efforts to obtain from the Foreign Office some other post, and she was never weary of bringing his claims before the notice of the Government, the public, and any influential friends who might be likely to help. Indeed the record of her diary during these years is one of continuous struggle on her husband's behalf, which is varied only by anxiety for his health.

"I am like a swimmer battling against strong waves," she writes to a friend about this time, "and I think my life will always be thus. Were I struggling only for myself, I should long before have tired; but since it is for my dear one's sake I shall fight on so long as life lasts. Every now and then one seems to reach the crest of the wave, and that gives one courage; but how long a time it is when one is in the depths!"

To another friend she wrote :

"We have dropped into our old Triestine lives. We have made our Opçina den very comfortable. We have taken the big room and Dick's old one, opened them, and shut the end one, which is too cold, and put in lamps, stoves, and stores and comforts of all kinds; in fact partly refurnished. I am much better, and can walk a little now; so I walk up half-way from Trieste on Saturday, Dick all the way; Sunday Mass in village, and walk; and Monday walk down. We keep all the week's letters for here (Opçina) and all the week's newspapers to read, and do our translations. I have begun *Ariosto*, but am rather disheartened. We have set up a *tir au pistolet* in the rooms, which are long enough (opened) to give twenty-two paces, and we have brought up some foils. The Triestines think us as mad as hatters to come up here, on account of the weather, which is 'seasonable'—*bora*, snow, and frozen fingers. I am interesting myself in the two hundred and twenty badly behaved Slav children in the village. Dick's *Lusiads* are making a stir. My Indian sketches and our Oberammergau have gone to the bad. My publisher, as I told you, took to evil ways, failed, and eventually died December 10. However, I hope to rise like a phœnix out of my ashes. The rest of our week is passed in fencing three times a week, twice a week Italian, twice a week German. Friday I receive the Trieste world from twelve noon to 6 p.m., with accompaniments of Arab coffee, cigarettes, and liqueurs. Dick is always grinding at literature as usual; so what with helping Dick (we are studying something together), literature, looking after the little *ménage*, and philanthropic business, Church work, the animals, and the poor, I am very happy and busy, and I think stronger; albeit I have little rest or *amusement*, according to the doctor's ideas. In fact I have a winter I love, a quiet Darby and Joan by our own fireside, which I so seldom get." [1]

The principal event at Trieste in 1881 appears to have been the arrival of the British squadron in July. Burton and his wife were always of a most hospitable nature; they would have spent their last penny in entertaining their friends. The first thing they did on the arrival of the squadron was to invite the captains and officers of every ship to an evening *fête champêtre*

[1] Letter to Miss Bishop from Opçina, January 17, 1881.

and ball at Opçina. In addition to this they sent out about eight hundred invitations to the captains and officers of the Austrian navy and other men-of-war anchored at Trieste, the officers of the Austrian regiments stationed there, the Governor and Staff, and the Austrian authorities, the Consular corps, and all their private friends, to the number of about one hundred and fifty of the principal people of Trieste. They turned the gardens of the little inn at Opçina into a sort of Vauxhall or Rosherville for the occasion. There were refreshment tents, and seats, and benches, and barrels of wine and beer, and elaborate decorations of flowers, and coloured lamps and flags, and no end of fireworks. When the eventful evening arrived, and everything was in full swing, the weather, which had been perfectly fine heretofore, broke up with the startling suddenness which is peculiar to the Adriatic. The heavens opened, and to the accompaniment of thunder and lightning the rain descended in torrents, flooding the tents, quenching the illuminations, and reducing the whole ground to a Slough of Despond. The guests naturally rushed for shelter to the little inn, which was much too small to accommodate them. The police made for the barrels of beer, and were soon incapable of keeping order, and a mob of villagers, who had assembled to witness the festivities from without, broke through the barricades, made a raid on the refreshment tent, smashed the dishes, and carried off all the best things to eat and drink. Burton took it very philosophically; but Isabel, overcome with vexation and disappointment, burst into tears. The sight, however, of the raiders soon turned her grief to anger. She pulled herself together, got a party of young braves, sallied forth into the grounds, and made a rush for the tent. With her little band she rescued all that was left of the food and drink, and then cleared away the furniture in the lower part of the inn, told the band to play, and set her guests dancing, while she rigged up an impromptu supper-room in the garret. This spirited conduct soon restored the chaos to something like order. The guests—the majority of whom were English—unconscious of the havoc which had been wrought, enjoyed themselves right merrily, and the party did not break up until five o'clock in the morning.

The British squadron, both officers and men, were well received at Trieste, and became most popular during their stay there. Isabel made great friends with the sailors, and she rescued one of them from what might have been a serious squabble. One day she saw a sailor picking the apples off a tree in the Austrian Admiral's garden, which overhung the road. The sentry came out, and a crowd of people assembled. Jack Tar looked at them scornfully, and went on munching his apple until they laid hands on him, when he gave a sweeping backhander, which knocked one or two of them over. Everything was ripe for a row, when Isabel stepped in between the combatants, and said to the sailor, "I am your Consul's wife, and they are trying to make you understand that these are the Austrian Admiral's apples, and you must not eat them." The sailor apologized, said he did not know he had done any wrong, and did not understand what they were all jabbering about; and he saluted and went. Then Isabel explained to the sentry, and generally poured oil on the troubled waters. The sailor told the story to his comrades, and thus she became very popular among them. The sailors liked Trieste so much that, when the squadron was to leave, eighteen of them did not join their ship; and when they were caught Isabel went and interceded for them, and begged the captain not to punish them severely. He said, "Oh no, the darlings; wait till I get them on board ship! I will have them tucked up comfortably in bed with nice hot grog." Whether her intercession availed is not related.

In August, 1881, the Burtons started on a trip somewhat farther afield than was their wont for short expeditions. They went up to Veldes, a lovely spot, where there was a good inn and first-rate fishing. Burton was absent without leave from the Foreign Office; and though he had left the Consulate in charge of the Vice-Consul, his conduct was, officially speaking, irregular, and both he and his wife were afraid of meeting any one they knew. The first person they saw at the inn was the Chaplain of the British Embassy at Vienna, who might have reported the absentee Consul to his Ambassador. Burton bolted up to bed to avoid him; but Isabel thought that the better plan would be to take the bull by the horns. So she went to the Chaplain, and made a frank confession that they were truants. He burst out laughing, and said, "My dear lady, I am doing exactly the same thing myself."

She then went upstairs, brought Burton down again, and the three had a convivial evening together.

After this they went on by stages to Ischl, where they parted company, Burton going to Vienna, and Isabel to Marienbad for a cure. Her stay at Marienbad she notes as mainly interesting because she made the acquaintance of Madame Olga Novikoff. Her cure over, with no good result, she joined her husband at Trieste. They stopped there one night to change baggage, and went across to Venice, where there was a great meeting of the Geographical Congress. Burton was not asked to meet his fellow-geographers, or to take any part in the Congress. The slight was very marked, and both he and his wife felt it keenly. It was only one more instance of the undying prejudice against him in certain quarters. They met many friends, including Captain Verney Lovett Cameron. In November Burton went with him to the west coast of Africa, to report on certain mines which Burton had discovered when Consul at Fernando Po. Isabel was anxious to accompany them; but it was the usual tale, "My expenses were not paid, and we personally hadn't enough money for two, so I was left behind."

The first part of 1882 Isabel spent without her husband, as he was absent on the Guinea coast. She fretted very much at his long absence, and made herself ill with disappointment because she was not able to join him. The following letter shows *inter alia* how much she felt the separation[1]:

[1] Letter to Miss Bishop from Trieste, December 5, 1881.

"I was so pleased you liked the scourging I gave the reviewers.[1] No one has answered me, and it has well spread. I don't know how they could. All Dick's friends were very glad. The Commentary is out, two vols. (that makes four out and four to come). The 'Reviewers Reviewed' is a postscript to the Commentary, and the Glossary is in that too. I wrote the 'Reviewers' at Duino in June last, and I enjoyed doing it immensely. I put all the reviews in a row on a big table, and lashed myself into a spiteful humour one by one, so that my usually suave pen was dipped with gall and caustic. You will have had my last, I think, from Marienbad. I then joined Dick at Vienna, where we spent a few days; and then went to Venice for the *fêtes*, which were marvellous, and the Queen was lovely. Then we came home, and had two charming, quiet, delicious months together; and to my joy he gave up dining out and dined at home *tête-à-tête* ; but of course it was overshadowed by the knowledge of the coming parting, which I feel terribly this time, as I go on getting older. We left together in the Cunarder *Demerara*. Her route was Trieste, Venice, Fiume, Patras, Gibraltar, England. By dropping off at Fiume I got ten days on board with him. He leaves her at Gibraltar about the 7th; goes to Cadiz, Lisbon, Madeira, and Axim on the West Coast. He has to change ship four times, and this is a great anxiety to me in this stormy weather.

---

[1] This refers to *Camoens : the Commentary, Life, and Lusiads*. Englished by R. F. Burton. Two vols. Containing a Glossary, and Reviewers Reviewed, by Isabel Burton. 1880.

God keep him safe! Once at Axim, the mines are all round the coast, and then I dread fever for him. He wishes to make a little trip to the Kong Mountains, and then I fear natives and beasts. Perhaps Cameron will be with him; but *entre nous* Cameron is not very solid, and requires a leading hand. If all goes well (D.V., and may He be merciful), we are to meet in London in March, and I hope we shall get a glimpse of you.

"I am, as you may think, fearfully sad. I have been nowhere; I neither visit, nor receive, nor go out. Men drink when they are sad, women fly into company; but I must fight the battle with my own heart, learn to live alone and work, and when I have conquered I will allow myself to see something of my friends. I dreaded my empty home without children or relatives; but I have braved the worst now. I am cleaning and tidying his room, putting each thing down in its own place; but I won't make it luxurious this time; I have learnt by experience."

Isabel passed the next three months at Trieste busily studying, writing, and carrying out the numerous directions contained in her husband's letters.

Early in April her doctor discovered that she had the germs of the internal complaint of which she ultimately died. She had noticed all the year that she had been getting weaker and weaker in the fencing-school, until one day she turned faint, and the fencing-master said to her, "Why, what's the matter with you? Your arms are getting quite limp in using the broadsword." She did not know what was the matter with her at the time; but soon after she became so ill that she had to take to her bed, and then her doctor discovered the nature of the malady. She did not go to the fencing-school any more after that. In the Life of her husband, speaking of this matter, Lady Burton says that her internal complaint possibly resulted from her fall downstairs in Paris in 1879; but in talking the matter over with her sister, Mrs. Fitzgerald, a year or two before her death, she recalled another accident which seems the more likely origin of her distressing malady. Once when she was riding alone in the woods in Brazil she was pursued by a brigand. As she was unarmed, she fled as fast as her horse would carry her. The brigand gave chase, and in the course of an hour's exciting ride Isabel's horse stumbled and threw her violently against the pommel of her saddle. Fortunately the horse recovered its footing, and she was able to get safely away from her pursuer; but the bruise was a serious one (though she thought little of it at the time), and many years later she came to the conclusion that this was the probable origin of her illness.

The third week in April she left Trieste for England to meet her husband, who was due at Liverpool in May. While she was in London she consulted an eminent surgeon on the subject of her illness, which was then at its beginning. He advised an operation, which he said would be a trifling matter. There is every probability, if she had consented, that she would have recovered, and been alive to this day. But she had a horror of the knife and anæsthetics. Nevertheless she would have braved them if it had not been for another consideration, which weighed with her most of all. She knew that an operation of this kind would lay her up for some time, and she would not be able to look after her husband on his return from his long absence. She was afraid too that the knowledge of her illness might worry him, so for his sake she refused the operation, and she kept the knowledge of her malady a secret from him. It is perhaps a little far-fetched to say that by doing this she sacrificed her life for her husband's sake, yet in a sense she may be said to have done so. Her first thought, and her only thought, was always of him, and it is literally true to say that she would at any moment cheerfully have laid down her life that he might gain.

Isabel went to Liverpool to meet Burton on his return from the west coast of Africa. He came back with Captain Lovett Cameron. There was a great dinner given at Liverpool to welcome the wanderers. The next day the Burtons went to London, where they stayed for a couple of months through the season, met many interesting people, and were entertained largely. On the last day of July they returned to Trieste.

In September Isabel went again to Marienbad for the baths, which did her no good. While there she wrote a letter to *Vanity Fair* anent a certain article which spoke of Burton and his " much-prized post." She took occasion to point out his public services, and to show that the "much-prized post" was "the poor, hard-earned, little six hundred a year, well earned by forty years' hard toil in the public service." On returning to Trieste, she entertained many friends who arrived there for the Exhibition, and after that settled down to the usual round again.

In October Burton was suddenly ordered by the Foreign Office to go to Ghazzeh in Syria in search of Professor Palmer, their old friend and travelling companion, who was lost in the desert. There was then a chance of his being still alive, though the bodies of his companions had been found. Burton's knowledge of the Bedawin and Sinai country was of course specially valuable in such a quest. He started at once.

After he had left Isabel went into retreat at the Convent della Osolini at Gorizia. The following were among her reflections at this period[1]:

"In retreat at last. I have so long felt the want of one. My life seems to be like an express train, every day bringing fresh things which *must* be done. I am goaded on by time and circumstances, and God, my first beginning and last end, is always put off, thrust out of the way, to make place for the unimportant, and gets served last and badly. This cannot continue. What friend would have such long-enduring patience with me? None! Certainly less a king! far less a husband! How then? Shall God be kept waiting until nobody else wants me? How ashamed and miserable I feel! How my heart twinges at the

---

[1] From her devotional book *Laméd*, pp. 28, 29.

thought of my ingratitude, and the poor return I make for such favours and graces as I have received! God has called me into retreat once more, perhaps for the last time. He has created an unexpected opportunity for me, since my husband has been sent to look for poor Palmer's body. I thought I heard Him cry, 'Beware! Do not wait until I drive you by misfortune, but go voluntarily into solitude, prepare for Me, and wait for Me, till I come to abide with you.'

"I am here, my God, according to Thy command; Thou and I, I and Thou, face to face in the silence. Oh, speak to my heart, and clear out from it everything that is not of Thee, and let me abide with Thee awhile! Not only speak, but make me understand, and turn my body and spirit and soul into feelings and actions, not words and thoughts alone.

"My health and nerves for the past three years have rendered me less practical and assiduous in religion than I was. Then I used to essay fine, large, good works, travel, write, and lead a noble and virile life. Now I am weaker, and feel a lassitude incidental to my time of life, which I trust may pass away. I am left at home to town life, and I seem to have declined to petty details, small works, dreaming, and making lists and plans of noble things not carried out. It looks like the beginning of the end.

"I ask for two worldly petitions, quite submitted to God's will: (1) That I may be cured, and that Dick and I may have good, strong health to be able to work and do good—if we are destined to live. (2) That if it be God's will, and not bad for us, we may get a comfortable independence, without working any more for our bread, and independent of any master save God."

Isabel returned to Trieste when her retreat was concluded; and soon after—much sooner than she expected—her husband returned to her.

When he reached Ghazzeh, Burton found Sir Charles Warren already in the field, and he did not want to be interfered with, so that Burton came home again and spent Christmas with his wife at Trieste. Thus ended 1882. Isabel notes: "After this year misfortunes began to come upon us all, and we have never had another like it."

Early next year the Burtons left their flat in Trieste, where they had been for over ten years. Something went wrong with the drainage for one thing, and Burton took an intense dislike to it for another; and when he took a dislike to a house nothing would ever induce him to remain in it. The only thing to do was to move. They looked all over Trieste in search of something suitable, and only saw one house that would do for them, and that was a palazzo, which then seemed quite beyond their means; yet six months later they got into it. It was a large house in a large garden on a wooded eminence looking out to the sea. It had been built in the palmy days of Trieste by an English merchant prince, and was one of the best houses in the place. It had a good entrance, so wide that it would have been possible to drive a

THE BURTONS' HOUSE AT TRIESTE.

[*Page* 638.

carriage into the hall. A marble staircase led to the interior, which contained some twenty large rooms, magnificent in size. The house was full of air and light, and the views were charming. One looked over the Adriatic, one over the wooded promontory, another towards the open country, and the fourth into gardens and orchards.

· The early part of 1883 was sad to Isabel by reason of her husband's failing health and her own illness. In May she went alone to Bologna, at her husband's request, for she then told him of the nature of her illness, to consult Count Mattei, of whom they had heard much from their friend Lady Paget, Ambassadress at Vienna. When she arrived at Bologna, she found he had gone on to Riola, and she followed him thither. Mattei's castle was perched on a rock, and to it Isabel repaired.

"First," she says, "I had to consult a very doubtful-looking mastiff; then appeared a tall, robust, well-made, soldierlike-looking form in English costume of blue serge, brigand felt hat, with a long pipe, who looked about fifty, and not at all like a doctor. He received me very kindly, and took me up flights of stairs, through courts, into a wainscoted oak room, with fruits and sweets on the table, with barred-iron gates and drawbridges and chains in different parts of the room, that looked as if he could pull one up and put one down into a hole. He talked French and Italian; but I soon perceived that he liked Italian better, and stuck to it; and I also noticed that, by his mouth and eyes, instead of fifty, he must be about seventy-five. A sumptuous dinner-table was laid out in an adjoining room, with fruit and flowers. I told him I could not be content, having come so far to see him, to have only a passing quarter of an hour. He listened to all my long complaints about my health most patiently, asked me every question; but he did not ask to examine me, nor look at my tongue, nor feel my pulse, as other doctors do. He said that I did not look like a person with the complaint mentioned, but as if circulation and nerves were out of order. He prescribed four internal and four external remedies and baths. I wrote down all his suggestions, and rehearsed them that he might correct any mistakes."[1]

After the interview with Count Mattei Isabel did not remain at Riola, but with all her medicines returned to Trieste. The remedies were not, however, of any avail.

In June Isabel presided over a *fête* of her Society for the Prevention of Cruelty to Animals, and made a long speech, in which she reviewed the work from the beginning, and the difficulties and successes. She wound up as follows:

"May none of you ever know the fatigue, anxiety, disgust, heartaches, nervousness, self-abnegation, and disappointments of this mission, and the small good drawn out of years of it; for so it seems to me. Old residents, and people living up the country, do say that you would not know the town to be the same it was eleven years ago, when I first came. They tell me

[1] *Life of Sir Richard Burton*, by Isabel his wife, vol. ii., p. 248.

there is quite a new stamp or horse, a new mode of working and treatment and feeling. I, the workwoman, cannot see it or feel it. I think I am always rolling a stone uphill. I know that you all hear something of what I have to put up with to carry it out—the opposition, and contentions, treachery, abuse, threats, and ridicule; and therefore I all the more cherish the friendly hand such a large assembly has gathered together to hold out to me to-day to give me fresh courage. You all know how fond I am of Trieste; but it is the very hardest place I ever worked in, and eleven years of it have pretty nearly broken me up. Nevertheless I shall always, please God, wherever I am, 'open my mouth for the dumb,' and adhere to my favourite motto: 'Fais ce que dois, advienne que pourra.'"

For the first time this summer Isabel and her husband found that swimming in the sea, which had been one of their favourite recreations at Trieste, no longer agreed with them, and they came reluctantly to the conclusion that their swimming must go the way of the fencing, and that the days of their more active physical exercises were over. For the first time also in all the twenty-two years of their married life they began to shirk the early rising, and now no longer got up at 3 or 4 a.m., but at the comparatively late hour of 6 or 6.30 a.m. In November Burton had a serious attack of gout, which gave him agonies of pain; and it was at last borne in upon him that he would have to make up his mind henceforth to be more or less of an invalid. Simultaneously Isabel was ill from peritonitis. There seemed to be a curious sympathy between the two, which extended to all things, even to their physical health. On December 6 Burton put the following in his diary in red ink: "*This day eleven years I came here. What a shame!*"

Early in 1884 Isabel came in for a small legacy of £500, which was useful to them at the time, as they were far from being well off, and had incurred many expenses consequent on their change of-house. She expended the whole of it in additional comforts for her husband during his illness, which unfortunately seemed to get more serious as time went on. In February he quite lost the use of his legs for eight months, which of necessity kept him much in the house. It was during this period that he began his great work *Alf Laylah wa Laylah*, or *The Arabian Nights*. When I say he began it, that is not strictly speaking correct, for he had been gathering material for years. He merely took in hand the matter which he had already collected thirty years before. He worked at it *con amore*, and it was very soon necessary to call in an amanuensis to copy his manuscript.

This year was uneventful. They were absent from Trieste a good deal on "cures" and short excursions. Burton's health gave him a great deal of trouble; but whenever he was well enough, or could find time from his official duties, he devoted himself to his translation of *The Arabian Nights*. Isabel also worked hard in connexion with it in another way. She had undertaken the financial part of the business, and sent out no less than thirty-four thousand circulars to people with a view to their buying copies of the book as it came out.

In January and February, 1885, Burton was so ill that his wife implored him to throw up the Consular Service, and live in a place which suited him, away from Trieste. Of course that meant that they would have to live in a very small way; for if they gave up their appointment at that time and forfeited the salary, they would have been very poor. Still, so impressed was Isabel that the winter in Trieste did not agree with her husband, that she said, "You must never winter here again"; but he said, "I quite agree with you there—we will never winter here again; but I won't throw up the Service until I either get Morocco or they let me retire on full pension." She then said, "When we go home again, that is what we will try for, that you may retire on full pension, which will be only six years before your time." Henceforth she tried for only two things: one, that he might be promoted to Morocco, because it was his pet ambition to be Consul there before he died; the other, failing Morocco, he should be allowed to retire on full pension on account of his health. Notwithstanding that she moved heaven and earth to obtain this latter request, it was never granted.

In the meantime they were busy writing together the index to *The Arabian Nights*. On Thursday, February 12, she said to him, "Now mind, to-morrow is Friday the 13th. It is our unlucky day, and we have got to be very careful."

When the morning dawned, they heard of the death of one of their greatest friends, General Gordon, which had taken place on January 26 at Kartoum; but the news had been kept from them. At this sad event Isabel writes, " We both collapsed together, were ill all day, and profoundly melancholy."

CHAPTER XXV

GORDON AND THE BURTONS

> Oh! bring us back once more
> The vanished days of yore,
> When the world with faith was filled;
> Bring back the fervid zeal,
> The hearts of fire and steel,
> The hands that believe and build.

THE mention of Gordon's death suggests that this would be the fittest place to bring to notice the relations which existed between him and the Burtons. Their acquaintance, which ripened into a strong liking and friendship, may be said to have existed over a period of ten years (from 1875 to 1885), from the time when Gordon wrote to ask Burton for information concerning Victoria Nyanza and the regions round about, to the day when he went to his death at Kartoum. Long before they met in the flesh, Gordon and Burton knew each other in the spirit, and Gordon thought he saw in Burton a man after his own heart. In many respects he was right. The two men were curiously alike in their independence of thought and action, in their chivalrous devotion to honour and duty, in their absolute contempt for the world's opinion, in their love of adventure, in their indifference to danger, in their curious mysticism and fatalism, and in the neglect which each suffered from the Government until it was too late. They were both born leaders of men, and for that reason indifferent followers, incapable of running quietly in the official harness. Least of all could they have worked together, for they were too like one another in some things, and too unlike in others. Burton saw this from the first, and later Gordon came to see that his view was the right one. But it never prevented either of them from appreciating the great qualities in the other.

The correspondence between Gordon and the Burtons was voluminous. Lady Burton kept all Gordon's letters, intending to publish them some day. I am only carrying out her wishes in publishing them here. Both Gordon and Burton were in the habit of writing quite freely on men and things, and therefore it has been found necessary to suppress some of the letters; but those given will, I think, be found of general interest.

The first letter Gordon wrote to Burton was about fifteen months after he had taken up the Governorship of the Equatorial Provinces. It was as follows:

"BEDDEN, SOUTH OF GONDOKORO [1] 23 MILES,
"*July* 17, 1875.

"MY DEAR CAPTAIN BURTON,

"Though I have not had the honour of meeting you, I hope you will not object to give me certain

[1] Gondokoro was the seat of Government of the Province of the Equator.

information which I imagine you are most capable of doing. I will first relate to you my proposed movements. At this moment I am just starting from this station for the South. You are aware that hitherto the Nile from about eighteen miles south of Gondokoro to the junction of it with the Unyame Hor (Apuddo, Hiameye, Dufte, or Mahadé, as different people call it) has been considered impassable and a torrential stream. Being very much bothered with the difficulties of the land route for this distance, I thought I would establish ports along the river, hoping to find it in steps with portions which might be navigable, instead of what it was supposed to be—viz. a continuous rapid. Happily I came on the river at the commencement of its rise at end of March, and found it navigable as far as Kerri, which is forty-six miles south of Gondokoro, and about forty miles north of the point where the Nile is navigable to the lake. As far south as one can see from Kerri the river looks good, for the highlands do not approach one another. I have already a station at Mahadé, and one at Kerri, and there remains for me to make another midway between Kerri and Mahadé, to complete my communication with the lake. I go very slowly, and make my stations as I proceed. I cannot reconnoitre between Kerri and Mahadé, but am obliged, when once I move, to move for a permanent object. If I reconnoitred, it would cost me as much time as if I was going to establish myself permanently, and also would alarm the natives, who hitherto have been quiet enough. I do not think that there are any properly so-called cataracts between Kerri and the lake. There may be bad rapids; but as the bed of the river is so narrow there will be enough water for my boats, and if the banks are not precipices I count on being able to haul my boats through. We have hauled them through a gap sixty-five yards wide at Kerri, where the Nile has a tremendous current. Now Kerri is below the junction of the Nile and the Asua; while Mahadé, where all agree the other rapids are, is above the junction; so that I may hope at Mahadé to have a less violent current to contend with, and to have the Asua waters in some degree cushioning up that current. I have little doubt of being able to take my steamer (the one constructed by Baker's[1] engineers at Gondokoro) up to Kerri, for I have already there boats of as great a draught or water. From Mahadé it is some one hundred and thirty miles to Magungo. About seventy miles south of Mahadé a split takes place in the river: one branch flows from east, another from west. I imagine that to north of the lake a large accumulation of aquatic vegetation has taken place, and eventually has formed this isle. Through this vegetation the Victoria Nile has cut a passage to the east, and the lake waters have done this to the west. Baker passed through a narrow passage from the lake to the Victoria Nile channel. From Magungo the Victoria Nile is said to be a torrent to within eighteen miles of Karuma Falls. Perhaps it is also in steps. Karuma Falls may be passable or not. And then we have Isamba and Ripon Falls. If they

---

[1] Sir Samuel Baker, whom Gordon succeeded as Governor of the tribes which inhabit the Nile Basin in 1874.

are downright cataracts, nothing remains but to make stations at them, and to have an upper and a lower flotilla. If they are rapids, there must be depth of water in such a river in the rainy season to allow of the passage of boats, if you have power to stem the current.

"I now come to Victoria Nyanza; and about this I want to ask you some questions—viz. What is the north frontier of Zanzibar? And have we any British interests which would be interfered with by a debouch of the Egyptians on the sea? Another query is, If the coast north of Equator does not belong to Zanzibar, in whose hands is it? Are the Arabs there refugees from the Wahhabees of Arabia?—for if so, they would be deadly hostile to Egypt. To what limit inland are the people acquainted with partial civilization, or in trade with the coast, and accordingly supplied with firearms? Could I count on virgin native tribes from Lake Baringo or Ngo to Mount Kenia—tribes not in close communication with the coast Arabs?

"My idea is, that till the core of Africa is pierced from the coast but little progress will take place among the hordes of natives in the interior. Personally I would wish a route to sea, for the present route is more or less hampered by other governors of provinces. By the sea route I should be free. The idea is entirely my own ; and I would ask you not to mention it, as (though you are a consul and I have also been one) you must know that nothing would delight the Zanzibar Consul better than to have the thwarting of such a scheme, inasmuch as it would bring him into notice and give him opportunity to write to F. O. I do not myself wish to go farther east than Lake Baringo or Ngo. But whether Egypt is allowed a port or not on the coast, at any rate I may be allowed to pass my caravans through to Zanzibar and to get supplies thence.

"When I contrast the comparative comfort of my work with the miseries you and other travellers have gone through, I have reason to be thankful. Dr. Kraft talks of the River Dana—debouching into sea under the name of river—as navigable from Mount Kenia. If so—and rivers are considered highways and free to all flags—I would far sooner have my frontier at Mount Kenia than descend to the lower lands.

"Believe me, with many excuses for troubling you,

"Yours sincerely,

"C. G. GORDON."

Burton, who possessed a great and personal knowledge of the Nile Basin and the tribes inhabiting it, cordially answered Gordon's letter, giving him full information and many valuable hints. Henceforward the two men frequently corresponded, and got to know one another very well on paper. The next letter of Gordon's which I am permitted to give was written the following year :

"LARDO, *October* 12, 1876.

"MY DEAR CAPTAIN BURTON,

"Thank you for your letter July 13, which I received proceeding from the Lake Albert to this place. I came down from Magungo here in eight days, and could have done it in six days. This is a great comfort to me, and I am proud of my road and of the herds of cattle the natives pasture along either side of it without fear. I have been up the Victoria Nile from Mrooli to near Urmdogani, and seen Long's lake—viz. Lake Mesanga. It is a vast lake, but of still shallow water. The river seems to lose itself entirely in it. A narrow passage, scarcely nine feet wide, joins the north end of the Victoria Nile near Mrooli; and judging from the Murchison Falls— which are rapids, not falls—I should say Victoria Lake and Victoria Nile contribute very little to the true Nile. The branch Piaggia saw is very doubtful. I could not find it, and the boatmen seem very hazy as to its existence. As for Gessi's[1] branch north of Albert Lake, I could not find that either. And, *entre nous*, I believe in neither of the two branches. The R. G. S. will have my maps of the whole Nile from Berber to Urmdogani on a large scale, and they will show the nature of the river. I go home on leave (D.V.) in January for six months, and then come out again to finish off. You would learn my address from Cox & Co., Craig's Court. I would be glad to meet you; for I believe you are not one of those men who bother people, and who pump you in order that they, by writing, might keep themselves before the world. If it was not such a deadly climate, you would find much to interest you in these parts; but it is *very deadly*. An Arab at Mtesa's[2] knows you very well. He gave the Doctor a letter for you. His name is either

---

[1] Romalus Gessi (Gessi Pasha), a member of Gordon's staff.
[2] Mtesa, King of Uganda.

Ahmed bin Hishim or Abdullah bin Habíb. I have had, *entre nous*, a deal of trouble, not yet over, with Mtesa, who, as they will find out, is a regular native. I cannot write this, but will tell you. Stanley knows it, I expect, by this time. The Mission will stay there (Mtesa's) about three months: that will settle them, I think.

"Believe me, with kind regards,
"Yours sincerely,
"C. G. Gordon."

Shortly after this, in December, Gordon determined to resign his official position and return to England, as he had great difficulty in adjusting matters, so far as finances were concerned, with the Governor-General at Kartoum. He went to Cairo, and announced his intention of going home to the Khedive (Ismail), who, however, induced him to promise that he would return to Egypt. Burton wrote to ask Gordon to come, on his journey back to England, round by way of Trieste, and talk over matters. Gordon replied as follows:

"On board 'Sumatra,' *December* 17, 1876.

"My dear Captain Burton,
"I received your kind note as I was leaving for Brindisi. I am sorry I cannot manage the Trieste route. I am not sure what will be my fate. Personally, the whole of the future exploration, or rather opening, of the Victoria Lake to Egypt has not a promising future to me, and I do not a bit like the idea of returning. I have been humbugged into saying

I would do so, and I suppose must keep my word. I, however, have an instinctive feeling that something may turn up ere I go back, and so feel pretty comfortable about it. I gave Gessi a letter to you. He is a zealous and energetic, sharp fellow. I shall not, however, take him back with me, even if I go. I do not like having a man with a family hanging on one.

"Believe me,
"Yours sincerely,
"C. G. GORDON."

Burton then wrote to Gordon, urging him to write a book on his experiences in Equatorial Africa, and asking what his intentions were about returning. In his reply Gordon first broaches the idea which he afterwards returned to again and again—namely, that Burton should take up work in Egypt.

"7, CECIL STREET, STRAND, *January* 12, 1877.

"MY DEAR CAPTAIN BURTON,

"Thank you for your kind note. Gessi wrote to me from Trieste, dating his letter only 'Trieste,' and I replied to that address, so I suppose the post-office know him. Yes; I am back, but I have escaped persecution. Wilson[1] I have heard nothing of. I have not the least intention of publishing anything.[2] My life and work there was a very humdrum one;

---

[1] Mr. Rivers Wilson.
[2] Nevertheless he permitted Dr. Birkbeck Hill to edit and publish his letters in 1881, which give a good account of his work in Central Africa.

and, unlike you, I have no store of knowledge to draw on. (I may tell you your book was thought by us all out in Africa as by far the best ever written.) I am not going back to H.H. It is a great pang to me, I assure you; but it is *hopeless, hopeless* work. Why do not you take up the work? You may not be so sensitive as I am.

"Good-bye, and believe me,
"Yours very truly,
"C. G. Gordon."

Gordon duly returned to Egypt, for the Khedive held him to his promised word. He was made Governor-General of the Soudan, Darfur, and the Equatorial Provinces, which were now reunited into one great whole. It was necessary for good administration that Gordon should have three governors under him, one for the Soudan proper, one for the Equatorial Provinces, and one for Darfur. As soon as Gordon had arranged matters with the Khedive and entered upon his Governor-Generalship he wrote to Burton, offering him the post of Governor-General of Darfur.

"Oomchanga, Darfur, *June* 21, 1877.

"My dear Captain Burton,

"You now, I see, have £600 a year, a good climate, quiet life, good food, etc., and are engaged in literary inquiries, etc., etc. I have no doubt that you are very comfortable, but I cannot think entirely satisfied with your present small sphere. I have therefore written to the Khedive to ask him to give you

Darfur as Governor-General, with £1,600 a year, and a couple of secretaries at £300 a year each. Darfur is *l'enfer*. The country is a vast sand plain, with but little water; the heat is very great; there is little shooting. The people consist of huge Bedawin tribes, and of a settled population in the larger villages. Their previous history under the Sultans would show them fanatical. I have not found them the least so; in fact I think them even less so than the Arabs of Cairo. If you got two years' leave from H.M.'s Government, you would lose nothing. You know the position of Darfur; its frontier through Wadi is only fifteen days from Lake Tchad. On the other side of Lake Tchad you come on another sultanate, that of Bowmon, and you then near the Gulf of Guinea. Darfur is healthy. You will (D.V.) soon have the telegraph to your capital, El Tascher. If the Khedive asks you, accept the post, and you will do a mint of good, and benefit these poor people. You will also see working out curious problems; you will see these huge tribes of Bedawins, to whom the Bedawin tribes of Arabia are as naught; you will trace their history, etc.; and you will open relations with Wadai, Baginni, etc. I know that you have much important work at the Consulate, with the ship captains, etc., and of course it would not be easy to replace you; but it is not every day you use your knowledge of Asiatics or of Arabia. Now is the time for you to make your indelible mark in the world and in these countries. You will be remembered in the literary world, but I would sooner be remembered in Egypt as having made Darfur. I hope, if his Highness writes to you,

you will ask for two years' leave and take the post as Governor-General. You are Commandant of Civil and Military and Finance, and have but very little to do with me beyond demanding what you may want.

"Believe me,

"Yours sincerely,

"C. G. Gordon."

Burton's reply was very characteristic:

"My dear Gordon,

"You and I are too much alike. I could not serve under you, nor you under me. I do not look upon the Soudan as a lasting thing. I have nothing to depend upon but my salary; and I have a wife, and you have not."

Perhaps too Burton was a little annoyed at Gordon apparently taking it for granted that he would jump at Darfur. Much as he loathed Trieste and the life of forced inaction there, he felt this might be to exchange the frying-pan for the fire. Pending Burton's answer, Gordon followed up his first letter by two more:

"Oomchanga, Darfur, *June* 27, 1877.

"My dear Burton,

"Thanks for your letter May 9, received to-day. I have answered. . . . *Would you be bothered with him?* I feel certain you would not. What is the use of such men in these countries; they are, as Speke was to you, infinitely more bother than use. Then why do you put him on me? I have had enough trouble with them already.

"You will have my letter about Darfur. I must say your task will not be pleasant; but you talk Arabic, which I do not; and you will have much to interest you, for most of the old Darfur families are of Mohammed's family.

"I dare say you wonder how I can get on without an interpreter and not knowing Arabic. I do not believe in man's free-will, and therefore believe all things are from God and preordained. Such being the case, the judgments or decisions I give are fixed to be thus or thus, whether I have exactly hit off all the circumstances or not. This is my raft, and on it I manage to float along, thanks to God, more or less successfully. I do not pretend my belief could commend itself to any wisdom or science, or in fact anything; but as I have said elsewhere, a bag of rice jolting along these roads could, if it had the gift of speech, and if it were God's will, do as well as I do. You may not agree with me. Keep your own belief. I get my elixir from mine—viz. that with these views I am comfortable, whether I am a failure or not, and can disregard the world's summary of what I do, or of what I do not do.

"Yours sincerely,
"C. G. GORDON."

"DARA, *July* 18, 1877.

"MY DEAR BURTON,

"I have got round to Dara *viâ* Toashia, and hope in four or five days to get to Tascher. The *soi-*

disant Sultan Haroun is said to have left Tamée. The people are very good. They have been driven into this revolt. Most of the tribes have given in their subscription. The Fors, or original natives of the land, are the only people partially in revolt. Dar For is the land of Fors, as Dar Fertit is the land of the Fertits. You would find much to interest you here, for the Ulemas are well-read people, and know the old history. I found a lot of chain armour here, just like the armour of Saladin's people, time of the Crusades, with old helmets, some embossed with gold. They were taken from the Sultan Ibrahim's bodyguard when he was killed. The sheep are wonderful; some with a regular mane. The people would delight in the interest you would take in them. When the Egyptians took the country here, they seized an ancient mosque for a mug. I have given it back and endowed it. There was a great ceremony, and the people are delighted. It is curious how these Arab tribes came up here. It appears those of Biernan and Bagerini came from Tripoli; the others came up the Nile. The Dar Fertit lies between these semi-Mussulman lands and the Negro lands proper. On the border are the Niam-Niam, who circumcise. I suppose they took it from these Arab tribes. I only hope you will come up. You will (D.V.) find no great trouble here by that time, and none of the misery I have had.

"Believe me,
      "Yours sincerely,
            "C. G. GORDON."

A few weeks later Burton's laconic refusal of Darfur reached Gordon. That Gordon was nettled a little is apparent from the opening paragraph of the following letter. But he was far too just not to understand; and so far from resenting Burton's frankness, as a lesser man might have done, this incident only served to make him appreciate his rare qualities the more:

"EN ROUTE TO BERBER, *October* 19, 1877.

"MY DEAR CAPTAIN BURTON,

"£1,600, or indeed £16,000, would never compensate a man for a year spent actively in Darfur. But I considered you, from your independence, one of Nature's nobility, who did not serve for money. Excuse the mistake—if such it is.

"I am now going to Dongola and Assouan, and thence to Massowah to see Johannis,[1] and then to Berberah *vis-à-vis* Aden, near your old friends the Somalis. (Now there is a government which might suit you, and which you might develop, paying off old scores by the way for having thwarted you; it is too far off for me to hope to do anything.) I then return to Kartoum, and then go to Darfur and return to Kartoum, and then go to the Lakes. Why do people die in these countries? Do not you, who are a philosopher, think it is due to moral prostration more than to the climate? I think so, and have done so for a long time. My assistant, Prout,[2] has been lingering on the

---

[1] Johannis, King of Abyssinia.
[2] Colonel Prout, of the American army, for some time in command of the Equatorial Provinces.

grave's brink for a long time, and I doubt if he will go up again. I have no fear of dying in any climate. 'Men now seek honours, not honour.' You put that in one of your books. Do you remember it? How true it is! I have often pirated it, and not acknowledged the author, though I believe *you* stole it. I see Wilson is now Sir Andrew. Is it on account of his father's decease? How is he? He wanted to come out, but he could not bear the fatigue. All these experiments of the King of the Belgians will come to grief, in spite of the money they have; the different nationalities doom them. Kaba Rega,[1] now that we have two steamers on Lake Albert (which, by the way, is, according to Mason, one hundred and twenty miles longer than Gessi made it), asks for peace, which I am delighted at; he never was to blame, and you will see that, if you read how Baker treated him and his ambassadors. Baker certainly gave me a nice job in raising him against the Government so unnecessarily, even on his own showing (*vide* his book *Ismaïlia*). *Judge justly.* Little by little we creep on to our goal—viz. the two lakes; *and nothing can stop us, I think.* Mtesa is very good friends, and agrees much more with us than with your missionaries. You know the hopelessness of such a task, till you find a St. Paul or St. John. Their representatives nowadays want so much a year and a contract. It is all nonsense; no one will stay four years out there. I would like to hear you hold forth

---

[1] King of Unyoro, a powerful and treacherous savage. Sir Samuel Baker attempted to depose him, but Kaba Rega maintained his power.

on the idol 'Livingstone,' etc., and on the slave-trade. Setting aside the end to be gained, I think that Slave Convention is a very just one in many ways towards the people; but we are not an over-just nation towards the weak. I suppose you know that old creature Grant, who for seventeen or eighteen years has traded on his wonderful walk. I am grateful to say he does not trouble me now. I would also like to discuss with you the wonderful journey of Cameron, but we are too far apart; though when you are at Akata or For, I shall be at Berenice or Suakin. It was very kind of you offering me Faulkner. Do you remember his uncle in R. N.? Stanley will give them some bother; they cannot bear him, and in my belief rather wished he had not come through safe. He will give them a dose for their hard speeches. He is to blame for *writing* what he did (as Baker was). These things may be done, but not advertised. I shall now conclude with kind regards,

"Yours sincerely,
"C. G. GORDON."

While Lady Burton was alone at Suez in the March of the following year (1878), waiting to meet her husband on his return from the expedition to Midian, Gordon arrived there. He of course hastened to make the acquaintance of Burton's wife. He stayed a week at Suez, and during that time Isabel and he saw one another every day. She found him "very eccentric, but very charming. I say eccentric, until you got to know and understand him." A warm friendship sprang up between the two, for they had much to talk about and much in common. They were both Christian mystics (I use the term in the highest sense); and though they differed on many points of faith (for Isabel held that Catholicism was the highest form of Christian mysticism, and in this Gordon did not agree with her), they were at one in regarding religion as a vital principle and a guiding rule of life and action. They were at one too in their love of probing

> Things more true and deep
> Than we mortals know.

With regard to more mundane matters, Gordon did not scruple to pour cold water on the Burtons' golden dream of wealth from the Mines of Midian, and frankly told Isabel that the "Midian Myth" was worth very little, and that Burton would do much better to throw in his lot with him. Isabel, however, did not see things in the same light, and she was confident of the future of Midian, and had no desire to go to Darfur. When Burton returned from Midian in April, and he and his wife went to Cairo at the request of the Khedive, they saw a good deal of Gordon again. He and Burton discussed affairs thoroughly—especially Egyptian affairs—and Gordon again expressed his regret that Burton did not see his way to joining him. When Burton was in London later in the year, he received the following letter from Gordon, in which he renewed his offer, increasing the salary from £1,600 to £5,000 a year.

CAIRO.
[*Page* 662.

"KARTOUM, *August* 8, 1878.

"MY DEAR BURTON,

"Please date, or rather put address on your letters. Thanks for yours of July 4, received to-day. I am very sorry Mrs. Burton is not well, but hope England has enabled her to regain her health. My arrangement is *letter for letter*. If you write, I will answer. I wish you could undertake the Government of Zeyla, Harar, and Berberah, and free me of the bother. Why cannot you get two years' leave from F. O., then write (saying it is my suggestion) to H.H., and offer it? I could give, say, £5,000 a year from London to your Government. Do do something to help me, and do it without further reference to me; you would lift a burthen off my shoulders. I have now to stay at Kartoum for the finances. I am in a deplorable state. I have a nasty revolt of Slandralus at Bahr Gazelle, which will cost me some trouble; I mean not to fight them, but to blockade them into submission. I am now hard at work against the slave caravans; we have caught fifteen in two months, and I hope by a few judicious hangings to stop their work. I hanged a man the other day for making a eunuch without asking H.H.'s leave. Emin Effendi, now Governor of Equator Province, is Dr. Sneitzer; but he is furious if you mention it, and denies that is his name to me; he declares he is a Turk. There is something queer about him which I do not understand; he is a queer fellow, very cringing in general, but sometimes bursts out into his natural form.

He came up here in a friendless state. He is perhaps the only riddle I have met with in life. He is the man Amspldt spoke to you about. Amspldt was a useless fellow, and he has no reason to complain of Emin Effendi. I have sent Gessi up to see after the slave-dealers' outbreak. He was humble enough. Good-bye! Kind regards to Mrs. Burton.

"Yours sincerely,
"C. G. GORDON."

Burton again refused, giving the same reasons as before, and reiterating his opinion that the existing state of affairs in the Soudan could not last. Gordon, seeing his decision was not to be shaken, acquiesced, and did not ask him again. Moreover he was losing faith in the Soudan himself. A few months later we have him writing as follows:

"KARTOUM, *November* 20, 1878.

"My DEAR BURTON,

"Thanks for your letter of October 6, received to-day. I have not forgotten the manuscript from Harar, nor the coins.

"I wish much I could get a European to go to Berberah, Zeyla, and Harar, at £1,200 or £1,500, a really good man. They keep howling for troops, and give me a deal of trouble. Our finances take up all my time; I find it best to look after them myself, and so I am kept close at work. We owe £300,000 floating debt, but not to Europeans, and our *present* expenditure exceeds revenue by £97,000.

"Rossit, who took your place in Darfur, died the other day there, after three and a half months' residence; he is a serious loss to me, for the son of Zebahr with his slave-dealers is still in revolt. Cairo and Nubia never take any notice of me, nor do they answer my questions.

"I have *scotched* the slave-trade, and Wyld of Jeddah says that scarcely any slaves pass over, and that the people of Jeddah are disgusted. It is, however, only *scotched*. I am blockading all roads to the slave districts, and I expect to make the slave-dealers now in revolt give in, for they must be nearly out of stores. I have indeed a very heavy task, for I have to do everything myself. Kind regards to Mrs. Burton and yourself.

"Believe me,
"Yours sincerely,
"C. G. GORDON.

"P.S.—Personally I am very weary and tired of the inaction at Kartoum, with its semi-state, a thing which bores me greatly."

The following year Burton's prescience proved true. The Soudan was "not a lasting thing," so far as Gordon was concerned. Ismail Khedive had abdicated, and Tewfik his son ruled in his stead ; and Gordon, dissatisfied with many things, finally threw up his post on account of the Slave Convention. Though he placed his resignation in the Khedive's hands, Tewfik begged him to undertake a mission to Abyssinia. While he was on the journey he wrote the following to Burton :

"EN ROUTE TO MASSOWAH, RED SEA,
"*August* 31, 1879.

"MY DEAR BURTON,

"Thanks for several little notes from you, and one from Mrs. Burton, and also for the papers you sent me. I have been on my travels, and had not time to write. An Italian has egged on Johannis to be hostile, and so I have to go to Massowah to settle the affair if I can. I then hope to go home for good, for the slave-hunters (thanks to Gessi) have collapsed, and it will take a long time to rebuild again, even if fostered by my successor. I like the new Khedive immensely; but I warn you that all Midian guiles will be wasted on him, and Mrs. Burton ought to have taken the £3,000 I offered her at Suez, and which she scoffed at, saying, 'You would want that for gloves.' Do you wear those skin coverings to your paws? I do not! No, the days of Arabian Nights are over, and stern economy now rules. Tewfik seeks 'honour, not honours.' I do not know what he will do with the Soudan; he is glad, I think (indeed feel sure), I am going. I was becoming a too powerful Satrap. The general report at Cairo was that I meditated rebellion even under Ismail the 'incurable,' and now they cannot imagine why I am so well received by the new Khedive.

    " Believe me,
     " Yours sincerely,
      " C. G. Gordon."

Gordon was not the only one who suffered by the change of Khedive. Burton, as Gordon had foretold, came to grief over the Mines of Midian, for Tewfik declined to be bound by any promise of his father; and though Burton went to Egypt to interview the Khedive, to see if he could do anything, his efforts were of no avail. Meanwhile Isabel, who had come to London mainly for medical treatment, was moving heaven and earth to see if she could induce the English Government to stir in the matter; but they naturally declined. Isabel wrote to Gordon, who had now come home from Egypt, on this and other matters. She received from him the following letters in answer to her request and inquiries concerning the state of affairs in Egypt:

       " U.S. Club, Pall Mall,
        " 4.2.80.

" My dear Mrs. Burton,

 " You write to an orb which is setting, or rather is set. I have no power to aid your husband in any way. I went to F. O. to-day, and, as you know, Lord —— is very ill. Well! the people there were afraid of me, for I have written hard things to them; and though they knew all, they would say naught. I said, 'Who is the personification of Foreign Office?' They said, 'X is.' I saw 'X'; but he tried to evade my question—*i.e.* Would F. O. do anything to prevent the Soudan falling into chaos? It was no use. I cornered him, and he then said, '*I am merely a clerk to register letters coming in and going out.*' So then I gave it up, and marvelled. I must say I was surprised to see such a thing; a great Government like ours governed by men who dare not call their souls their own. Lord —— rules them with a rod of iron. If your husband would understand that F. O. at present is Lord —— (and he is *ill*), he would see that I can do nothing. I have written letters to F. O. that would raise a corpse; it is no good. I have threatened to go to the French Government about the Soudan; it is no good. In fact, my dear Mrs. Burton, I have done for myself with this Government, and you may count me a feather, for I am worth no more. Will you send this on to your husband? He is a first-rate fellow, and I wish I had seen him long ago (scratch this out, for he will fear I am going to borrow money); and believe me, my dear Mrs. Burton (pardon me about Suez),

"Yours sincerely,
"C. G. GORDON."

"HÔTEL TAUCAN, LAUSANNE,
"12.3.80.

"MY DEAR MRS. BURTON,

"Excuse my not answering your kind note of 5.3.80 before; but to be quiet I have come abroad, and did not have a decided address, so I only got your letter to-day. I will come and see you when I (D.V.) come home; but that is undecided. Of course your husband failed with Tewfik. I scent carrion a long way off, and felt that the hour of my departure from Egypt had come, so I left quietly. Instead of A (Ismail), who was a good man, you have B (Tewfik), who may be good or bad, as events will allow him. B is the true son of A; but has the inexperience of youth, and may be smarter. The problem working out in the small brains of Tewfik is this: 'My father lost his throne because he scented the creditors. The Government only cared for the creditors; they did not care for good government. So if I look after the creditors, I may govern the country as I like.' No doubt Tewfik is mistaken; but these are his views, backed up by a ring of pashas. Now look at his Ministry. Are they not aliens to Egypt? They are all slaves or of low origin. Put their price down:

Riaz Pasha, a dancing-boy of Abbas Pasha, value	350
A slave, Osman, Minister of War, turned out by me	350
Etc., etc., etc., each—five . . 350 =	1,750
	2,450

So that the value of the Ministry (which *we* think an enlightened one) is £490. What do they care for the country? Not a jot. We ought to sweep all this lot out, and the corresponding lot at Stamboul. It is hopeless and madness to think that with such material you can do anything. Good-bye. Kind regards to your husband.

"Believe me,
"Yours sincerely,
"C. G. GORDON."

"PARIS, 2.4.80.

"MY DEAR MRS. BURTON,

"Thanks for your telegram and your letter. Excuse half-sheet (economy). No, I will not write to Cairo, and your letters are all torn up. I am going to Brussels in a few days, and after a stay there I come over to England. I do not like or believe in Nubar. He is my horror; for he led the old ex-Khedive to his fall, though Nubar owed him everything. When Ismail became Khedive, Nubar had £3 a month; he now owns £1,000,000. Things will not and cannot go straight in Egypt, and I would say, 'Let them glide.' Before long time elapses things will come to a crisis. The best way is to let all minor affairs rest, and to consider quietly how the ruin is to fall. It must fall ere long. United Bulgaria, Syria France, and Egypt England. France would then have as much interest in repelling Russia as we have. Supposing you got out Riaz, why, you would have Riaz's brother; and if you got rid of the latter, you would have Riaz's nephew. Le plus on change, le plus c'est la même chose. We may, by stimulants, keep the life in them; but as long as the body of the people are unaffected, so long will it be corruption in high places, varying in form, not in matter. Egypt is usurped by the family of the Sandjeh of Salonique, and (by our folly) *we* have added a ring of Circassian pashas. The whole lot should go; they are as much strangers as we would be. Before we began muddling we had only to deal with the Salonique family; now we have added the ring, who say, '*We are Egypt.*' We have made Cairo a second Stamboul. So much the better. Let these locusts fall together. As well expect any reform, any good sentiment, from these people as water from a stone; the extract you wish to get does not and cannot exist in them. Remember I do not say this of the Turkish peasantry or of the Egyptian-born poor families. It is written, Egypt shall be the prey of nations, and so she has been; she is the servant; in fact Egypt does not really exist. It is a nest of usurpers.

"Believe me,
"Yours sincerely,
"C. G. GORDON."

A day or two after the date of this last letter Gordon returned to London, and went several times to see Isabel, who was ill in lodgings in Upper Montagu Street, and very anxious about her husband and the Midian Mines. Gordon's prospects too were far from rosy at this time, so that they were companions in misfortune. They discussed Egypt and many things. Isabel writes: "I remember on April 15, 1880, he asked me if I knew the origin of the Union Jack, and he sat down on my hearth-rug before the fire, cross-legged, with a bit of paper and a pair of scissors, and he made me three or four Union Jacks, of which I pasted one in my journal of that day; and I never saw him again."[1] She also writes elsewhere: "I shall never forget how kind and sympathetic he was; but he always said, 'As God has willed it, so will it be.' That was the burden of his talk: 'As God has willed it, so will it be.'"

In May Burton wrote to Lord Granville, pointing out that Riaz Pasha was undoing all Gordon's anti-slavery work, and asking for a temporary appointment as Slave Commissioner in the Soudan and Red Sea, to follow up the policy of anti-slavery which Gordon had begun. This Lord Granville refused.

Gordon went to many places—India, China, the Cape—and played many parts during the next three years; but he still continued to correspond with Isabel and her husband at intervals, though his correspondence referred mainly to private matters, and was of no public interest. In 1883 he wrote the following to Burton from Jerusalem, anent certain inquiries in which he was much interested:

"JERUSALEM, *June* 3, 1883.

"MY DEAR BURTON,

"I have a favour to ask, which I will begin with, and then go on to other subjects. In 1878 (I think) I sent you a manuscript in Arabic, copy of the

---

[1] *Life of Sir Richard Burton*, by Isabel his wife, vol. ii., p. 177.

My dear Burton

Thanks for your note. 24.11.
I am just back from Ireland studying the question

I have read Allen's letter, I do not think he meant anything of course one cannot judge for I have not seen Mrs Burton's letter to which he replied

However one thing is sure that the Foreign Office will do nothing in this matter, for the present

Are you not coming to England with Mrs Burton. How do you know Malet attached us he wrote to me most kindly the other day

Excuse haste with kind regards to Mrs Burton. Believe me
Yours sincerely
C E S——

[Page 672.

manuscript you discovered in Harar. I want you to lend it to me for a month or so, and will ask you in sending it to register it. This is the favour I want from you. I have time and means to get it fairly translated, and I will do this for you. I will send you the translation and the original back; and if it is worth it, you will publish it. I hope you and Mrs. Burton are well. Sorry that £ s. d. keep you away from the East, for there is much to interest here in every way, and you would be useful to me as an encyclopædia of oriental lore; as it is, Greek is looked on by me as hieroglyphics.

"Here is result of my studies: The whole of the writers on Jerusalem, with few exceptions, fight for Zion on the Western Hill, and put the whole Jerusalem in tribe Benjamin! I have worked this out, and to me it is thus: The whole question turns on the position of En-shemesh, which is generally placed, for no reason I know of, at Ain Hand. I find Kubbat el Sama, which corresponds to Bæthsamys of the Septuagint, at the north of Jerusalem, and I split Jerusalem by the Tyropœan Valley (*alias* the Gibeon of Eden, of which more another time).

"Anyway one can scarcely cut Judah out of Jerusalem altogether; yet that is always done, except by a few. If the juncture is as I have drawn it, it brings Gibeon, Nob, and Mizpah all down too close to Jerusalem on the Western Hills. This is part of my studies. Here is the Skull Hill north of the City (traced from map, ordnance of 1864), which I think is the Golgotha; for the victims were to be slain on north of altar, not west, as the Latin Holy Sepulchre. This hill is close to the old church of St. Stephen, and I believe that eventually near here will be found the Constantine churches.

"I have been, and still am, much interested in these parts, and as it is cheap I shall stop here. I live at Ain Karim, five miles from Jerusalem. There are few there who care for antiquities. Schink, an old German, is the only one who is not a bigot. Have you ever written on Palestine? I wondered you never followed up your visit to Harar; that is a place of great interest. My idea is that the Pison is the Blue Nile, and that the sons of Joktan were at Harar, Abyssinia, Godjam; but it is not well supported.

"The Rock of Harar was the platform Adam was moulded on out of clay from the Potter's Field. He was then put in Seychelles (Eden), and after Fall brought back to Mount Moriah to till the ground in the place he was taken from. Noah built the Ark twelve miles from Jaffa, at Ain Judeh; the Flood began; the Ark floated up and rested on Mount Baris, afterwards Antonia; he sacrificed on the Rock (Adam was buried on the Skull Hill, hence the skull under the cross). It was only 776 A.D. that Mount Ararat of Armenia became the site of the Ark's descent. Korán says Al Judi (Ararat) is holy land. After Flood the remnants went east to Plain of Shimar. Had they gone east from the Al Judi, near Mosul, or from Armenian Ararat, they could never have reached Shimar. Shem was Melchizedek, etc., etc.

"With kind regards to Mrs. Burton and you, and the hope you will send me the manuscript,
"Believe me,
"Yours sincerely,
"C. G. GORDON.

"P.S.—Did you ever get the £1,000 I offered you on part of ex-Khedive for the Mines of Midian?"

Some six months after the date of this letter Gordon left England for the Soudan, and later went to Kartoum, with what result all the world knows. Burton said, when the Government sent Gordon to Kartoum, they failed because they sent him alone. Had they sent him with five hundred soldiers there would have been no war. It was just possible at the time that Burton might have been sent instead of Gordon; and Isabel, dreading this, wrote privately to the Foreign Office, unknown to her husband, to let them know how ill he then was.

The Burtons were profoundly moved at the death of Gordon; they both felt it with a keen sense of personal loss. Isabel relates that in one of the illustrated papers there was a picture of Gordon lying in the desert, his Bible in one hand, his revolver in the other, and the vultures hovering around. Burton said, "Take it away! I can't bear to look at it. I have had to feel that myself; I know what it is." But upon reflection Burton grew to disbelieve in Gordon's death, and he died believing that he had escaped into the desert, but disgusted at his betrayal and abandonment he would never let himself be discovered or show himself in

England again. In this conviction Burton was of course mistaken; but he had formed it on his knowledge of Gordon's character.

I am aware that this chapter dealing with Gordon and his letters is something of an interpolation, and has little to do with the main thread of the story; but Lady Burton wished it to be so, and its irrelevance may be pardoned for the sake of the light it throws upon the friendship which existed between three very remarkable personages, each curiously alike in some respects, and in others widely dissimilar.

CHAPTER XXVI

THE SWORD HANGS

(1885—1890)

> Life is no holiday: therein
> Are want and woe and sin,
> Death with nameless fears; and over all
> Our pitying tears must fall.
>
> The hour draws near, howe'er delayed or late,
> When, at the Eternal Gate,
> We leave the words and works we call our own,
> And lift void hands alone
>
> For love to fill. Our nakedness of soul
> Brings to that gate no toll:
> Giftless we come to Him who all things gives;
> And live because He lives.
> WHITTIER.

IN May, 1885, Isabel started with her husband for England. They travelled together as far as Venice, and here, as often, they parted, and went their separate ways. Burton was ordered to go by sea for his health, and his wife arranged to proceed by land. She went round by way of Bologna, and thence travelled *viâ* Milan and Paris, and arrived in London on June 2. Her husband joined her twelve days later.

They had two objects in coming to London at this time—one was to consult physicians concerning Burton's health, the other to make arrangements concerning *The Arabian Nights*. The production of this book may be described as a joint affair; for though the lion's share of the work of translating, writing, and correcting proofs devolved upon Burton alone, the financial part of the work fell upon his wife, and that it was a big thing no one who has had any experience of writing or publishing would deny. There were several editions in the field; but they were all abridged or "Bowdlerized" ones, adapted more or less for "family and domestic reading." Burton's object in bringing out this great work was not only to produce a literal translation, but to reproduce it faithfully in the Arabian manner. He preserved throughout the orientation of the verses and figures of speech instead of Anglicising them. It is this, combined with his profound oriental scholarship, his fine old-world style, and the richness, variety, and quaintness of his vocabulary, which has given to his original edition its unique value.

In Burton the immortal tales had at last found a translator who would do them justice, and who was not afraid of prejudices of Anglo-Saxon Puritanism. Burton's view of this matter is sufficiently expressed in the following speech: "I do not care a button about being prosecuted; and if the matter comes to a fight, I will walk into court with my Bible and my Shakspeare and my Rabelais under my arm, and prove to them that before they condemn me they must cut half of *them* out, and not allow them to be circulated to the public."[1] He expressed his views in this matter to his wife; and though at his wish she did not read the original edition of *The Arabian Nights*, she set to work to help him in every way that she could. In fact it may be truly said that it was she who did all the difficult work of evading the "vigilance" of certain persons, and of arranging for the publication of this important book. In order that her husband's original text might be copyrighted, she herself brought out an expurgated edition, which was called the "Household Edition." By this means she was enabled to copyright three thousand pages of her husband's original text, and only excluded two hundred and fifteen. She says, "Richard forbade me to read these pages until he blotted out with ink the worst words, and desired me to substitute not English but Arab society words, which I did to his complete satisfaction." Of course to bring out a work of this kind, and to bear the whole burden of the labour and initial expense of it, was no ordinary task, and it is to Isabel's efforts and to her marvellous business capacity that the credit of publishing the book is due. From a financial point of view the Burtons had no reason to regret their venture. At the beginning a publisher had offered Burton £500 for the book; but Isabel said, "No, let me do it." It was seventeen months' hard work, and during that time they had to find the means for printing and binding and circulating the volumes as they came out. The Burtons were their own printers

---

[1] He actually compiled a book of quotations from the Bible and Shakspeare for use in case of need, which he called *The Black Book*.

and their own publishers, and they made between September, 1885, and November, 1888, sixteen thousand guineas, six thousand of which went towards the expenses of publishing and ten thousand guineas into their own pockets. Isabel writes, "It came just in time to give my husband the comforts and luxuries and freedom which gilded the last five years of his life. When he died there were four florins left, which I put into the poor-box."

They had a very pleasant season in London. They were mainly occupied in preparing *The Arabian Nights*; but their labours over for the day, they went out in society a great deal. Perhaps the most noteworthy event at this time was that Isabel made a long speech at St. James's Hall at a meeting for the purpose of appealing to the Pope for a Circular Letter on the subject of the protection of animals. The meeting was in vain.

The first volume of *The Arabian Nights* came out on December 12, 1885, and the sixteenth volume, the last of the Supplementals, on November 13, 1888. Thus in a period of three years they produced twenty-two volumes—namely, ten Originals, six Supplementals, and Lady Burton's six volumes of the Household Edition.

In October, 1885, they went down to Hatfield on a visit to Lord and Lady Salisbury. A week before this Burton, having heard that Sir John Drummond Hay, Consul at Morocco, was about to retire, applied for the post. It was the one thing that he had stayed on in the Consular Service in the hope of obtaining. He wrote a letter to the Foreign Secretary, which was backed up by about fifty of the best names in England, whom his wife had canvassed; and indeed it seemed that the post was as good as assured to him. In the third week in November Burton started for Morocco in order to spy out the promised land, or rather the land which he hoped would have been his. Isabel was left behind to bring out some volumes of *The Arabian Nights*. She brought them out up to the seventh volume, and then made ready to join her husband at Gibraltar on his way to Tangiers in January. She says *à propos* of her labours in this respect: "I was dreadfully spied upon by those who wished to get Richard into trouble about it, and once an unaccountable person came and took rooms in some lodgings which I took after Richard left, and I settled with the landlord that I should leave or that person should not have the rooms, and of course he did not have any hesitation between the two, and I took the whole of the rooms during my stay."

In January, 1886, just as she was leaving London, she received a telegram from her husband saying that there was cholera at Gibraltar, and she could get no quarantine there, and would not be allowed to land. But she was not a woman to be stopped; so she at once telegraphed to Sir John Ayde, who was then commanding Gibraltar, and asked if he would allow a Government boat to take her off the P. & O. and put her straight on the Morocco boat. He telegraphed back, "Yes," whereat she rejoiced greatly, as she wanted especially to reach her husband in time for them to celebrate their Silver Wedding together. When she arrived at Gibraltar, Burton, who was staying there, came off in a boat to meet her, and they called together on Sir John Ayde to thank him for his kindness. A few days later the news came to them that the Government had at last recognized Burton's public services. It came in the form of a telegram addressed to " Sir Richard Burton." Isabel says : " He tossed it over to me, and said, 'Some fellow is playing me a practical joke, or else it is not for me. I shall not open it, so you may as well ring the bell and give it back again.' " His wife said, " Oh no ; I shall open it if you don't." So it was opened. It was from Lord Salisbury, conveying in the kindest terms that the Queen, at his recommendation, had made him K.C.M.G. in reward for his services. He looked very serious and quite uncomfortable, and said, " Oh, I shall not accept it." She said, " You had better accept it, Jemmy, because it is a certain sign that they are going to give you the place—Tangiers, Morocco."

There is only one thing to be said about this honour—it came too late. Too late for him, because he had never at any time cared much for these things. " Honour, not honours " was his motto ; and now the recognition of his services, which might have been a great encouragement ten or fifteen years earlier, and have spurred him on to fresh efforts, found him broken by sickness, and with life's zest to a great extent gone. Too late for her, because her only pleasure in these things was that they reflected credit upon her husband ; and if he did not appreciate them, she did not care. Yet of course she was glad that at last there had come some return for her unceasing efforts, and some admission, though tardy, of the services which her husband had rendered. It was a sign too that the prejudice against him in certain quarters was at last lived down. She wrote to a friend [1]:

"You will have seen from the papers, and I know what pleasure it will give you, that the Conservatives on going out made Dick Sir Richard Burton, K.C.M.G. . . . The Queen's recognition of Dick's forty-four years of service was sweetly done at last, sent for our Silver Wedding, and she told a friend of mine that she was pleased to confer something that would include both husband and wife."

The Burtons crossed over to Morocco from Gibraltar in a flat-bottomed cattle-tug, only fit for a river; and as the sea was exceedingly heavy, and the machinery had stopped, the sailors said for want of oil, the seas washed right over the boat, and the passage was prolonged from two hours to five. They made many excursions round about Tangiers; but on the whole they were disappointed with Morocco. They disliked Tangiers itself, and the Consulate seemed to them a miserable little house after their palazzo at Trieste. Lady Burton had expected to find Tangiers a second Damascus; but in this she was sorely disappointed. She wrote to a friend from there, "Trieste will seem like Paris after it. It has none of the romance or barbaric splendour of Damascus. Nevertheless," she says, "I would willingly have lived there, and put out all my best capabilities, if my husband could have got

[1] Letter to Miss Bishop from Tangiers, Morocco, February 16, 1886.

the place he wanted, and for which I had employed every bit of interest on his side and mine to obtain." They received a great deal of hospitality in Tangiers, and inspected the place and the natives thoroughly. Most of the people looked forward to welcoming them.

On their departure they went to Genoa, which they reached after a rough voyage, and thence they proceeded by easy stages to Trieste. Lady Burton arrived home alone at ten o'clock in the evening; and as she was accustomed to be met by a crowd of friends on her return, she was surprised to find no one to meet her. When she got to the house, their absence was explained. Three telegrams were handed to her. The first was, "Father very ill; can you come?" the second was, "Father died to-day"; the third, "Father buried to-day at Mortlake." As her friends were unaware of her address the telegrams had not been forwarded, and they had kept away, so as not to intrude on her grief. The blow was not altogether unexpected, for Mr. Arundell had been ill for some time; but it was none the less severe, for she had always been devotedly attached to her father, and his house had been made a rallying-point for them when they were wont to return home.

They remained at Trieste three months, during which time the English colony presented them with a silver cup and congratulations on their hardly earned honours. Then, as Burton had to consult a particular manuscript which would supply two volumes of his "Supplemental" *Arabian Nights*, they left again for England. On their return to London they took up their work where they had left it a few months before. In July they had the mortification of finding that Lord Rosebery had given away the coveted post of Morocco, which had been as good as promised to them by Lord Salisbury, to some one else. It was during their few months' absence from England that the change of Government had taken place, and Lord Salisbury's brief-lived Administration of 1886 had yielded place to a Liberal Government. Such are the vicissitudes of official life. Had Lord Salisbury been in office, Sir Richard would probably have got Morocco. It was perhaps all for the best that he did not get the post, although it was a sore disappointment to them at the time. Even Lady Burton came to take this view. She writes: "I sometimes now think that it was better so, and that he would not have lived so long had he had it, for he was decidedly breaking up. The climate did not appear to be the one that suited him, and the anxiety and responsibilities of the post might have hurried on the catastrophe. . . . It was for the honour of the thing, and we saw for ourselves how uneasy a crown it would be."

Perhaps there was another reason too, for when Lady Burton remonstrated a Minister wrote to her in friendly chaff: "We don't want to annex Morocco, and we know that you two would be Emperor and Empress in about six months." This was an evident allusion to the part which they had played during their brief reign at Damascus. At Trieste there was no room for the eagles to soar; their wings were clipped.

Seeing that the last hope was over, and the one post

which Sir Richard Burton had coveted as the crown of his career was denied to him, his wife set to work to induce the Government to allow him to retire on his pension four years before his time. She had good grounds for making this request, for his health was breaking, and this last disappointment about Morocco seemed to have broken him even more. When he told her that it was given to another man, he said, " There is no room for me now, and I do not want anything ; but I have worked forty-four years for nothing. I am breaking up, and I want to go free." So she at once set to work to draw up what she called " The Last Appeal," enumerating the services which her husband had rendered to his country, and canvassing her friends to obtain the pension. The petition was backed as usual by forty-seven or fifty big names, who actively exerted themselves in the matter. It was refused, notwithstanding that public feeling and the press seemed unanimously in favour of its being granted. The ground on which it was refused, apparently, was that it was contrary to precedent, and that it was not usual ; but then the case was altogether an unusual one, and Sir Richard Burton was altogether an unusual man. Even supposing that there had been a difficulty about giving him the full Consular pension, it would have been easy for the Government, if they had been so minded, to have made up to him the sum—only a few hundred pounds a year—from the Civil List, on the ground of his literary and linguistic labours and services. It should be added that this petition was refused both by Liberal and Conservative Governments, for Lord

LADY BURTON IN 1887.

Salisbury's second Administration came into office before the Burtons left England. But there was this difference: whereas Lord Rosebery reprimanded Burton for his frequent absence from his post, Lord Salisbury was very indulgent in the matter of leave. He recognized that Burton's was an exceptional case, and gave him exceptional privileges.

They remained in London until the end of the year, and on January 4, 1887, they left England for Cannes, where they spent a few pleasant weeks, rejoicing in the sun and blue sea and sky. They enjoyed a good deal of society at Cannes, where they met the Prince of Wales and many friends. On Ash Wednesday occurred the earthquake which made such a commotion on the Riviera at that time, and of which Sir Richard Burton gave the following account:

"A little before 6 a.m., on the finest of mornings, with the smoothest of seas, the still sleeping world was aroused by a rumbling and shaking as of a thousand express trains hissing and rolling along, and in a few minutes followed a shock, making the hotel reel and wave. The duration was about one minute. My wife said to me, 'Why, what sort of express train have they got on to-day?' It broke on to us, upheaving and making the earth undulate, and as it came I said, 'By Jove! that is a good earthquake.' She called out, 'All the people are rushing out into the garden undressed; shall we go too?' I said, 'No, my girl; you and I have been in too many earthquakes to show the white feather at our age.' 'All right,' she answered; and I turned round and went to sleep again."

The result of the earthquake was a great and sudden exodus from Cannes, and indeed from all the Riviera. Visitors fled in panic, but Sir Richard and Lady Burton went about their usual business, and were amused at seeing the terrified people rush off to the railway-station, and the queer garments in which they were clad. Shortly after Lady Burton was terribly frightened from another cause. Her husband had an epileptic fit, and it was some time before she and the doctors could bring him round again. Henceforth it became necessary for them to have always with them a resident doctor. They both of them disliked the idea of having a stranger spying about them very much; but it was inevitable, for the epilepsy was a new development, and as Burton says, "My wife felt, though she had successfully nursed me through seven long illnesses since our marriage, that this was a case beyond her ken." So Dr. Ralph Leslie was telegraphed for, and came out from England to Cannes, where he joined them. Then commenced what they called their *Via Crucis* to Trieste. Lady Burton thus describes her troubles at that time:

"On February 23 we were shaken to a jelly by the earthquakes—three strong shocks and three weeks of palpitating earth in the Riviera. On February 26 my poor darling Dick had an epileptic fit, or, more properly speaking, an epileptiform convulsion, which lasted about half an hour, and endangered his life. I had six doctors and two nurses, and we watched and tended him for fifteen days; and I telegraphed for an English doctor to England by express, who came, and lives and travels with us, as Richard insisted on coming to Trieste, not to England, and will return with us. It took us, *after his arrival*, twenty-eight days to accomplish the twenty-eight hours of express between Cannes and Trieste in toil, anguish, and anxiety. We arrived April 5 at home in rest and comfort. He has been making daily progress to health. He is now out walking with his doctor. We had a consultation a few days ago. He will always require *great care and watching* all his life—diet and internal health; must not climb, as his heart is weak, nor take Turkish baths, nor overwork; and he may so live fifteen years, but he may die any moment of heart disease. And I need not say that I shall never have a really happy, peaceful moment again. In the midst of this my uncle,[1] who was like my father to me, was found dead in his bed. Then I have had a bad lip and money losses, and altogether a bad time of it."[2]

At Trieste Burton led the life of a confirmed invalid, and his wife attended him with unfailing devotion, which was in no way abated by the presence of the resident doctor—" a disagreeable luxury," as she called him. They used to sit a good deal under their favourite linden tree in the garden and receive visitors. Burton's love for his wife, always deep, though never demonstrative, seems to have shown itself more at this time; and in the few remaining years he came to lean on her more and more, making her his *confidante* in all things. In June they celebrated the Jubilee of Queen

[1] The late Lord Gerard.
[2] Letter to Miss Bird from Trieste, April 10, 1887.

Victoria, and, owing to her husband's illness, nearly all the arrangements fell upon Lady Burton. It was she who drew up the address which was sent to Her Majesty, and she also prepared the speech to deliver in case her husband was too unwell to attend the public dinner in celebration of the event. As Lady Burton has been accused of being such a bigoted Roman Catholic, it is only fair to mention that on this auspicious occasion she accompanied her husband to the official service in the Anglican Church. Her loyalty to her Queen was unswerving. She was not required to make the speech, as Burton was well enough to be carried down to the dinner, where he delivered the oration. It was the only occasion on which he ever wore his Order of St. Michael and St. George. The effort was so great that he had to be carried upstairs again the moment his speech was over.

The rest of 1887 was chiefly taken up by a dreary record of failing health. The Burtons went away for a summer holiday as usual, and during their absence from Trieste many English Royalties arrived there with the squadron; but they were unable to receive them. On their return Dr. Leslie had to leave them, and his place was supplied by another doctor. It became more than ever necessary that a medical man should be in attendance, for Lady Burton seemed to suffer in sympathy with her husband, and as he got worse she became worse too. She writes about this time: "I am unable to take anything which might be called a walk. Driving was sometimes very painful to him, and it would not have been safe to let him go alone." It was one of her sorest trials that she could not minister to her husband as formerly; but disease had laid its hand on her too. Their life at Trieste at this time was naturally uneventful. Instead of getting up, as they used to do, and beginning their labours in the small hours of the morning, the Burtons now rose at seven, and did as much literary work as they could until nine, when the doctor would come in. At twelve o'clock they had breakfast, and after that the time was devoted either to more literary work or recreation. At four they would receive any friends who came to see them. At half-past seven they dined, no longer at the hotel as formerly, but at home; and at nine o'clock they retired to rest. It was about this time that Sir Richard finished the last volume of his "Supplemental" *Arabian Nights*. The weather was so bad at Trieste, and his health so uncertain, that the Foreign Office again gave him leave.

He and his wife came by a roundabout route to England, and saw many old friends. On October 15 they went down to Folkestone, where they stayed a few days with his relatives. They crossed on October 26 to Boulogne. It was Sir Richard's last visit to England; he never saw his country again.

At Boulogne they visited once more the old haunts where they had met for the first time years ago, and renewed acquaintance with the scenes of their vanished youth. It is worthy of notice how often husband and wife went to Boulogne together during their married life. It seemed as though the place was endeared to them by the recollection that it was here that they had first come together. From Boulogne they went to Switzerland, where they passed Christmas. When they were at Montreux they celebrated their wedding day (January 22), and the people in the hotel overwhelmed them with presents and flowers and pretty speeches. Lady Burton says, "I got quite choky, and Richard ran away and locked himself up." A rather ludicrous incident occurred here. They were expecting a visit from the famous Elisée Réclus. Lady Burton prepared herself to receive him with honour, and she had beforehand been warned of his little peculiarities. Suddenly the door was thrown open, and some one was announced whose name she did not catch. She greeted the new-comer with effusion, saying, "Dear Monsieur Réclus, I am so delighted to make your acquaintance; such a pleasure to know such a distinguished man." Her greeting was acknowledged with equal effusion by her visitor, who then proceeded to pull a key out of his pocket, and went up to the clock. Lady Burton was somewhat surprised, but she put it down to a great man's peculiarity; so she went on talking to him, and explaining the pleasure which it would give Sir Richard to make his acquaintance, when the door was opened again, and the servant announced, "Monsieur Réclus." The man she had been talking to was the clock-winder.

From Montreux they toured about Switzerland for some few weeks, and in March they returned again to Trieste, where they remained off and on until November.

During the summer Burton's health, fortified by

continual change of air and scene, improved a good deal. The Foreign Office was most indulgent in the amount of liberty which it gave to him. Lord Salisbury was now at the head of affairs; and though the Government did not see their way to allowing Burton to retire on full pension, they granted him what was almost the same thing—frequent and extended leaves; and it must be remembered too the time of his Consular service was now fast drawing to a close. Lady Burton always said that, next to Lord Derby, Lord and Lady Salisbury were their best friends. About this time Lady Salisbury wrote to her:

"HATFIELD HOUSE, HATFIELD, HERTS, *July* 21, 1889.

"MY DEAR LADY BURTON,

"I am very glad to hear so good an account of you and Sir Richard. We are here as busy as usual at this time of year. We have had great doings for the Shah, who is still in this country. He dined and slept here one night about a fortnight ago, and we had a garden-party for him next day. He behaved very well, and gives me the idea of being an able man; though whether he will think England a stronger friend than Russia remains to be seen. I sometimes fear he will carry away a greater idea of our riches and luxury than of our strength, but *qui vivra, verra.*

"We are now up to our lips in a royal marriage. It is to take place next Saturday, and will I dare say be a very pretty sight. The young lady [1] is very happy

[1] The Duchess of Fife.

by all accounts, and looks quite radiant. Politics are pretty quiet, and there are as few mistakes made as you can expect in the fourth year of a Government. I think we are rather losing in London, but are gaining in other places. On the whole all things are very quiet. With kind regards to Sir Richard,

"Believe me,
"Yours very sincerely,
"G. SALISBURY."

In November the Burtons started, *via* Brindisi, for Malta, where they passed a pleasant month, met many friends, and enjoyed themselves very much. From Malta they went to Tunis, and renewed their acquaintance with the Bedawin and the Arab tents. It was their last glimpse of the desert life which they loved so well. Among other places they visited the ruins of Carthage, and made as many excursions into the interior as it was possible, considering the state of Sir Richard's health. From Tunis they went by train to Algiers, starting on the journey at 5.15 on a cold January morning. When they reached Algiers, they were delighted with it at first; but they soon tired. Even an expedition to the baths of Hammám R'irha did not reconcile them to the place, and they left it early in March, going by boat to Marseilles, and then travelling homewards by way of the Riviera to Genoa, and thence to Venice. They crossed to Trieste the following day, having been absent more than four months.

They remained at Trieste until July 1, when they

A NATIVE LADY, TUNIS. [*Page* 694.

started for their last summer trip. The heat in Trieste during July and August is almost insupportable. They went to Innsbruck, Zurich, Davos Platz, Regatz, and other places. They were counting the months to the day when Burton would complete his term in the Consular Service, and would be permitted to retire on his pension. From Zurich Lady Burton wrote to a friend [1]:

"We go back (D.V.) September 1 or thereabouts, stay three months, and then winter in Greece and Constantinople. In March Dick's service is ended, and between that and August we pack up, settle our affairs, and come home for good. In one sense I am glad, because he yearns for a little flat in London; we shall be in the land of good advice and nourishment; and, God willing, I shall have brought him home safe and sound after thirty years' perils and dangers by health and land and sea. On the other hand, it is a wrench to give up my nice home. I have the whole of the second and top floor now, and I have made it so pretty, and I love Trieste and the life of my friends. I don't know how I shall concentrate myself and my belongings into a vulgar little flat—on small means. If you see any flat likely to suit us, let me know."

It was during this time in Switzerland that Burton made his wife his literary executrix. He called her into his room one day, and dictated to her a list of private papers which he wished to be burned in the event of his death, and gave her three signed documents, one of which ran as follows:

[1] Letter to Miss Bishop, July 21, 1890.

"In the event of my death, I bequeath especially to my wife, Isabel Burton, every book, paper, or manuscript, to be overhauled and examined by her only, and to be dealt with entirely at her own discretion, and in the manner she thinks best, having been my sole helper for thirty years.

(Signed) " RICHARD F. BURTON."

On September 7 they returned to Trieste together for the last time. They were both very much better for the good air in Switzerland, and settled down again to their quiet literary life, full of occupations for the present and plans for the future. Lady Burton was especially busy during these six weeks in helping her husband to sort and arrange his manuscripts and papers, and he worked as usual at three or four books at a time, especially his *Scented Garden*, which was now nearing completion.

I should like to interpolate here a beautiful and characteristic letter Lady Burton wrote, on October 10, to a friend, Madame de Gutmansthal-Benvenuti, who had just lost her husband :

"You need no letter from me to tell you how my heart is grieving for you, and with you, in this greatest trial woman can ever know—the trial before which my own head is ever bowed down, and my heart shrinking from in terror. And it has fallen on you, my best and dearest friend. But you have such consolations. He was a religious man, and died with the Sacraments, and you are sure of a happy meeting, just as if he had gone on a journey to wait for you ; but *more surely to meet* than if he had gone on an earthly journey. You have your dear children to live for, and that must now be your *only* thought, and taking care of your health for that purpose. All of us, who love you, are thinking of you and praying for you."

Ten days later the trial she so much dreaded had come upon her. And here for a space Lady Burton will speak in her own words.

CHAPTER XXVII

THE SWORD FALLS

1890

> Life is a sheet of paper white,
> Whereon each one of us may write
> His word or two, and then comes night.
>
> LOWELL.

"LET me recall the last happy day of my life. It was Sunday, October 19, 1890. I went out to Communion and Mass at eight o'clock, came back, and kissed my husband at his writing. He was engaged on the last page of *The Scented Garden*, which had occupied him seriously only six actual months, not thirty years, as the press said. He said to me, 'To-morrow I shall have finished this, and I promise you that I will never write another book on this subject. I will take to our biography.' And I said, 'What a happiness that will be!' He took his usual walk of nearly two hours in the morning, breakfasting well.

"That afternoon we sat together writing an immense number of letters, which, when we had finished, I put on the hall table to be posted on Monday morning. Each letter breathed of life and hope and happiness; for we were making our preparations for a delightful voyage to Greece and Constantinople, which was to last from November 15 to March 15. We were to return to Trieste from March 15 till July 1. He would be a free man on March 19, and those three months and a half we were to pack up, make our preparations, wind up all our affairs, send our heavy baggage to England, and, bidding adieu to Trieste, we were to pass July and August in Switzerland, arrive in England in September, 1891, look for a little flat and a little cottage, unpack, and settle ourselves to live in England.

"The only difference remarkable on this particular Sunday, October 19, was, that whereas my husband was dreadfully punctual, and with military precision as the clock struck we had to be in our places at the table at half-past seven, he seemed to dawdle about the room putting things away. He said to me, 'You had better go in to table'; and I answered, 'No, darling, I will wait for you'; and we went in together. He dined well, but sparingly; he laughed, talked, and joked. We discussed our future plans and preparations, and he desired me on the morrow to write to Sir Edmund Monson, and several other letters, to forward the preparations. We talked of our future life in London, and so on. About half-past nine he got up and went to his bedroom, accompanied by the doctor and myself, and we assisted him at his toilet. I then said the night prayers to him, and whilst I was saying them a dog began that dreadful howl which the superstitious say denotes a death. It disturbed me so dreadfully that I got up from the prayers, went out of the room, and called the porter to go out and see what was the matter with the dog. I then returned, and finished the prayers, after which he asked me for a novel. I gave him Robert Buchanan's *Martyrdom of Madeleine*. I kissed him and got into bed, and he was reading in bed.

"At twelve o'clock, midnight, he began to grow uneasy. I asked him what ailed him, and he said, 'I have a gouty pain in my foot. When did I have my last attack?' I referred to our journals, and found it was three months previously that he had had a real gout, and I said, 'You know that the doctor considers it a safety-valve that you should have a healthy gout in your feet every three months for your head and your general health. Your last attack was three months ago at Zurich, and your next will be due next January.' He was then quite content; and though he moaned and was restless, he tried to sleep, and I sat by him magnetizing the foot locally, as I had the habit of doing, to soothe the pain, and it gave him so much relief that he dozed a little, and said, 'I dreamt I saw our little flat in London, and it had quite a nice large room in it.' Between whiles he laughed and talked and spoke of our future plans, and even joked.

"At four o'clock he got more uneasy, and I said I should go for the doctor. He said, 'Oh no, don't disturb him; he cannot do anything.' And I answered, 'What is the use of keeping a doctor if he is not to be called when you are suffering?' The doctor was there in a few moments, felt his heart and pulse, found him in perfect order—that the gout was healthy. He gave him some medicine, and went back to bed. About half-past four he complained that there was no air. I flew back for the doctor, who came and found him in danger. I went at once, called up all the servants, sent in five directions for a priest, according to the directions I had received, hoping to get one; and the doctor, and I and Lisa[1] under the doctor's orders, tried every remedy and restorative, but in vain.

"What harasses my memory, what I cannot bear to think of, what wakes me with horror every morning from four till seven, when I get up, is that for a minute or two he kept on crying, 'Oh, Puss, chloroform—ether —or I am a dead man!' My God! I would have given him the blood out of my veins, if it would have saved him; but I had to answer, 'My darling, the doctor says it will kill you; he is doing all he knows.' I was holding him in my arms, when he got heavier and heavier, and more insensible, and we laid him on the bed. The doctor said he was quite insensible, and assured me he did not suffer. I trust not; I believe it was a clot of blood to the heart.

"My one endeavour was to be useful to the doctor, and not impede his actions by my own feelings. The doctor applied the electric battery to the heart, and kept it there till seven o'clock; and I knelt down at his left side, holding his hand and pulse, and prayed my heart out to God to keep his soul there (though he might be dead in appearance) till the priest arrived. I should say that he was insensible in thirty minutes from the time he said there was no air.

"It was a country Slav priest, lately promoted to be

[1] Lady Burton's maid, now dead.

our parish priest, who came. He called me aside, and told me that he could not give Extreme Unction to my husband, because he had not declared himself; but I besought him not to lose a moment in giving the Sacrament, for the soul was passing away, and that I had the means of satisfying him. He looked at us all three, and asked if he was dead, and we all said no. God was good, for had he had to go back for the holy materials it would have been too late, but he had them in his pocket, and he immediately administered Extreme Unction—'*Si vivis,*' or '*Si es capax,*' 'If thou art alive'—and said the prayers for the dying and the departing soul. The doctor still kept the battery to the heart all the time, and I still held the left hand with my finger on the pulse. By the clasp of the hand, and a little trickle of blood running under the finger, I judged there was a little life until seven, and then I knew that . . . I was alone and desolate for ever." [1]

I have given the foregoing in Lady Burton's own words, as unfortunately a fierce controversy has raged round her husband's death-bed, and therefore it is desirable to repeat her testimony on the subject. This testimony was given to the world in 1893, when all the witnesses of Sir Richard Burton's death were living, and it was never publicly contradicted or called into question until December of last year (1896), eight months after Lady Burton's death, when Miss Stisted's book made its appearance. In consequence of the attack made upon

---

[1] *Life of Sir Richard Burton*, by Isabel his wife, vol. ii., pp. 410-414. This work was published in May, 1893.

Lady Burton by her niece, which has been repeated and echoed elsewhere, it is necessary to defend Lady Burton on this point, since she is no longer able to defend herself. But I should like to reiterate that the question of Sir Richard Burton's religion did not enter into the original scheme of this book. I only approach it now with reluctance, and that not so much for the purpose of arguing as to what was Sir Richard Burton's religion (that was a matter for himself alone) as of upholding the good faith of his wife. In view also of the peculiar bitterness of the *odium theologicum*, perhaps it may be permitted me to say at the outset that I have no prejudice on this subject. I am not a Roman Catholic, and therefore cannot be accused of approaching the controversy with what Paley was wont to call an "antecedent bias."

In this I have the advantage of Miss Stisted, who appears to be animated by a bitter hostility not only against her aunt but against the Church of Rome. In her book she asserts that Sir Richard Burton died before the priest arrived on the scene, and that the Sacrament of Extreme Unction was administered to a corpse. She also goes on to say:

> The terrible shock of so fatal a termination to what seemed an attack of little consequence, would have daunted most Romanists desirous of effecting a death-bed conversion. It did not daunt Isabel. No sooner did she perceive that her husband's life was in danger, than she sent messengers in every direction for a priest. Mercifully, even the first to arrive, a man of peasant extraction, who had just been appointed to the parish, came too late to molest one then far beyond the reach of human folly and superstition. But Isabel had been too well trained by

the Society of Jesus not to see that a chance yet remained of glorifying her Church—a heaven-sent chance which was not to be lost. Her husband's body was not yet cold, and who could tell for certain whether some spark of life yet lingered in that inanimate form? The doctor declared that no doubt existed regarding the decease, but doctors are often mistaken. So, hardly had the priest crossed the threshold than she flung herself at his feet, and implored him to administer Extreme Unction. The father, who seems to have belonged to the ordinary type of country-bred ecclesiastic so common abroad, and who probably in the whole course of his life had never before availed himself of so startling a method of enrolling a new convert, demurred. There had been no profession of faith, he urged; there could be none now, for—and he hardly liked to pronounce the cruel words—Burton was dead. But Isabel would listen to no arguments, would take no refusal; she remained weeping and wailing on the floor, until at last, to terminate a disagreeable scene, which most likely would have ended in hysterics, he consented to perform the rite. Rome took formal possession of Richard Burton's corpse, and pretended, moreover, with insufferable insolence, to take under her protection his soul. From that moment an inquisitive mob never ceased to disturb the solemn chamber. Other priests went in and out at will, children from a neighbouring orphanage sang hymns and giggled alternately, pious old women recited their rosaries, gloated over the dead, and splashed the bed with holy water; the widow, who had regained her composure, directing the innumerable ceremonies. . . . After the necessary interval had elapsed, Burton's funeral took place in the largest church in Trieste, and was made the excuse for an ecclesiastical triumph of a faith he had always loathed.[1]

These statements of Lady Burton and Miss Stisted have been placed one after another, in order that the dispassionate reader may be able to judge not only of their conflicting nature, but of the different spirit which

[1] Miss Stisted's Life of Burton, pp. 409-414.

animates them. Lady Burton writes from her heart, reverently, as a good woman would write of the most solemn moments of her life, and of things which were to her eternal verities. Would she be likely to perjure herself on such a subject? Miss Stisted writes with an unconcealed animus, and is not so much concerned in defending the purity of her uncle's Protestantism as in vilifying her aunt and the faith to which she belonged. It may be noted too that Miss Stisted has no word of womanly sympathy for the wife who loved her husband with a love passing the love of women, and who was bowed down by her awful sorrow. On the contrary, with revolting heartlessness and irreverence, she jeers at her aunt's grief and the last offices of the dead. We may agree with the doctrines of the Church of Rome, or we may not; the solemn rites may be unavailing, or they may be otherwise; but at least they can do no harm, and the death-chamber should surely be sacred from such vulgar ribaldry! Good taste, if no higher consideration, might have kept her from mocking the religious convictions of others.

Miss Stisted's indictment of Lady Burton on this point falls under three heads:

First, that Sir Richard was dead before the priest arrived.

Secondly, that he was never a Catholic at all, and so his wife acted in bad faith.

Thirdly, that he "loathed" the Catholic religion.

It is better to deal with these charges *seriatim*.

With regard to the first, we have the positive and public testimony of Lady Burton, which was never contradicted during her lifetime, to the effect that her husband was alive when the Sacrament of Extreme Unction was administered to him. As, however, this testimony has been publicly called in question, though not until eight months after her death, we obtained through the kindness of the Baroness Paul de Ralli, a friend of Lady Burton at Trieste, the following written attestation from the priest who attended Sir Richard Burton's death-bed, and who is still living:

Declaration.[1]

"On October 20, 1890, at six o'clock in the morning, I was called in to assist at the last moments of Sir Richard Burton, British Consul.

"Knowing that he had been brought up, or born in, the Evangelical religion, before repairing to his house I went to see Dr. Giovanni Sũst, the Provost of this Cathedral, in order to find out from him what I was to do in the matter. He replied that I should go, and act accordingly as the circumstances might seem to require.

"So I went.

"Entering into the room of the sick man, I found him in bed with the doctor and Lady Burton beside him.

"At first sight it seemed that I was looking, not at a sick man, but rather at a corpse. My first question was, 'Is he alive or dead?' Lady Burton replied that he was still living, and the doctor nodded his head, to confirm what she had said.

"And in fact the doctor was seated on the bed hold-

[1] Translated from the Italian.

ing in his hands the hand of Sir Richard Burton to feel the beat of his pulse, and from time to time he administered some *corroborante*,[1] or gave an injection. Which of these two things he did I cannot now recollect, but it was certainly one or the other of them. These are things which one would certainly not do to a corpse, but only to a person still living; or if these acts were performed with the knowledge that the person in question was already dead, they could not be done without laying oneself open to an accusation of deception, all the more reprehensible if put in operation at such a solemn moment.

"In such a case all the responsibility would fall upon the doctor in charge, who with a single word, or even a sign given secretly to the priest, would have been able to prevent the administration of the Holy Sacrament of Extreme Unction.

"The second observation which I made to Lady Burton was one concerning religion—namely, 'That whoever was of the Evangelical persuasion could not receive the Holy Sacraments in this manner.'

"To this observation of mine she answered that some years ago he had received Extreme Unction, being, if I mistake not, at Cannes, and that on this occasion he had abjured the heresy and professed himself as belonging to the Catholic Church. On such a declaration from Lady Burton, I did that which a minister of God ought to do, and decided to administer to the dying man the last comforts of our holy religion. As it seemed to me that there was not much time to

[1] A tonic, a strengthening restorative.

lose, I wished to administer the Extreme Unction by means of one single anointing on the forehead, as is done in urgent cases; but Lady Burton said that death was not so imminent; therefore she begged me to carry out fully the prescribed ceremony of Extreme Unction.

"This completed, together with the other customary prayers for the dying, I took my departure. I returned to the house of the Provost, Dr. Süst, and laid everything before him, and he said I had done quite right.

"In a certificate of death drawn up by the Visitatore dei Morti,[1] Inspector Corani, in the register, under the head of religion, is written 'Catholic.' The funeral also was conducted according to the rites of the Catholic Church. I am convinced that Sir Richard Burton really became a Catholic, but that outwardly he did not wish this to be known, having regard to his position as a Consul to a Government of the Evangelical persuasion; and I have built up the hope that the innumerable prayers for her husband's conversion and good works of his pious wife Lady Burton will have been heeded by that Lord who said unto us, 'Pray, and your prayers shall be answered,' and that his soul will now have been received by the good God, together with that of the saintly lady his wife.

"One question I permit myself to ask of those who have now published the Life of Sir Richard Burton, which is this, 'Why did they not publish it during the lifetime of Lady Burton? Who better than she would

---

[1] An official (generally a physician) who visits the dead, and assures himself that the death is real, and not an apparent one.

have been able to enlighten the world on this point of much importance? Why publish it now when she is no longer here to speak?'

"Trieste, January 12, 1897,
"PIETRO MARTELANI,
"Formerly Parish Priest of the B.V. del Soccorso, now Prebendary and Priest of the Cathedral of Trieste."[1]

---

[1] The Baroness Paul de Ralli, who procured the above attestation from the priest, sent it in the first instance to Cardinal Vaughan, together with the following letter:

"TRIESTE, AUSTRIA, *January* 19, 1897.
"MY LORD CARDINAL,
"There has lately been published a so-called 'true' Life of the late Sir Richard Burton, written by his niece. Since my letter to *The Catholic Times*, which appeared in the issue of December 24, it has been pointed out to me that it would be well if I could procure a written attestation of the priest who gave Extreme Unction to the late Sir Richard Burton. I am authorized by Monseigneur Sterk to place in the hands of your Eminence the enclosed manuscript, written by Monseigneur Martelani, who is now Prebendary of the Cathedral here. As an intimate friend of the Burtons, I beg to say that everything said about the life of the Burtons at this place in the 'true' life has been written from dictation, and, furthermore, that I could name the authoress's informant, which makes the book worthless for those who know the source from which the authoress has gathered her information—the same source which has made Lady Burton's life hideous from the day of her husband's death to the time she left this place. As regards those who claim to have known all about Sir Richard Burton—'They knew the man well,' etc.—allow me to point out that the exoteric subtleties of his character were only exceeded by the esoteric; and to what an extent this is true is only known to those who were at the same time his friends and his wife's intimate friends, of whom there are several here beside myself. My position at the Villa Gosslett was perhaps a little exceptional. Having come here from England in 1875 after my marriage, I was looked upon by the Burtons as a sort of ex-subject of theirs.
"Believe me to be, my Lord Cardinal,
"Yours faithfully,
"CATHERINE DE RALLI."

I am further able to state that the gross travesty of Lady Burton's grief—"her weeping and wailing on the floor," etc., etc.—is the outcome of a malevolent imagination, from which nothing is sacred, not even a widow's tears. Lady Burton bore herself through the most awful trial of her life with quietude, fortitude, and resignation.

And now to turn to the second charge—to wit, that Sir Richard was never a Catholic at all ; from which, if true, it follows that he was in fact " kidnapped " by his wife and the priest on his death-bed.

If this charge did not involve a suggestion of bad faith on the part of Lady Burton, I should have ignored it ; for I hold most strongly that a man's religion is a matter for himself alone, a matter between himself and his God, one in which no outsider has any concern. Burton himself took this view, for he once said : " My religious opinion is of no importance to anybody but myself. No one knows what my religious views are. I object to confession, and I will not confess. My standpoint is, and I hope ever will be, the Truth, as far as it is in me, known only to myself."[1] This attitude he maintained to the world to the day of his death ; but to his wife he was different. Let me make my meaning quite clear. I do not say Burton was a Catholic or that he was not ; I offer no opinion. But what I do assert with all emphasis is that *he gave his wife reason to believe that he had become a Catholic*; and in this matter she acted in all good faith, in accordance with the highest dictates of her conscience and her duty.

[1] Speech at the Anthropological Society, London, 1865.

Gorizia 15'z February 1877)

Should my husband Richard Burton be in his deathbed unable to speak — perhaps strong dead, and that he may wish and have the grace to retract & recant his former errors and to join the Catholic Church and also receive the Sacraments of Penance Extreme Unction & Holy Eucharist — he might perhaps be able to sign this paper or make the Sign of the Cross to show his wish. Richard F. Burton

Burton knew how strongly his wife felt on this subject, and how earnest were her convictions. He knew that his conversion to Catholicism was her daily and nightly prayer. These considerations probably weighed with him when he signed the following paper (reproduced in facsimile on the opposite page). He signed it on the understanding that she was to keep it secret till he was a dying man :

"GORIZIA, *February* 15, 1877.

"Should my husband, Richard Burton, be on his death-bed unable to speak—I perhaps already dead—and that he may wish to have the grace to retract and recant his former errors, and to join the Catholic Church, and also to receive the Sacraments of Penance, Extreme Unction, and Holy Eucharist, he might perhaps be able to sign this paper, or make the sign of the cross to show his need.

(Signed) "RICHARD F. BURTON."

I do not analyse the motives which led Burton to sign this paper. He may have done it merely to satisfy his wife (for, from the Agnostic point of view, the Sacraments would not have mattered much either way), or he may have done it from honest conviction, or from a variety of causes, for human motives are strangely commingled ; *but that he did sign it there is no doubt.* Lady Burton, at any rate, took it all in good faith, and acted accordingly in sending for the priest ; the priest, on receiving her assurance, acted in good faith in administering to Sir Richard Burton the last rites of the Church ; and the Bishop of Trieste also acted in good faith in conceding to him a Catholic funeral. It is difficult to see how any of them could have acted otherwise.

Lastly, it has been asserted that Sir Richard Burton "loathed" the Roman Catholic Church; and though he was indifferent to most religions, he entertained a "positive aversion" to this one, and therefore to "kidnap" him on his death-bed was peculiarly cruel. I have read most of Burton's writings, and it is true, especially in his earlier books, that he girds against what he conceives to be certain abuses in the Roman Catholic Church and her priesthood in out-of-the-way countries; but then he attacks other forms of Christianity and other religions too. He had a great hatred of cant and humbug under the cloak of religion, and denounced them accordingly. There is nothing remarkable in this. We all denounce cant and humbug in the abstract, often most loudly when we are humbugs ourselves. If Burton attacked Christianity more than other religions, and Catholicism more than other forms of Christianity, he probably did so because they came more in his way. His religious acts generally appear to have been guided by the principle of "When one is at Rome, do as Rome does." He was a Mohammedan among Mohammedans, a Mormon among Mormons, a Sufi among the Shazlis, and a Catholic among the Catholics. One thing he certainly was not in his later years—a member of the Church of England. He was baptized and brought up in the Anglican Communion. He entered at Trinity College, Oxford, and he joined the Indian army as a member of the Church of

England; but when he was at Goa in 1847 he left off "sitting under" the garrison chaplain and betook himself to the Roman Catholic chapel, and availed himself of the ministrations of the Goanese priest. From that time, except officially, he never seems to have availed himself of the services of the Church of England. I do not unduly press the point of his attendance at the Roman Catholic chapel at Goa, for it may simply have meant that Burton merely went to the chapel and worshipped as a Catholic among Catholics, just as when he was at Mecca he worshipped as a Mohammedan among Mohammedans; but it tells against the theory that he "loathed" Catholicism, as the same necessity did not exist at Goa as at Mecca. It was a purely voluntary act on his part. Henceforward it would seem that, so far from being prejudiced against Catholicism, Burton was always coquetting with it; and if he took any religion seriously at all, he may be said to have taken this one seriously. The following facts also go to prove this theory. He married a Catholic wife, of whose strong religious views he was well aware. Before the marriage he signed a paper to the effect that his children, if any, should be brought up in the Roman Catholic faith. He obtained and used the following letter from Cardinal Wiseman, with whom he was on friendly terms:

"LONDON, *June* 28, 1856.

"DEAR SIR,

"Allow me to introduce to you Captain Burton, the bearer of this note, who is employed by Government to make an expedition to Africa, at the head of a little band of adventurers. Captain Burton has been highly spoken of in the papers here; and I have been asked to give him this introduction to you as a Catholic officer.

"I am, dear Sir,
"Yours sincerely in Christ,
"N. CARD. WISEMAN.

"COLONEL HAMMERTON," etc., etc., etc.

He habitually wore a crucifix, which his wife had given him, next his skin; he championed the cause of the Catholic converts in Syria; and when staying with his wife's family, he would frequently attend a service in a Roman Catholic church, and behave in all things as a Catholic worshipper. I am not saying that these things prove that Burton was a Catholic, but they afford strong presumptive evidence that he had leanings in the direction of Catholicism; and undoubtedly they go to prove that he did not "loathe" the Catholic religion. One thing is certain, he was too much of a scholar to indulge in any vulgar prejudice against the Roman Catholic Church, and too much of a gentleman to insult her priests.

After all there is nothing inherently improbable in Burton's conversion to Catholicism. Most of his life had been spent in countries where Catholicism is practically the only form of Christianity; and such a mind as his, if on the rebound from Agnosticism, would be much more likely to find a refuge in the bosom of the Roman Catholic Church than in the half-way house of Evangelical Protestantism. To a temperament like Burton's, steeped in Eastern mysticism and Sufiism, Catholicism would undoubtedly have offered strong attractions; for the links between the highest form of Sufiism and the Gospel of St. John, the *Ecstasis* of St. Bernard, and other writings of the Fathers of the Church who were of the Alexandrian school, are well known, and could hardly have been ignored by Burton, who made a comparative study of religions.

This, however, is by the way, and has only an indirect bearing on his wife's action. She, who knew him best, and from whom he had no secrets, believed that, in his later years at least, her husband was at heart a Catholic. He gave her ample grounds for this belief, and she acted upon it in all good faith. That he may have deceived her is possible, though not probable; but that she would have deceived a priest of her Church at the most solemn moment of her life, and on one of the most sacred things of her religion, is both impossible and improbable. The whole nature of the woman, her transparent truthfulness, her fervent piety, rise up in witness against this charge, and condemn it. And to what end would she have done this thing? No one knew better than Lady Burton that there is One whom she could not deceive; for with her the things invisible were living realities, and the actualities of this life were but passing things which come and fade away.

BOOK III
WIDOWED
(1890—1896)

"*El Maraa min ghayr Zaujuhá mislahá tayarán maksús el Jenáhh.*"
("The woman without her husband is like a bird with one wing"

CHAPTER I

THE TRUTH ABOUT "THE SCENTED GARDEN"

> Now I indeed will hide desire and all repine,
> And light up this my fire that neighbours see no sign:
> Accept I what befalls by order of my Lord,
> Haply he too accept this humble act of mine.
>
> ALF LAYLAH WA LAYLAH
(Burton's "Arabian Nights").

SIR RICHARD BURTON'S funeral was attended by a great crowd of mourners and representatives of every class in Trieste. The Austrian authorities accorded him military honours, and the Bishop of Trieste conceded all the rites of the Church. His remains were laid, with much pomp and circumstance, in their temporary resting-place—a small chapel in the burial-ground—until his widow could take them back with her to England. The funeral over, Lady Burton returned to her desolate house—a home no longer, for the loved presence which had made the palazzo a home, as it would have made a home to her of the humblest hut on earth, was gone for ever. The house was but an empty shell. Sir Richard Burton's death had been so sudden and unexpected that none of Lady Burton's near relatives, her sisters, were able to reach her in time; and though they had telegraphed to her offering to come at once, she had replied asking them not to undertake the journey. And so it came about that, in this hour of sorest trial, she was absolutely alone. She had no one to turn to in her grief; she had no children's love to solace her; she had no son to say, "Mother, lean on me"; no daughter to share her sorrow. Friends she had in plenty, and friends such as the world rarely gives, but they could not intrude their sympathy overmuch at such a time as this. Moreover, she had concentrated all her affections on her husband; she had lived so entirely for him, and in him, that she had not formed any of those intimate friendships in which some women delight. She had, in short, put all her earthly happiness in one frail barque, and it had foundered.

Hitherto we have followed her through her wedded life, that beautiful union which was more like a poem than an ordinary marriage. We have seen how the love which she bore her husband had sanctified her life, and his, lifting it above and beyond the ordinary love of men and women, glorifying all things, even her meanest tasks, for they were done in love's holy name. We have seen how she knew no fear, spared herself no pain, heeded no rebuff in the service of the man she loved. We have followed her in journeyings often, in perils of sea, in perils of robbers, in perils of the heathen, in perils of the wilderness, in weariness and sorrow, in watchings often, in hunger and thirst, and besides these things that were without, bearing those secret sorrows—"my beloved secret cross," she called them—which are known only to the soul and its God. We have seen all this, the full, perfect, glorious life which she lived by the side of the man she loved ; in the brief survey of the few broken years left to her on earth, we shall henceforth see her alone— alone, yet not alone, for the Divine love went with her, and with her also was ever present the memory of an earthly love, a love purified and holy, growing nearer and nearer to the love of the perfect day.

If we were to search the wide world over, ransack history, dive deep into the annals of the past, I doubt if there would be found any more perfect example of unselfish love than that which is exemplified in the wedded life of this woman. With her it was always "Richard only." It is with this thought in our minds that we approach her crowning act of self-sacrifice, her last supreme offering on the altar of her love. I refer to the act whereby she deliberately sacrificed the provision her husband had made for her, and faced poverty, and the contumely of her enemies, for the sake of his fair memory.

Lady Burton's first act after her husband's death was to lock up his manuscripts and papers to secure them against all curious and prying eyes—a wise and necessary act under the circumstances, and one which was sufficient to show that, great though her grief was, it did not rob her for one moment of her faculties. As soon as her husband's funeral was over, she went back to his rooms, locked the door securely, and examined carefully all his books and papers, burning those which he had desired to be burnt, and sorting and classifying the others. Among the manuscripts was Sir Richard's translation of the notorious *Scented Garden, Men's Hearts to Gladden, of the Shaykh el Nafzawih,* which he had been working at the day before his death, completed all but one page, and the proceeds of which he had told his wife were to form her jointure. As his original edition of *The Arabian Nights* had brought in £10,000 profit, the *Scented Garden,* beside which *The Arabian Nights* was a "baby tale," might reasonably have been expected to have produced as much, if not more. Indeed, a few days after Sir Richard's death, a man offered Lady Burton six thousand guineas down for the manuscript as it stood, and told her that he would relieve her of all risk and responsibility in the matter. She might, therefore, easily have closed with this offer without any one being the wiser, and if she had been inclined to drive a bargain, she would doubtless have had no difficulty in securing double the price. As her husband's death had reduced her to comparative poverty, the temptation to an ordinary woman, even a good and conscientious woman, would have been irresistible; she could have taken the money, and have quieted her conscience with some of those sophistries which we can all call to our aid on occasion. But Lady Burton was not an ordinary woman, and the money side of the question never weighed with her for one moment. How she acted at this crisis in her life is best told by herself.

"My husband had been collecting for fourteen years

The Truth about "The Scented Garden"

information and materials on a certain subject. His last volume of *The Supplemental Nights* had been finished and out on November 13, 1888. He then gave himself up entirely to the writing of this book, which was called *The Scented Garden*, a translation from the Arabic. It treated of a certain passion. Do not let any one suppose for a moment that Richard Burton ever wrote a thing from the impure point of view. He dissected a passion from every point of view, as a doctor may dissect a body, showing its source, its origin, its evil, and its good, and its proper uses, as designed by Providence and Nature, as the great Academician Watts paints them. In private life he was the most pure, the most refined and modest man that ever lived, and he was so guileless himself that he could never be brought to believe that other men said or used these things from any other standpoint. I, as a woman, think differently. The day before he died he called me into his room and showed me half a page of Arabic manuscript upon which he was working, and he said, 'To-morrow I shall have finished this, and I promise you after this I will never write another book upon this subject. I will take to our biography.' I told him it would be a happy day when he left off that subject, and that the only thing that reconciled me to it was, that the doctors had said that it was so fortunate, with his partial loss of health, that he could find something to interest and occupy his days. He said, 'This is to be your jointure, and the proceeds are to be set apart for an annuity for you'; and I said, 'I hope not; I hope you will live to spend it like the other.' He said, 'I am afraid it will make a great row in England, because *The Arabian Nights* was a baby tale in comparison to this, and I am in communication with several men in England about it.' The next morning, at 7 a.m., he had ceased to exist. Some days later, when I locked myself up in his rooms, and sorted and examined the manuscripts, I read this one. No promise had been exacted from me, because the end had been so unforeseen, and I remained for three days in a state of perfect torture as to what I ought to do about it. During that time I received an offer from a man whose name shall be always kept private, of six thousand guineas for it. He said, 'I know from fifteen hundred to two thousand men who will buy it at four guineas, *i.e.* at two guineas the volume; and as I shall not restrict myself to numbers, but supply all applicants on payment, I shall probably make £20,000 out of it.' I said to myself, 'Out of fifteen hundred men, fifteen will probably read it in the spirit of science in which it was written; the other fourteen hundred and eighty-five will read it for filth's sake, and pass it to their friends, and the harm done may be incalculable.' 'Bury it,' said one adviser; 'don't decide.' 'That means digging it up again and reproducing at will.' 'Get a man to do it for you,' said No. 2; 'don't appear in it.' 'I have got that,' I said. 'I can take in the world, but I cannot deceive God Almighty, who holds my husband's soul in His hands.' I tested one man who was very earnest about it: 'Let us go and consult So-and-so'; but he, with a little shriek of horror, said, 'Oh, pray don't let me have anything to do with it; don't let my name get mixed up in it, but it is a beautiful book I know.'

"I sat down on the floor before the fire at dark, to consult my own heart, my own head. How I wanted a brother! My head told me that sin is the only rolling stone that gathers moss; that what a gentleman, a scholar, a man of the world may write when living, he would see very differently to what the poor soul would see standing naked before its God, with its good or evil deeds alone to answer for, and their consequences visible to it for the first moment, rolling on to the end of time. Oh for a friend on earth to stop and check them! What would he care for the applause of fifteen hundred men now— for the whole world's praise, and God offended. My heart said, 'You can have six thousand guineas; your husband worked for you, kept you in a happy home, with honour and respect for thirty years. How are you going to reward him? That your wretched body may be fed and clothed and warmed for a few miserable months or years, will you let that soul, which is part of your soul, be left out in cold and darkness till the end of time, till all those sins which may have been committed on account of reading those writings have been expiated, or passed away perhaps for ever? Why, it would be just parallel with the original thirty pieces of silver!' I fetched the manuscript and laid it on the ground before me, two large volumes' worth. Still my thoughts were, Was it a sacrilege? It was his *magnum opus*, his last work that he was so proud of, that was to have been finished on the awful morrow—that never came. Will he rise up in his grave and curse me or bless me? The thought will haunt me to death, but Sadi and El Shaykh el Nafzawih, who were pagans, begged pardon of God and prayed not to be cast into hell fire for having written them, and implored their friends to pray for them to the Lord, that He would have mercy on them. And then I said, 'Not only not for six thousand guineas, but not for six million guineas will I risk it.' Sorrowfully, reverently, and in fear and trembling, I burnt sheet after sheet, until the whole of the volumes were consumed."[1]

As to the act itself I am not called upon to express any opinion. But there can be no two opinions among fair-minded people as to the heroism, the purity, and the sublime self-sacrifice of the motives which prompted Lady Burton to this deed. Absolutely devoted to her husband and his interests as she had been in his lifetime, she was equally jealous of his honour now that he was dead. Nothing must tarnish the brightness of his good name. It was this thought, above all others, which led her to burn *The Scented Garden*. For this act the vials of misrepresentation and abuse were poured on Lady Burton's head. She was accused of the "bigotry of a Torquemada, the vandalism of a John Knox." She has been called hysterical and illiterate. It has been asserted that she did it from selfish motives, "for the sake of her own salvation, through the promptings of a benighted

[1] Lady Burton's letter to *The Morning Post*, June 19, 1891.

religion," for fear of the legal consequences which might fall upon her if she sold the book, for love of gain, for love of notoriety, for love of "posing as a martyr," and so on, and so on. She was publicly vilified and privately abused, pursued with obscene, anonymous, and insulting letters until the day of her death. In fact, every imputation was hurled at her, and she who might have answered all her persecutors with a word, held her peace, or broke it only to put them on another track. It was not merely the act itself which caused her suffering; it was the long persecution which followed her from the day her letter appeared in *The Morning Post* almost to the day she died. How keenly she felt it none but those who knew her best will ever know. A proud, high-spirited woman, she had never schooled herself to stay her hand, but generally gave her adversaries back blow for blow; but these cowardly attacks she bore in silence, nay more, she counted all the suffering as gain, for she was bearing it for the sake of the man she loved.

And this silence would never have been broken, and the true reasons which led Lady Burton to act as she did would never have been told to the world, had it not been that, after her death, a woman, whom she had never injured by thought, word, or deed, has seen fit to rake up this unpleasant subject again, for the purpose of throwing mud on her memory, impugning her motives, and belittling the magnitude of her sacrifice. It is solely in defence that the truth is now told.

I have never read Sir Richard's translation of *The*

Scented Garden, for the simple reason that there is none in existence (notwithstanding all that has been said to the contrary); the only two copies were destroyed by his widow. But I have read another translation of the book, mainly the work of a man who was also an Orientalist and a distinguished soldier, which, though doubtless inferior to Burton's, is more than sufficient to give one full knowledge of the character of the book. I have read also Burton's original and unexpurgated edition of *Alf Laylah wa Laylah* and his Terminal Essay, including the Section which is omitted in all later editions, and certain other unpublished notes of his on the same subject. Lady Burton also talked with me freely on the matter. I know therefore of what I speak, and am not in the same position as Lady Burton's latest accuser, who declares with quite unnecessary emphasis that she has never read *The Arabian Nights,* and of course never saw the burnt manuscript of *The Scented Garden.* She is therefore obviously disqualified to express any opinion on the subject.

So far as I can gather from all I have learned, the chief value of Burton's version of *The Scented Garden* lay not so much in his translation of the text, though that of course was admirably done, as in the copious notes and explanations which he had gathered together for the purpose of annotating the book. He had made this subject a study of years. For the notes of the book alone he had been collecting material for thirty years, though his actual translation of it only took him eighteen months. The theme of *The Scented*

Garden is one which is familiar to every student of Oriental literature. Burton, who was nothing if not thorough in all he undertook, did not ignore this. In fact, one may say that from his early manhood he had been working at it, as he commenced his inquiries soon after his arrival in India. Lady Burton, it will be seen, says he " dissected a passion from every point of view, as a doctor may dissect a body, showing its source, its origin, its evil, and its good, and its proper uses, as designed by Providence and Nature " ; that is, Burton pursued his inquiries on this subject in the same spirit as that which has animated Kraft-Ebbing and Moll, and other men of science. But from what I have read in *The Arabian Nights* and elsewhere, it seems to me that Burton's researches in this direction were rather of an ethnological and historical character than a medical or scientific one. His researches had this peculiarity, that whereas most of the writers on this subject speak from hearsay, Burton's information was obtained at first hand, by dint of personal inquiries. Thus it came about that he was misunderstood. For a man, especially a young soldier whose work is not generally supposed to lie in the direction of scientific and ethnological investigation, to undertake such inquiries was to lay himself open to unpleasant imputations. People are not apt to distinguish between scientific motives and unworthy ones, and so Burton found it. His contemporaries and comrades in India did not understand him, and what people do not understand they often dislike. In his regiment he soon incurred odium, and a cloud of prejudice enveloped him. Unfortunately, too, he was not overwise ; and he had a habit of telling tales against himself, partly out of bravado, which of course did not tend to improve matters. People are very apt to be taken at their own valuation, especially if their valuation be a bad one. It must not be supposed that I am giving countenance, colour, or belief to these rumours against Burton for a moment : on the contrary, I believe them to be false and unjust ; but false and unjust though they were, they were undoubtedly believed by many, and herein was the gathering of the cloud which hung over Burton's head through the earlier part of his official career. To prove that I am not drawing on my own imagination with regard to this theory, I quote the following, told in Burton's own words :—

"In 1845, when Sir Charles Napier had conquered and annexed Sind, . . . it was reported to me that Karachi, a townlet of some two thousand souls, and distant not more than a mile from camp. . . . Being then the only British officer who could speak Sindi, I was asked indirectly to make inquiries, and to report upon the subject ; and I undertook the task on the express condition that my report should not be forwarded to the Bombay Government, from whom supporters of the conqueror's policy could expect scant favour, mercy, or justice. Accompanied by a Munshi, Mirza Mohammed Hosayn Shiraz, and habited as a merchant, Mirza Abdullah the Bushiri passed many an evening in the townlet, visited all the porneia, and obtained the fullest details, which were duly dispatched to Government House. But the 'Devil's Brother' presently quitted Sind, leaving in his office my unfortunate official ; this found its way with sundry other reports to Bombay, and produced the expected result. A friend in the secretariat informed me that my summary dismissal had been formally proposed by one of Sir Charles Napier's successors, whose decease compels me *parcere sepulto*, but this excess of outraged modesty was not allowed." [1]

Burton was not dismissed from the Service, it is true, but the unfavourable impression created by the incident remained. He was refused the post he coveted—namely, to accompany the second expedition to Mooltan as interpreter ; and seeing all prospect of promotion at an end for the present, he obtained a long furlough, and came home from India under a cloud. Evil rumour travels fast ; and when he went to Boulogne (the time and place where he first met Isabel), there were plenty of people ready to whisper ill things concerning him. When he returned to India two years after, notwithstanding his Mecca exploit, he found prejudice still strong against him, and nothing he could do seemed to remove it. His enemies in India and at home were not slow to use it against him. One can trace its baleful influence throughout his subsequent career. Lady Burton, whose vigilance on her husband's behalf never slept, and who would never rest until she confronted his enemies, got to know of it. When I know not, in what way I know not, but the fact that sooner or later she did get to know of it is indisputable. How she fought to dispel

[1] Vol. X. *Arabian Nights*, Terminal Essay, Section D, pp. 205, 206, 1886.

this cloud none but herself will ever know. Official displeasure she could brave, definite charges she could combat; but this baseless rumour, shadowy, indefinite, intangible, ever eluded her, but eluded her only to reappear. She could not grasp it. She was conscious that the thing was in the air, so to speak, but she could not even assume its existence. She could only take her stand by her husband, and point to his blameless life and say, " You are all the world to me; I trust you and believe in you with all my heart and soul." And in this her wisdom was justified, for at last the calumny died down, as all calumnies must die, for lack of sustenance.

When *The Arabian Nights* came out, at which she had worked so hard to manage the business arrangements, Lady Burton did not read the book throughout; she had promised her husband not to do so. She had perhaps a vague idea of some of its contents, for she raised objections. He explained them away, and she then worked heart and soul to ensure its success. The success which the book achieved, and the praise with which it was greeted, were naturally gratifying to her, and did much to dispel any objections which she might have had, especially when it is remembered that this book yielded profits which enabled her to procure for her husband every comfort and luxury for his declining years. It has been urged against her that she was extravagant because, when Burton died, only four florins remained of the £10,000 which they had netted by *The Arabian Nights*; but when it is borne in mind that she spent every penny upon her husband and not a penny upon herself, it is not possible that the charge of extravagance can be maintained against her—certainly not in a selfish sense.

When Burton took to translating *The Scented Garden*, he acquainted his wife to some extent with its contents, and she objected. But he overcame her objections, as he had done before, and the thought that the money would be needed to maintain her husband in the same comfort as he had enjoyed during the last few years weighed down her scruples; besides which, though she had a general idea that the book was not *virginibus purisque*, she had no knowledge of its real character. When therefore she read it for the first time, in the lonely days of her early widowhood, with the full shock of her sudden loss upon her, and a vivid sense of the worthlessness of all earthly gain brought home to her, she naturally did not look at things from the worldly point of view. She has told with graphic power how she sat down with locked doors to read this book, and how she read it through carefully, page by page; and it must be remembered that it was not Burton's translation alone which she read, but also the notes and evidence which he had collected on the subject. Then it was that the real nature of its contents was brought home to her, and she determined to act. It has been said that she only "half understood" what she read. Alas! she understood but too well, for here was the nameless horror which she had tried to track to earth leaping up again and staring her in the face. She knew well enough what interpretations her husband's enemies—those enemies whom even the grave does not silence—would place upon this book; how they would turn and twist it about, and put the worst construction upon his motives, and so blur the fair mirror of his memory. Burton wrote as a scholar and an ethnologist writing to scholars and ethnologists. But take what precautions he would, sooner or later, and sooner rather than later, the character of his book would ooze out to the world, and the ignorant world judges harshly. So she burnt the manuscript leaf by leaf; and by the act she consummated her life sacrifice of love.

I repeat that her regard for her husband's memory was her supreme reason for this act. That there were minor reasons is not denied: she herself has stated them. There was the thought of the harm a book of this kind might do; there was the thought of her responsibility to God and man; there was the thought of the eternal welfare of her husband's soul. She has stated, "It is my belief that by this act, if my husband's soul were weighed down, the cords were cut, and it was left free to soar to its native heaven." It is easy to sneer at such a sentiment as this, but the spiritual was very real with Lady Burton. All these minor considerations, therefore, weighed with her in addition to the greatest of them all. On the other hand, there came to her the thought that it was the first time she had ever gone against her husband's wishes, and now that he was dead they were doubly sacred to her. The mental struggle which she underwent was a terrible one: it was a conflict which is not given to certain lower natures to know, and not knowing it, they can neither understand nor sympathize. I make bold to say that the sacrifice which she made, and the motives which prompted her to make it, will stand to her honour as long as her name is remembered.

There remain two other considerations: the first is—Why did she make this act known to the world at all? Surely it would have been better from every point of view to have veiled it in absolute secrecy. She has given the answer in her own words: "I was obliged to confess this because there were fifteen hundred men expecting the book, and I did not quite know how to get at them; also I wanted to avoid unpleasant hints by telling the truth." In other words, there was a large number of Burton's supporters, persons who had subscribed to *The Arabian Nights*, and all his literary friends, with whom he was in constant communication, who knew that he was working at *The Scented Garden*, and were eagerly expecting it. Lady Burton burned the manuscript in October, 1890; she did not make her public confession of the act in *The Morning Post* until June, 1891, nearly nine months after the event. During all this time she was continually receiving letters asking what had become of the book which she knew that she had destroyed. What course was open to her? One answer suggests itself: send a circular or write privately to all these people, saying that the book would not come out at all. But this was impossible because she did not know all of "the little army of her husband's admiring subscribers"; she neither knew their names nor their addresses; and apart from the endless worry and difficulty of answering letters which such a course would have entailed, a garbled version of the facts would be sure to have leaked out, and then she would have had to contradict the misstatements publicly. Or perhaps spurious copies of *The Scented Garden* professing to be Sir Richard's translation might have been foisted upon the public, and she would have been under the necessity of denouncing them. So she argued that it was best to have the thing over and done with once for all, to make a clean breast of it, and let the world say what it pleased. In this I cannot but think that she was right, though she often said, "I have never regretted for a moment having burned it, but I shall regret all my life having made it known publicly, though I could hardly have done otherwise. I did not know my public, I did not know England." Here I think she was wrong in confusing England with a few anonymous letter-writers and scurrilous persons; for however opinions may differ upon the act itself, its wisdom or unwisdom, all right-thinking people honoured her for the sacrifice which she had made. They would have honoured her even more if they had known that she had done it for the sake of her husband's name!

Her latest and most malevolent accuser, Miss Stisted, has also urged against her that by this act she conveyed a "wrong impression concerning the character of the book," and so cast a slur upon her husband's memory. A wrong impression! The ignorance and animus of this attack are obvious. The character of the manuscript was well known: it was the translation of a notorious book.

The story of Burton's inquiries in this unpleasant field was known too, if not to the many at least to the few, and his enemies had not scrupled to place the worst construction on his motives. His wife knew this but too well, and she fought the prejudice with sleepless vigilance all the years of her married life, and by this last act of hers did her best to bury it in oblivion. Surely it is cruelly unjust to say that it was she who cast the slur!

And now to refer to another matter. Miss Stisted animadverts on Lady Burton's having sold the library edition of *The Arabian Nights* in 1894 "with merely a few excisions absolutely indispensable." "Coming as it did so soon," she says, "after her somewhat theatrical destruction of *The Scented Garden*," this act "could not be permitted to pass unchallenged." She not only charges Lady Burton with inconsistency, but hints at pecuniary greed, for she mentions the sum she received. Yet there was nothing inconsistent in Lady Burton's conduct in this connexion. On the contrary, it is one more tribute to her consistency, one more proof of the theory I have put forward in her defence, for the excisions which Lady Burton made were only those which referred to the subject which was the theme of *The Scented Garden*. Lady Burton was no prude: she knew that ignorance is not necessarily innocence. She knew also that her husband did not write as "a young lady to young ladies"; but she drew the line at a certain point, and she drew it rigidly. By her husband's will she had full power to bring out any editions she might please of *The Arabian Nights* or any other book of his. She therefore sanctioned the library edition with certain excisions, and the reasons which prompted her to make these excisions in *The Arabian Nights* were the same as those which led her to burn *The Scented Garden.*

CHAPTER II

THE RETURN TO ENGLAND

(1890—1891)

> Not yet, poor soul! A few more darksome hours
> And sore temptations met and overcome,
> A few more crosses bravely, meekly carried,
> Ere I can proudly call the tried one home.
> Nerve then thy heart; the toil will soon be done,
> The crown of self-denial nobly earned and won.
> *From Lady Burton's Devotional Book "Tan."*

LADY BURTON remained at Trieste three months after her husband's death. We have seen how she spent the first weeks of her bereavement, locked up with his manuscripts and papers. During that time she would see no one, speak to no one. When her work was done, all her husband's wishes as to the disposal of his private papers carried out, and the manuscripts duly sorted and arranged, she came out from her seclusion, and put herself a little in touch with the world again. She was deeply touched at the sympathy which was shown to her. The Burtons had been so many years at Trieste, and were so widely known there and respected, that Sir Richard's death was felt as a public loss. A eulogy of Sir Richard was delivered in the Diet of Trieste, and the House adjourned as a mark of respect to his memory. The city had three funeral requiems for him, and hundreds of people in Trieste, from the highest to the lowest, showed their sympathy with his widow. Her friends rallied round her, for they knew that her loss was no ordinary one, and she had consigned to the grave all that made life worth living for to her. Nor was this sympathetic regard confined to Trieste alone; the English press was full of the "dead lion," and the dominant note was that he had not been done justice to while he was alive. Lady Burton was greatly gratified by all this, and she says a little bitterly: "It shows how truly he was appreciated except by the handful who could have made his life happy by success."

Her first public act after her husband's death was a defence of his memory. She had fought so hard for him when living that it seemed only natural to her to go on fighting for him now that he was beyond the reach of praise or blame. Colonel Grant had written a letter to *The Times* anent an obituary notice of Sir Richard Burton, in which he defended Speke, and spoke of the "grave charges" which Speke communicated against Burton to his relatives and to the Geographical Society. Lady Burton saw this letter some time after it appeared. She knew well enough what it hinted at, and she lost no time in sending a reply wherein she defended her husband's character, and prefaced her remarks with the characteristic lines:

> He had not dared to do it,
> Except he surely knew my lord was dead.

Lady Burton had soon to face, in these first days of her widowhood, the problem of her altered circumstances. With her husband's death his salary as a Consul came to an end, and there was no pension for his widow. For the last three or four years, since they had netted £10,000 by *The Arabian Nights*, the Burtons had been living at the rate of £3,000—£4,000 a year, and had kept up their palazzo at Trieste and a large staff of servants, in addition to continually travelling *en prince*, with all the luxuries of the best hotels, servants, and a resident doctor who always accompanied them. Lady Burton had sanctioned this expenditure because she wished, as she said, to give her husband every comfort during his declining days. Moreover, Burton had looked forward to *The Scented Garden* to replenish his exchequer. Now Lady Burton found herself face to face with these facts: the whole of the money of *The Arabian Nights* was gone, her husband's salary was gone, *The Scented Garden* was gone, and there was nothing left for her but a tiny patrimony. It was therefore necessary that she should rouse herself to a sense of the position. She did so without delay. She determined as far as possible to carry out the plans which she and her husband had made when they were looking forward to his retirement from the Consular service; that is to say, she determined to leave Trieste, to return to London, take a little flat, and occupy herself with literary work. It was a sore pang to her to give up the beautiful home on which she had expended so much care and taste, and to part with her kind friends at Trieste, many of whom she had known for eighteen years. At Trieste she was a personage. Every one knew her and loved her. She knew well enough that when she came back to London after such a long absence, except by a few faithful friends, she might be forgotten and overlooked in the rush and hurry of modern life. Nevertheless her course was plain; she had but one desire; that was to get away from Trieste as quickly as might be, take her husband's remains with her, and lay them to rest in English soil, a rest which she hoped to share with him before long.

After her husband's funeral at Trieste, Lady Burton's first step should have been the dismissal of her household, except one or two servants. She did not feel equal to this, however, and difficulties arose which are touched on in the following letter:

"From the time I lost my all, my earthly god of thirty-five years, in two hours, I have been like one with a blow on the head. I cannot write about him; I must tell of myself. Having been eighteen years in Trieste, it was difficult to leave so many dependent on me, so many friends to bid farewell, so many philanthropic works to wind up the affairs of, and I had to settle twenty rooms full of things I could not throw away. It took me fourteen weeks to do it. During that time I swam in a sea of small horrors—wickedness, treachery, threats; but my Triestine friends stuck to me. The authorities behaved nobly, and I pulled through and got off." [1]

[1] Letter to Madame de Gutmansthal-Benvenuti, from London, March 1, 1891.

The next few months were busy ones for Lady Burton. It is hard under any circumstances to break up a home of eighteen years, and harder still when it has to be done as economically and expeditiously as possible. She placed out all her old and trusted servants; she endeavoured to find friends to take on the care of many of the aged and poor people who were more or less dependent on her; she wound up the institutions of which she was President; she paid her debts, and said good-bye to all her friends. She refused to sell any of the furniture or effects of the home she had loved so well. She said it would be like selling her friends. So she packed the few things she thought she would want to furnish her flat in London, and all her husband's and her own personal effects, his library and manuscripts, and she gave away the rest of the furniture where she thought it would be useful or valued. These duties occupied her fourteen weeks in all, and she worked every day early and late, the only break in her labours being her frequent visits to the *chapelle ardente* where the remains of her husband were reposing, preparatory to being carried to England. The only comfort to her in this time of sorrow was a visit from her cousin, Canon Waterton of Carlisle, a scholarly and cultured ecclesiastic, who, in addition to providing her with spiritual consolation, also gave her much valuable advice as to the disposition of the books and manuscripts. In order to guard against any misconception, however, I should like to add that Canon Waterton did not come to Trieste until some time after *The Scented Garden* had been burned. That act, in spite of all that has been said to the contrary, was entirely Lady Burton's own act, influenced by no priest, layman, or any person whatever. She spoke of it afterwards as a secret between herself and the dead husband.

So this year (1890), the saddest in Lady Burton's life, came to an end. On January 20, 1891, she caused her husband's remains to be removed from the chapel and conveyed on board the Cunard steamer *Palmyra*. She herself was going to England by the quicker route overland.

Her work now being done, a few days later Lady Burton left Trieste for the last time. The evening before her departure twenty of her friends came up to spend the last hours with her. She walked round every room, recalling her life in her happy home. She visited every nook and cranny of the garden; she sat under the linden tree where she and her husband had spent so many quiet hours, and she gazed at the beautiful views for the last time. This went on till the time came for her to leave. Many friends came to accompany her to the station. When she arrived she found that she had to face quite a demonstration. All the leading people in Trieste and the authorities of the city, all the children of the orphanage in which she had taken so keen an interest, all the poor whom she had helped, and all her private friends, who were many, were there to bid her good-bye and offer her flowers. She says: "It was an awful trial not to make an exhibition of myself, and I was glad when the train steamed out; but for a whole hour, ascending the beautiful road close to the sea and Miramar and

Trieste, I never took my misty eyes off Trieste and our home where I had been so happy for eighteen years."

On arriving in England, Lady Burton's first care was to go and see Sir Richard's sister and niece, Lady and Miss Stisted, and acquaint them with the circumstances of her husband's death, and her intentions. We will draw a veil over that meeting. She then went on to London and stayed at the Langham Hotel, intending to remain there a few days until she could find a lodging. At the Langham her three sisters were waiting for her.

Two days after her arrival in London, Lady Burton went to see about a monument to her husband. This monument has been already described, and it is unnecessary to repeat the description at any length here. Suffice it to say that it is a tomb, shaped like an Arab tent, of dark Forest of Dean stone, lined inside with white Carrara marble. The tent is surmounted by a large gilt star, and over the flap door is a white marble crucifix. The fringe is composed of gilt crescents and stars. The door supports an open book of white marble: on one page is an inscription to Sir Richard Burton; the opposite page was then left blank. Lady Burton had the tomb fitted up with an altar and other accessories, so as to make it as much like a *chapelle ardente* as possible, while preserving its Eastern character. There was room in the tent for two coffins, those of her husband and herself. Finding that her purse was too slender to carry out this somewhat elaborate design, Lady Burton was encouraged by her friends to ask for a public subscription, with the result that she received the greater part of the money, but the appeal was not responded to as it might have been.

She found that, owing to the state of the weather, the monument could not be completed for some months, but she selected the site in Mortlake Cemetery, the spot which she and her husband had chosen many years before, and had the ground pegged out. The next day, though very ill, she, with her sister Mrs. Fitzgerald, went down to Liverpool to meet her husband's remains, which were arriving by sea. Lord and Lady Derby, who had always been her kind friends, had arranged everything for her, and the next morning Lady Burton went on board ship. She says, "I forgot the people when I saw my beloved case, and I ran forward to kiss it." It was taken to the train, and Lady Burton and her sister travelled by the same train to Mortlake, where they arrived that evening. The coffin was conveyed by torchlight to a temporary resting-place in the crypt under the altar of the church, where it remained until the tent was erected. The same evening Lady Burton returned to London, and, her work being done, the reaction set in. She broke down and took to her bed that night, where she remained for many weeks. She says: "I cannot describe the horror of the seventy-six days enhanced by the fog, which, after sunlight and air, was like being buried alive. The sense of desolation and loneliness and the longing for him was cruel, and it became

> The custom of the day
> And the haunting of the night.

My altered circumstances, and the looking into and facing my future, had also to be borne."

In the meantime her friends, notably the Dowager Lady Stanley of Alderley, the Royal Geographical and other Societies, had not been idle, and her claims had been brought before the Queen, who was graciously pleased to grant Lady Burton a pension of £150 a year from the Civil List. This pension, which she enjoyed to the day of her death, came to her as a surprise, and was not due to any effort of her own. She would never have asked anything for herself: the only thing she did ask for was that the nation should help her in raising a monument to her husband's honour; but, as we have seen, the nation was somewhat lukewarm on that point.

At the end of April Lady Burton recovered sufficiently to leave the hotel, and joined her sister, Mrs. Fitzgerald. She was chiefly occupied during the next few months in looking out for a house, and in completing the arrangements for her husband's final resting-place. About the middle of June the tent was finished. Sir Richard Burton's remains were transferred from the crypt under the church to the mausoleum where they now rest. At the funeral service Lady Burton occupied a *prie-dieu* by the side, and to the right was Captain St. George Burton, of the Black Watch, a cousin of Sir Richard. There was a large gathering of representatives of both families and many friends. The widow carried a little bunch of forget-me-nots, which she laid on the coffin. This simple offering of love would doubtless have been far more acceptable to the great explorer than the "wreath from Royalty" the absence of which his latest biographer so loudly deplores.

When the ceremony was over, Lady Burton went away at once to the country for a ten days' rest to the Convent of the Canonesses of the Holy Sepulchre, New Hall, Chelmsford, where she had been educated, and which had received within its walls many of the Arundells of Wardour. She left New Hall much refreshed and invigorated in mind and body, and for the next month was busy arranging a house which she had taken in Baker Street. She moved into it in September, 1891, and so entered upon the last chapter of her life.

CHAPTER III

THE TINKLING OF THE CAMEL'S BELL

(1891—1896)

Friends of my youth, a last adieu! haply some day we meet again;
Yet ne'er the self-same men shall meet; the years shall make us other men:

The light of morn has grown to noon, has paled with eve, and now farewell!
Go, vanish from my Life as dies the tinkling of the Camel's bell.

RICHARD BURTON (*The Kasidah*).

THE next few months Lady Burton mainly occupied herself by arranging in her new house the things which she had brought with her from Trieste. When all was finished, her modest quarters in Baker Street were curiously characteristic of the woman. Like many of the houses in her beloved Damascus, the one in Baker Street was unpretentious, not to say unprepossessing, when viewed from without, but within totally different, for Lady Burton had managed to give it an oriental air, and to catch something of the warmth and colouring of the East. This was especially true of her little drawing-room, which had quite an oriental aspect. Eastern curtains veiled the windows, the floor was piled with Persian carpets, and a wide divan heaped with cushions and draped with bright Bedawin rugs ran along one side of the room. There were narghílehs and chibouques, and cups of filigree and porcelain for the dispensing of delectable Arab coffee. Quaint brackets of Morocco work, Eastern pictures, portraits, Persian enamels, and curios of every description covered the walls. The most striking object in the room was a life-size portrait of Sir Richard Burton, dressed in white, with a scarlet cummerbund, flanked on either side by a collection of rare books, most of them his works. Many other relics of him were scattered about the room; and all over the house were to be found his books and pictures, and busts of him. In fact, she made a cult of her husband's memory, and there were enough relics of him in the house to fill a little museum.

In this house Lady Burton settled down with her sister, Mrs. Fitzgerald, to her daily life in England, which was mostly a record of work—arduous and unceasing work, which began at 10.30 in the morning, and lasted till 6.30 at night. Sometimes, indeed, she would work much later, far on into the night, and generally in the morning she would do a certain amount of work before breakfast, for the old habit of early rising clung to her still, and until her death she never broke herself of the custom of waking at five o'clock in the morning. At the top of her Baker Street house Lady Burton built out a large room, or rather loft. It was here she housed her husband's manuscripts, which she knew, as she used to say, "as a shepherd knew his sheep." They lined three sides of the room, and filled many packing-cases on the floor. To this place she was wont to repair daily, ascending a tortuous staircase, and finally getting into the loft by means of a ladder. Later she had to abandon this steep ascent, but so long as it was possible she scaled the ladder daily, and would sit on a packing-case surrounded by her beloved manuscripts for hours together.

Lady Burton was scarcely settled in Baker Street before her sister (the one next to her in age), Mrs. Smyth Pigott, of Brockley Court, Somerset, died. She had to go down to Weston-super-Mare for the funeral. When that was over she came back to Baker Street, where she remained over Christmas. She wrote to a friend of hers about this time:

"I dream always of my books and the pile of work. I am worrying on as well as I can with my miscellaneous writing. Fogs have kept us in black darkness and pea-soup thickness for five days without a lift, and with smarting eyes and compressed head I have double work at heart. I passed Christmas night in the Convent of the Holy Souls. I went in my cab—the streets were one sheet of ice—and two flambeaux on each side. In Regent's Park the fog was black and thick. We had communion and three masses at midnight. It was too lovely: in the dead silence a little before midnight you heard the shepherd's pipe, or reed, in the distance, and echo nearer and nearer, and then the soft, clear voices burst into 'Glory be to God in the Highest,' and this was the refrain all through the service. I passed the time with our Lord and my darling, who had many masses said for him in London and all over England that night. I am better and have stronger nerves, and am perhaps more peaceful."[1]

[1] Letter to Miss Bishop, December 27, 1891.

In January, 1892, Lady Burton went down to her cottage at Mortlake, which she called "Our Cottage." In taking this house she had followed the plan which her husband when living had always adopted, of having a retreat a little way from their work, where they could go occasionally for rest and change. They had intended to follow this plan when they settled down in London. Another motive drew Lady Burton to Mortlake too: this cottage was close to the mausoleum of her husband, and she could visit it when she chose. It was a tiny cottage, plainly but prettily furnished. Most of her relics and curios were housed at Baker Street, and this place had few associations for her beyond those which connected it with her husband's grave. The cottage was covered with creepers outside, and trees grew all round it. She had a charming little garden at the back, in which she took a good deal of pride; and when the summer came she had a big tent erected in the garden, and would sit there for many hours together, doing her work and frequently taking her meals out there. She had always lived an outdoor life, and this tent recalled to her the days in the East. Here, too, she received a great many friends who found their way down to Mortlake; she was fond of asking them to come and take tea with her in her tent. From this arose a silly rumour, which I mention only to contradict, that Lady Burton was in the habit of receiving her visitors in her husband's tomb, which, as we have seen, was also fashioned like an Arab tent, though of stone.

Lady Burton stayed down at Mortlake for a few

months, and came back to Baker Street in March, 1892, where she remained for two or three months.

For the first year of her life in England she lived like a recluse, never going out anywhere except on business or to church, never accepting an invitation or paying visits; but about this time she gradually came out of her seclusion, and began to collect around her a small circle of near relatives and friends. Always fond of society, though she had now abjured it in a general sense, she could not live alone, so in addition to the companionship of her favourite sister Mrs. Fitzgerald, who lived with her and shared all her thoughts, she widened her circle a little and received a few friends. She was fond of entertaining, and gave many little informal gatherings, which were memorable from the grace and charm of the hostess. Lady Burton was always a picturesque and fascinating personality, but never more so than in these last years of her life. She possessed a fine and handsome presence, which was rendered even more effective by her plain black dress and widow's cap, with its long white veil which formed an effective background to her finely cut features. She reminded me of some of the pictures one sees of Mary Stuart. I do not think the resemblance ceased altogether with her personal appearance, for her manners were always queenly and gracious; and when she became interested in anything, her face would light up and her blue eyes would brighten, and one could see something of the courage and spirit which she shared in common with the ill-fated queen. She was a most accomplished woman and a clever linguist. She could write and speak fluently French, Italian, Arabic, and Portuguese. German she knew also, though not so well, and she had more than a smattering of Yiddish. She was well-read in the literature of all these (save Yiddish, of course), yet never was a woman less of a "blue-stocking." She was a brilliant talker, full of wit and charm in her conversation, and there was nothing she liked better than to relate, in her inimitable way, some of her many adventures in the past. In fact, though singularly well-informed on all the current questions of the hour, one could see that her heart was ever in the past, and her thoughts seldom strayed far from her husband. Thus it came about, after his death as in his life, she devoted herself wholly to glorifying his name, and I do not think it is any disparagement to Sir Richard Burton to say that his personality would never have impressed itself upon the public imagination in the way it did, if it had not been for the efforts of his wife.

In the summer of this year Lady Burton went to Ventnor, and also paid a few visits, and in the autumn she stayed at Ascot with her sister Mrs. Van Zeller, whose husband had just died. In November she went to Mortlake, where she settled down in earnest to write the biography of her husband, a work which occupied her eight months. When once she began, she worked at it morning, noon, and night, from early till late, and except for a flying visit to Baker Street for Christmas, she never ceased her labours until the book was finished at the end of March, 1893. She wrote to a friend at this time:

"I finished the book last night, and have never left Mortlake. It has taken me eight months. I hope it will be out the end of May. I do not know if I can harden my heart against the curs,[1] but I can put out my tongue and point my pen and play pussy cat about their eyes and ears. I am to have six months' rest, but you know what that means."[2]

Lady Burton received a substantial sum from the publishers for the book, and it was published in May. The success which it achieved was immediate and unqualified, and, what is more, deserved, for with all its faults it is a great book—the last great work in the life of the woman who never thought of self, and her supreme achievement to raise aloft her husband's name. Its success was very grateful to Lady Burton's heart, not on her own account, but her husband's; in fact, it may be said to have gilded with brightness the last years of her life. She felt now that her work was done and that nothing remained. She wrote to a friend early in the New Year (1894)[3]:

"I have had my head quite turned by the great success of my book. First came about a hundred half-nasty, or wholly nasty, critiques; then the book made its way. I had three leading articles, over a thousand charming reviews, and have been inundated with the loveliest letters and invitations. . . . With my earnings I am embellishing his mausoleum, and am putting up in honour of his poem, *Kasidah*, festoons

---

[1] Burton's enemies.
[2] Letter to Miss Bishop from Mortlake, March 25, 1893.
[3] Letter to Madame de Gutmansthal-Benvenuti, January 10, 1894.

of camel bells from the desert, in the roof of the tent where he lies, so that when I open or shut the door, or at the elevation of the Mass, the 'tinkling of the camel bell' will sound just as it does in the desert. On January 22 I am going down to pass the day in it, because it is my thirty-third wedding day, and the bells will ring for the first time. I am also carrying out all his favourite projects, and bringing out by degrees all his works hitherto published or unpublished, as of the former only small quantities were published, and these are mostly extinct. If God gives me two years, I shall be content. I live in my little *chaumière* near the mausoleum on the banks of the Thames for the six good months of the year, and in my warm dry home in London six bad months, with my sister. You cannot think how the picture of Richard by you was admired at the Grosvenor Gallery, and I put your name over it. I have now got it home again, and I thought he smiled as I brought him back in the cab for joy to get home. . . . There is a great wax-work exhibition in England which is very beautifully done (Tussaud's). They have now put Richard in the Meccan dress he wore in the desert. They have given him a large space with sand, water, palms, and three camels, and a domed skylight, painted yellow, throws a lurid light on the scene. It is quite life-like. I gave them the real clothes and the real weapons, and dressed him myself. When it was offered to him during his life, his face beamed, and he said, 'That will bring me in contact with the people.'"

The other works of Sir Richard's which Lady Burton

brought out after the Life of her husband included *Il Pentamerone* and *Catullus*. She also arranged for a new edition of his *Arabian Nights*, and she began what she called the "Memorial Library," which was mainly composed of the republication of half-forgotten books which he had written in the days before he became famous. She also recalled, at great pecuniary sacrifice to herself, another work which she thought was doing harm to his memory, and destroyed the copies.

Upon the publication of the Life of her husband, Lady Burton was overwhelmed with letters from old acquaintances who had half-forgotten her, from tried and trusted friends of her husband and herself, and from people whom she had never known, but who were struck by the magnitude of her self-sacrificing love. All these letters were pleasant. But she also received a number of letters of a very doubtful nature, which included begging letters and applications requesting to see her from quacks and charlatans of different kinds, who by professing great admiration for her husband, and veneration for his memory, thought they would find in Lady Burton an easy prey. In this they were mistaken. Although generous and open-hearted as the day, she always found out charlatans in the long run. She used to say she "liked to give them rope enough." Unfortunately, though, it must be admitted that Lady Burton had the defects of her qualities. Absolutely truthful herself, she was the last in the world to suspect double-dealing in others, and the result was that she sometimes misplaced her confidence, and put her trust in the wrong people. This led her into difficulties which she would otherwise have avoided.

The publication of the Life of her husband seemed also to arouse a number of dormant animosities, and it led, among other things, to a large increase in the number of abusive and insulting letters which she received from anonymous writers, chiefly with regard to her burning of *The Scented Garden.* They gave her great pain and annoyance. But many approved of her action, and among others who wrote to her a generous letter of sympathy was Lady Guendolen Ramsden, the daughter of her old friends the Duke and Duchess of Somerset. I give Lady Burton's reply because it shows how much she appreciated the kindness of her friends:

"*October* 31, 1893.

"My dear Lady Guendolen,

"I cannot tell you what pleasure your very kind letter gave me. I feared that you and all your family had forgotten me long ago. I was, and so was Richard, very much attached to the Duke and Duchess; they always made us welcome, they always made us feel at home. I delighted in the Duke—so clever, so fascinating, and he was my *beau idéal* of a gentleman of the Old School, whilst the kindness of heart, the high breeding, and the wit of the Duchess attached us both greatly to her. You were such a very young girl that I knew you the least, and yet you are the one to be kind to me now. The ones I knew best were poor Lord St. Maur and Lady Ulrica. Let me now thank you for speaking so truly and handsomely of my dear husband, and your kindness and sympathy with me and my work. It is quite true! If you knew what a small section of people have made me suffer, and the horrible letters that they have written me, you would feel sorry to think that there were such people in the world, and when I reflect that it was that class of people who would have received the manuscript with joy, I know how right I was to burn it. It was not the *learned* people, as you imagine, who regret this, because there was no learning to be gained in it. My dear husband did it simply to fill our purse again. The people who were angry were the people who loathe good, and seek for nothing but that class of literature. My husband had no vicious motive in writing it; he dissected these things as a doctor would a body. I was calculating what effect it would have on the mass of uneducated people who *might* read it. I did receive many beautiful letters on the subject, and the papers have more or less never let me drop, but often much blame. I was so astonished to find myself either praised or blamed; it seemed to me the natural thing for a woman to do; but I see now how mistaken I was to have confessed it, and to imagine it was my duty to confess, which I certainly did. I know that he, being dead, would not have wished it published; if so, why did he leave it to me? . . . You are quite right; it has pleased me more than I can say that you should approve and confirm my ideas, and I am so thankful that the Life has succeeded. I got my best reward in a review which said that 'Richard Burton's widow might comfort herself, as England now knew the man inside and out, that she had lifted every cloud from his memory, and his fame would shine as a beacon in all future ages.' I remember so well the party at Lady Margaret Beaumont's. I can shut my eyes and see the whole dinner-table; we were twenty-five in party. And I remember well also the party at Bulstrode. If I am alive in the summer, I shall be only too glad to pass a few days with you at Bulstrode, if you will let me. I feel that a talk to you would carry me back to my happy days.

"Believe me, with warmest thanks,
"Yours sincerely,
"Isabel Burton."

After the publication of the Life of her husband Lady Burton spent most of her time at Baker Street, with intervals at Mortlake, and a few visits to friends, including Lady Windsor, Lord Arundell of Wardour, Lady Guendolen Ramsden at Bulstrode, and Canon Waterton at Carlisle. The year which followed (1894) may be said to have been her last active year, and it was the pleasantest year of her life in England. The success which had attended her book had brought her more into contact with the world than she had been at any time since her husband's death, and she saw that there was a field of usefulness still before her. This was the year in which she saw most friends, entertained most, and went about most. Her health, never good, seemed to rally, and she was far less nervous than usual. She may be said about this time to have taken almost to literature as a profession, for she worked at it eight hours every day, in addition to keeping up a large correspondence, chiefly on literary and business matters. She went frequently to the play, got all the new books, and kept herself well in touch with the current thought of the day. She was not in sympathy with a good deal of it, and her way of expressing her opinions was delightfully frank and original. Despite her abiding sense of her loss, there was nothing morbid about Lady Burton. She was bright and cheerful, full of interest in things, and perfectly happy in the society of her dearly loved sister.

I think that here one might mention a few characteristics of Lady Burton. She was always very generous, but her generosity was not of the kind which would commend itself to the Charity Organization Society. For instance, she had an incurable propensity of giving away to beggars in the street. She never let one go. The result was that she frequently returned home with an empty purse; indeed, so aware was she of her weakness, she took out little money with her as a rule, so that she might not be tempted too far. When people remonstrated with her on this indiscriminate almsgiving, she used to say, "I would rather give to ten rogues than turn one honest man away; I should be amply repaid if there were one fairly good one amongst them." She was very fond of children—that is, *en bloc*; but she did not care to be troubled with them at too close quarters. She often took out the poor children of the Roman Catholic schools to treats on Wimbledon Common. She would hire drags, and go up there for the afternoon with them. She never forgot them at Christmas, and she would always set aside a day or two for buying them toys. Her way of doing this was somewhat peculiar. She had been so used to buying things of itinerant vendors in the streets abroad that she could not break herself of the habit in England. So, instead of going to a toy shop, she used to take a four-wheel cab, and drive slowly down Oxford Street and Regent Street; and whenever she came across a pedlar with toys on a tray, she would pull up her cab and make her purchases. These purchases generally took a good deal of time, for Lady Burton had been so much in the habit of dealing at bazars in the East that she was always under the impression that the pedlars in England asked double or treble what they really thought they would get. The result was a good deal of bargaining between her and the vendors. She used to make wholesale purchases; and during her bargaining, which was carried on with much animation, a crowd assembled, and not infrequently the younger members of it came in for a share of the spoils.

To the day of her death she always felt strongly on the subject of the prevention of cruelty to animals, and indeed engaged in a fierce controversy with Father Vaughan on the subject of vivisection. She was never tired of denouncing the "barbarism of bearing-reins," and so forth. When she went out in a cab, she invariably inspected the horse carefully first, to see if it looked well fed and cared for; if not, she discharged the cab and got another one, and she would always impress upon the driver that he must not beat his horse under any consideration when he was driving her. She would then get into the cab, let the window down, and keep a watch. If the driver forgot himself so far as to give a flick with his whip, Lady Burton would lunge at him with her umbrella from behind. Upon the cabby remonstrating at this unlooked-for attack, she would retort, "Yes, and how do you like it?" On one occasion though she was not consistent. She took a cab with her sister from Charing Cross Station, and was in a great hurry to get home. Of course she impressed as usual upon the Jehu that he was not to beat his horse. The horse, which was a wretched old screw, refused, in consequence, to go at more than a walking pace; and as Lady Burton was in a hurry to get back, and was fuming with impatience inside, she at last forgot herself so far as to put her head out of the window and cry to the driver, "Why don't you beat him? Why don't you make him go?"

In politics Lady Burton described herself as a progressive Conservative, which, being interpreted, would seem to signify that, though she was intensely conservative with regard to the things which she had at heart, such as religion and the importance of upholding the old *régime*, she was exceedingly progressive in smaller matters. Her views on social questions especially were remarkably broad, and it may safely be said that there never was a woman who had less narrowness or bigotry in her composition. She was fond of saying, "Let us hear all sides of the question, for that is the only way in which we can hope to arrive at the truth."

I should like to add a few words as to her spiritual life, because it entered so profoundly into all that she said and did, that no record of her would be complete which ignored it. We have seen how in every crisis of her life, through all her perils, trials, and difficulties, she turned instinctively to that Source where many look for strength and some find it. Lady Burton was one of those who found it: though all else might fail her, this consolation never failed. In her fervent faith is to be found the occult force which enabled her to dare all things, hope all things, endure all things. We may agree with her religious views or not, but we are compelled to admit their power to sustain her through life's battle. The secret of her strength was this: to her the things spiritual and invisible—which to many of us are unreal, however loudly we may profess our belief in them—were living realities. It is difficult for some of us perhaps, in this material, sceptical world of ours, to realize a nature like hers. Yet there are many such, and they form the strongest proof of the living force of Christianity to-day. "Transcendental," the world remarks, with a sneer. But who is there among us who would not, an he could, exchange uncertainty and unrest for the possession of a peace which the world cannot give? There are some natures who *can* believe, who *can* look forward to a prize so great and wonderful as to hold the pain and trouble of the race of very small account when weighed against the hope of victory. Lady Burton was one of these; she had her feet firm set upon the everlasting Rock. The teaching of her Church was to her divinest truth. The supernatural was real, the spiritual actual. The conflict between the powers of light and the powers of darkness, between good angels and evil angels, between benign influences and malefic forces, was no figure of speech with her, but a reality. In these last years of her life more especially the earthly veil seemed to have fallen from her eyes. She seemed to have grasped something of the vision of the servant of Elisha, for whom the prophet prayed: "*Lord, I pray Thee, open his eyes, that he may see. And the Lord opened the eyes of the young man; and he saw: and, behold, the mountain was full of horses and chariots of fire round about Elisha.*"

Because of all this, because her religion was such an actuality to her, is, I think, due half the misunderstandings which have arisen with regard to Lady Burton's attitude towards so-called "spiritualism." She always held that Catholicism was the highest form of spiritualism—using the word in its highest meaning—and from this attitude she never wavered. She had lived much in the East, and had come much into contact with oriental occult influences, but what she saw only served to convince her more of the truths of her religion. Lady Burton was a Christian mystic, not in the vulgar sense of the word, but only in the sense that many devout and religious women have been Christian mystics too. Like Saint Catherine of

Sienna, Saint Teresa, and other holy women, she was specially attracted to the spiritual and devotional aspect of the Catholic Faith. Neither did her devotion to the spiritual element unfit her for the practical side of things: quite the contrary. Like Saint Teresa, side by side with her religious life, she was a remarkably shrewd woman of business. It need scarcely be added that between so-called "spiritualism" as practised in England and the Catholicism of Lady Burton there was a great gulf fixed, and one which she proved to be unbridgable. This lower form of spiritualism, to use her own words, "can only act as a decoy to a crowd of sensation-seekers, who yearn to see a ghost as they would go to see a pantomime." Such things she considered, when not absolutely farcical, worked for evil, and not for good. As she wrote to a friend:

"That faculty you have about the spirits, though you may ignore it, is the cause of your constant misfortunes. I have great experience and knowledge in these matters. As soon as you are happy these demons of envy, spite, and malicious intention attack you for evil ends, and ruin your happiness to get hold of your body and soul. Never practise or interest yourself in these matters, and debar them from your house by prayer and absolute non-hearing or seeing them. . . . Do not treat my words lightly, because I have had experience of it myself, and I had untold misfortune until I did as I advise you. The more God loves you, the more will this spirit hate and pursue you and want you for his own. Drive him forth and resist him. . . . There is a spiritualism (I hate the word!)

that comes from God, but it does not come in this guise. This sort is from the spirits of evil."[1]

I have dwelt on this side of Lady Burton's character in order to contradict many foolish rumours. During the last years of her life in England, when her health was failing, she was induced against her better judgment to have some dealings with certain so-called "spiritualists," who approached her under the plea of "communicating" with her husband, thus appealing to her at the least point of resistance. Lady Burton told her sister that she wanted to see "if there was anything in it," and to compare it with the occultism of the East. In the course of her inquiries she unfortunately signed certain papers which contained ridiculous "revelations." On thinking the matter over subsequently, the absurdity of the thing struck her. She came to the conclusion that there was nothing in it at all, and that, as compared with the occultism of the East, this was mere *kindergarten*. She then wished to recall the papers. She was very ill at the time, and unable to write herself; but she mentioned the matter to her sister at Eastbourne a short time before her death, and said, "The first thing I do when I get back to London will be to recall those silly papers." She was most anxious to return to London for this purpose; but the day after her return she died. Mrs. Fitzgerald at once communicated Lady Burton's dying wishes to the person in whose charge the papers were, and requested

[1] Letter of Lady Burton written from Trieste to Mrs. Francis Joly, April 17, 1890.

that they should not be published. But with a disregard alike for the wishes of the dead and the feelings of the living, the person rushed some of these absurd "communications" into print within a few weeks of Lady Burton's death, and despite all remonstrance was later proceeding to publish others, when stopped by a threat of legal proceedings from the executors.

Early in 1895 Lady Burton was struck down with the prevailing epidemic of influenza; and though she rallied a little after a month or two, she never recovered. She was no longer able to walk up and down stairs without assistance, or even across the room. Her decline set in rapidly after this illness; for the influenza gave a fresh impetus to her internal malady, which she knew must be fatal to her sooner or later. She remained in Baker Street a sad invalid the first six months of the year, and then she recovered sufficiently to be removed to Eastbourne for a change. It was in July that I saw her last, just before she left for Eastbourne. She asked me to come and see her. I went one Sunday afternoon, and I was grieved to see the change which a few months had worked in her. She was lying on a couch in an upper room. Her face was of waxen whiteness, and her voice weak, but the brave, indomitable spirit shone from her eyes still, and she talked cheerfully for a long time about her literary labours and her plans and arrangements for some time ahead.

At Eastbourne she took a cottage, and remained there from September, 1895, to March 21, 1896. It was evident to her sister and all around her that she was fast failing; but whenever she was well enough she did some work. At this time she had begun her autobiography. When she was free from pain, she was always bright and cheerful, and enjoyed a joke as much as ever.

Early in the New Year, 1896, she became rapidly worse, and her one wish was to recover sufficiently to go home. One of the last letters she ever wrote was to her friend Madame de Gutmansthal-Benvenuti:

"I never forget you, and I wish our thoughts were telephones. I am very bad, and my one prayer is to be able to get home to London. The doctor is going to remove me on the first possible day. I work every moment I am free from pain. You will be glad to hear that I have had permission from Rome for Mass and Communion in the house, which is a great blessing to me. I have no strength to dictate more."[1]

The second week in March Lady Burton rallied a little, and the doctor thought her sufficiently well to be removed to London. She accordingly travelled on March 21. She was moved on a bed into an invalid carriage, and was accompanied by her sister, who never left her side, and the doctor and a priest. She was very cheerful during the journey; and when she got to Victoria, she said she felt so much better that she would walk along the platform to the cab. Mrs. Fitzgerald got out first; but on turning round to help her sister, she found that she had fainted. The doctor administered restoratives; and when she

[1] Holywell Lodge, Eastbourne, March 12, 1896.

had recovered a little, she was carried to a cab, and driven to her house in Baker Street.

Towards the evening she seemed better, and was glad to be back in her familiar surroundings again. She kept saying to her sister, "Thank God, I am at home again!" She had a haunting fear latterly at Eastbourne that she would not have the strength to come home. By this time it was of course known that she could not possibly recover, and the end would only be a question of a little time. But that evening no one thought that death was imminent. During the night, however, she grew worse.

The next morning (Passion Sunday, March 22) her sister saw a great change in her. She asked her what she wished, and Lady Burton answered, "It depends on you whether I receive the Last Sacraments." The priest was summoned at once, and administered Extreme Unction and the Holy Viaticum. She followed all the prayers, and was conscious to the last. When all was over, she bowed her head and whispered, "Thank God." A smile of peace and trusting came over her face, and with a faint sigh she breathed her last. She had heard the "tinkling of his camel's bell."

She was buried in the little cemetery at Mortlake one bright spring afternoon, when all Nature seemed waking from its winter sleep. She was laid to rest in the Arab tent by the side of him whom she had loved so dearly, there to sleep with the quiet dead until the great Resurrection Day. She was buried with all the rites of her Church. The coffin was taken down to Mort-

THE ROOM IN WHICH LADY BURTON DIED.

THE ARAB TENT AT MORTLAKE.   [*Page* 770.

lake the evening before, and rested before the altar in the little church all night. The next morning High Mass was celebrated in the presence of her relatives and friends; and after the Benediction, the procession, headed by the choir singing *In Paradiso*, wound its way along the path to the mausoleum, where the final ceremony took place. As the door was opened, the camel bells began to tinkle, and they continued ringing throughout the ceremony. They have never rung since. The door of the tent is now closed, and on the opposite page of the marble book which sets forth the deeds and renown of her husband are written these words only:

Isabel his Wife.

INDEX

A

ABD EL KADIR, 386, 396, 507
Acre, St. Jean d', 489
Adelsberg Caves, the, 546
Aden, 74, 570
Alderley, Dowager Lady Stanley of, 747
Alexandria, 365, 621
Alford, Lady Marian, 529
Algiers, 694
Almack's, fancy ball at, 26
Anthropological Society, dinner to Burton, 230
Anti-Lebanon, 371
Antioch, the Patriarch, Primate of, 432
Arneh, Druze wedding at, 453
Arundell, Blanche, 63, 88, 96, 556
—— Blanche Lady, 6, 439
—— Mr., death of, 684
—— Mrs., her opposition to Lady Burton's marriage, 151; her death, 530
Arundells of Wardour, family history, 1-10
Austria, Emperor and Empress of, 545; the Court of, 545
Auvergne, Princess de la Tour d', 361
Ayde, Sir John, 681

B

BA'ALBAK, 430
Bahia, 342
Balme, Col de, 127.
Barbacena, 281
—— Vicomte and Vicomtesse, 259
Beaconsfield, Lord, 614, 621, 623
Beatson, General, 79
Beaumont, Lady Margaret, 760
Beg, Omar, 412
Beyrout, 367
Bird, Dr., 155, 166
—— Miss Alice, 166, 689
Bishop, Miss, 683, 695, 751, 755
Blanc, Mont, 124
Bludán, 427 *et seq.*; news of the recall, 499
Bologna, 639
Bombay, 73; journey to, 554, 572; the Towers of Silence, 586; the Hindú Smáshán, 588
—— Government remove Burton's name from Army List, 175

Boulogne, life at, 40 *et seq.*, **555**; last visit to, 691
Brazil, 244 *et seq.*
—— Emperor and Empress of, 259
British Association meeting at Bath, 1864, 228
Bull-fight at Lisbon, a, 233
Bülow, Madame von, 552
Burton, Captain St. George, **747**
Byculla, races at, 576

C

CAMERON, Captain Verney Lovett, 631, 635
Candahar, **624**
Carnival at Venice, **114**
Carthage, 694
Cazalem, 597, 599
Cenis, Mont, ascent of, 117
Chambord, Comte de (Henri V.), 113, 115, **610**
Chamounix, 124
Chavannes, Comtesse de, 115
Cheron, Chevalier de St., 113
Chillon, 130
Citta Vecchia, 535
Clarendon, Lord, 352, 513, 623
Clifford, Isabel, 14
Constable, Sir Clifford and Lady, 157
Copsey, Mr. Charles, 284
Crawford, Rev. John, **522**
Cruz, Santa, 198

D

DAHOMÉ, King of, 226
Damascus, 372, 375
Dead Sea, 483
Derby, Lord, 230, 508, 623, 693; and Lady, 746
Digby, Hon. Jane, El Mezráb, 393
—— Lord, 393, 395

Dublin, 229
Dudley, Georgina Lady, 545

E

EASTBOURNE, 768
Eldridge, Consul-General, 520
Ellenborough, Lady, 389, 393, 459, **507**
Elliot, Sir Henry, 493, 522; letter to Lady Burton, 516
Elphinstone Point, 593
Entre Rios, 275
Eu, Comte and Comtesse d', 258
Extreme Unction, Sacrament of, administered to Sir Richard Burton, 702, 706

F

FERNANDO Po, 175
Fisherwomen of Boulogne, the, **44**
Fitzgerald, Mrs., 15, 634, 746, 750, 753, 767, 769
Fiume, 546
Florence, 110, 544
Frankel, Rev. E. B., **522**
Funchal, 189
Furze Hall, 17

G

GENEVA, 120
Genoa, 102
Gerard, Elizabeth, 14
—— Lord, 8, 183, 355, 689
—— Monica Lady, 173
Germany, the Empress Frederick of, 545
Ghazis, the, 410
Ghazzeh, 636, **638**
Gibraltar, 681
Giram, Cape, 193

Index

Gladstone, Mr. W. E., 551
Goa, 594 *et seq.*, 713
Gobat, Bishop, 481
Golconda, 585
Gordon, General, 644, 645; letters from, 646 *et seq.*; his death at Kartoum, 644, 675
Gordon, Mr. and Mrs., 294
Gorizia, 610
Grant, Colonel, 740
Granville, Lord, 456, 465, 508, 516, 531, 532, 621; his reasons for Burton's recall, 520, 528
Grindlay's fire, 178
Gutmansthal-Benvenuti, Mme. de, 696, 742, 755, 769
Gypsy forecast, a, 21

H

HAMMERTON, Colonel, 714
Harar in Somaliland, 73
Havre, 136
Hawthorne, General, 338
Hay, Sir J. D., 680
Henri V. (Comte de Chambord), 113, 115, 610
Honfleur, 137
Houghton, Lord, 177, 355, 551
Howard, Cardinal, 543
Hunt, Mr. Holman, 481
Hyderabad, 580; the Nizam of, 580 *et seq.*

I

ICELAND, 529, 552
Ideal lover, the, 37
Ireland, a trip to, 229
Ismail, Khedive, and the Mines of Midian, 610 *et seq.*, 621
Italy, Queen of, 558

J

JAFFA, 367, 470
James, Miss, 522
Jayrûd, 407
Jeddah, 563
Jerusalem, 471
Joly, Mrs. Francis, 767
Jowett, Professor, 551
Juiz de Fóra, 277
Jung, Sir Salar, 580

K

KARACHI, 730
Karla Caves, 578
Karyatayn, 412
Kazeh, 143
Kebir, Amir el, 583
Kennedy, Mr., 466

L

LAGÔA DOURADA, 285
Laguna, 200
Lanauli, 578
Lausanne, 131
Layard, Sir Henry, 182
Lebanon, 370
—— Cedars of, 432
Lee, Dr., 284
Leghorn, 110
Leighton, Sir Frederick, 354, 376; his picture of Sir Richard Burton, 551
Lentaigne, the convict philanthropist, 229
Leslie, Dr. Ralph, 688, 690
Lever, Charles, 530, 532, 580
Levis, Duc de, 115
Lido, the, 114
Lipizza, the Emperor of Austria's stud farm at, 546
Lisbon, 231

Llandaff, Lord (Mr. Henry Matthews), 548
Lytton, Lord and Lady, 233, 624

M

MACHICO, 192
Madeira, 190
Máhábáleshwar, 591, 593, 594
Malta, 694
Marianna, 302
Marienbad, 631, 635
Martelani, Pietro, 709
Mátherán, 577
Mattei, Count, 639
Meade, Sir Richard, 585
Mecca, 69, 565, 713
Midian, the Mines of, 610, 621
Mijwal, Shaykh, 394
Milan, 558
Milnes, Monckton (Lord Houghton), 81, 179
Mitford, Mr., 468
Monson, Sir Edmund, 699
Montagu, Lady Mary Wortley, 361
Montanvert, 125
Montreux, 692
Mormons, Burton's book on the, 180
Morocco, 643, 680, 682, 685
Morro Velho, 295 *et seq.*
Mortlake, Lady Burton's cottage at, 752
—— Cemetery, 228; burial of Sir Richard Burton, 746, 747; burial of Lady Burton, 770
Mukhtára, 449
Murchison, Sir Roderick, 355

N

NAPIER, Sir Charles, 730
Napoleon, Louis, 396
—— some relics of, 181

Nazareth, 486; the riot at, 487
Nevill, Major and Mrs., 580
New Hall (Convent), 17, 748
Nice, 100
Novikoff, Madame Olga, 631

O

OBERAMMERGAU, the Passion Play at, 623, 627
Opçina, 542; ball at, 627
Orotava, 201
Ouchy, 131
"Ouida," 537, 544
Ouro Branco, 328
—— Preto, 305

P

PAGET, Sir Augustus and Lady, 543, 639
Palmer, Mr. E. H., 430
—— Professor, 636
Palmerston, Lord, 177
Palmyra, 403 *et seq.*
Paris, 97; after the Franco-German War, 556; Lady Burton's fall downstairs, 616
Pasarni Ghát, 592
Perrochel, Vicomte de, 414, 421
Perry, Sir William, 533
Persigny, Duchesse de, 383
Petropolis, 258, 273, 339
Pico Arriere, 193
Pigott, Mrs. Smyth, 96, 751
Pisa, 109
Poissardes, Carolina, "Queen" of the, 44, 58, 556
Poonah, 579, 592
Port Said, 561
Portugal, a trip to, 230
Procopio, Com. Mariano, 277
Prout, Colonel, 659

Index

Q

QUEEN, the, makes Burton K.C.M.G., 682; grants pension to Lady Burton, 747

R

RALLI, Baroness Paul de, 706, 709
Ramsden, Lady Guendolen, 758
Réclus, Elisée, 692
Richards, Mr. Alfred Bates, 605
Rio de Janeiro, 244
Riviera, the earthquake in the, 1887, 687
Rome, 544
Rosebery, Lord, 685, 687
Royal Geographical Society and Speke, 144
Russell, Lady John, 177
—— Lord John, 175, 227

S

SABARÁ, 315
Safed, 491
Salahíyyeh, 376, 454
Salisbury, Lord and Lady, 614, 623, 682, 685, 687; letters from Lady Salisbury, 618, 622, 693
Santos, 230, 248
São João, 283
—— Paulo, 248
Scented Garden, The, 696, 698; truth about, 719 *et seq.*; burning of, 726
Schwartzenburg, Prince, 393
Scott, Rev. J. Orr, 522
Seão, Senhor Nicolão, 334
Shazlis, the, 496, 521
Sitt Jumblatt, the, 449
Smith, Mr. W. H., 623; letter from, 623
Somerset, Duke and Duchess of, 552, 758

Spain, Maria Theresa, ex-Queen of, 547
Speke, Lieut., 73, 140-144, 228, 355, 740
Spezzia, 107
Stafford, Lord, 468
Stanhope, Lady Hester, 361, 393, 426
Stanley, Lord, 230, 351
Stisted, Lady, 745
—— Miss, 393, 745; her impeachment of Lady Burton, 510 *et seq.*, 702, 736
Suez, 602, 612
Swinburne, Algernon, 354
Symmonds, Mr., 302

T

TABÚT or Múharram, Feast of, 575
Tanganyika, Lake, 142
Tangiers, 683
Teneriffe, 198 *et seq.*; the Peak of, 210
Thornton, Sir Edward and Lady, 247
Tiberias, Lake of, 491
Treloar, Captain, 301, 338
Trieste, 531, 535 *et seq.*, 604 *et seq.*, 616 *et seq.*; Burton a confirmed invalid, 689; his death at, 700
Tunis, 694
Tupper, Martin, 619
Tyrwhitt-Drake, Mr. Charles, 473, 546, 547

U

USAGARA Mountains, 141

V

VARDEN, Dr., 490
Vaughan, Cardinal, 709

Veldes, 630
Venice, 112, 533, 559; Geographical Congress at, 631
Vevey, 130
Vienna, **544**

W

WAHI, 592
Wales, the Prince of, 585, 687
Wali, the, 372, 391, 392; his daughter's wedding, **459**, **464**; his dispute with Burton, **517**
Warren, Sir Charles, **638**
Waterton, **Canon, 743, 760**

Wikar Shums Ool Umárá, the, 582
Wilson, Miss Ellen, 435
—— Sir Andrew, 660
Windsor, Lady, **760**
Wiseman, Cardinal, 713
Wright, **Rev. W.,** 522
Wuld Ali, 461
Würtemberg, Duke of, 560

Z

ZEBEDANI, 437
Zeller, Mrs. Van, **15**, **754**
Zenobia, 419

www.ingramcontent.com/pod-product-compliance
Lightning Source LLC
Chambersburg PA
CBHW031955300426
44117CB00008B/773